C-1247   CAREER EXAMINATION SERIES

This is your
PASSBOOK for...

Detective Investigator

Test Preparation Study Guide
Questions & Answers

COPYRIGHT NOTICE

This book is SOLELY intended for, is sold ONLY to, and its use is RESTRICTED to individual, bona fide applicants or candidates who qualify by virtue of having seriously filed applications for appropriate license, certificate, professional and/or promotional advancement, higher school matriculation, scholarship, or other legitimate requirements of education and/or governmental authorities.

This book is NOT intended for use, class instruction, tutoring, training, duplication, copying, reprinting, excerption, or adaptation, etc., by:

1) Other publishers
2) Proprietors and/or Instructors of "Coaching" and/or Preparatory Courses
3) Personnel and/or Training Divisions of commercial, industrial, and governmental organizations
4) Schools, colleges, or universities and/or their departments and staffs, including teachers and other personnel
5) Testing Agencies or Bureaus
6) Study groups which seek by the purchase of a single volume to copy and/or duplicate and/or adapt this material for use by the group as a whole without having purchased individual volumes for each of the members of the group
7) Et al.

Such persons would be in violation of appropriate Federal and State statutes.

PROVISION OF LICENSING AGREEMENTS – Recognized educational, commercial, industrial, and governmental institutions and organizations, and others legitimately engaged in educational pursuits, including training, testing, and measurement activities, may address request for a licensing agreement to the copyright owners, who will determine whether, and under what conditions, including fees and charges, the materials in this book may be used them. In other words, a licensing facility exists for the legitimate use of the material in this book on other than an individual basis. However, it is asseverated and affirmed here that the material in this book CANNOT be used without the receipt of the express permission of such a licensing agreement from the Publishers. Inquiries re licensing should be addressed to the company, attention rights and permissions department.

All rights reserved, including the right of reproduction in whole or in part, in any form or by any means, electronic or mechanical, including photocopying, recording, or by any information storage and retrieval system, without permission in writing from the Publisher.

Copyright © 2025 by
National Learning Corporation

212 Michael Drive, Syosset, NY 11791
(516) 921-8888 • www.passbooks.com
E-mail: info@passbooks.com

PASSBOOK® SERIES

THE *PASSBOOK® SERIES* has been created to prepare applicants and candidates for the ultimate academic battlefield – the examination room.

At some time in our lives, each and every one of us may be required to take an examination – for validation, matriculation, admission, qualification, registration, certification, or licensure.

Based on the assumption that every applicant or candidate has met the basic formal educational standards, has taken the required number of courses, and read the necessary texts, the *PASSBOOK® SERIES* furnishes the one special preparation which may assure passing with confidence, instead of failing with insecurity. Examination questions – together with answers – are furnished as the basic vehicle for study so that the mysteries of the examination and its compounding difficulties may be eliminated or diminished by a sure method.

This book is meant to help you pass your examination provided that you qualify and are serious in your objective.

The entire field is reviewed through the huge store of content information which is succinctly presented through a provocative and challenging approach – the question-and-answer method.

A climate of success is established by furnishing the correct answers at the end of each test.

You soon learn to recognize types of questions, forms of questions, and patterns of questioning. You may even begin to anticipate expected outcomes.

You perceive that many questions are repeated or adapted so that you can gain acute insights, which may enable you to score many sure points.

You learn how to confront new questions, or types of questions, and to attack them confidently and work out the correct answers.

You note objectives and emphases, and recognize pitfalls and dangers, so that you may make positive educational adjustments.

Moreover, you are kept fully informed in relation to new concepts, methods, practices, and directions in the field.

You discover that you are actually taking the examination all the time: you are preparing for the examination by "taking" an examination, not by reading extraneous and/or supererogatory textbooks.

In short, this PASSBOOK®, used directedly, should be an important factor in helping you to pass your test.

DETECTIVE INVESTIGATOR

DUTIES:
The work involves responsibility for investigating crimes and offenses in violation of law. The incumbent secures and reports facts and information by interview, observation and investigation. This position is characterized by the performance of extensive field activities concerned with gathering information for use in criminal proceedings. The work is performed under the general supervision of a higher ranking officer.

An employee in this class performs initial investigative steps pertaining to complaints received by the Police Department and/or District Attorney's Office. In organized crime or other complex investigations, the incumbent performs duties after conference with a Detective Investigator or the direction and under the supervision of a Senior Detective Investigator or other administrative supervisor. Performs undercover and general investigative work. Interrogates and takes statements from witnesses to crimes. Inspects scene of a suspected crime for evidence and reports the nature of the findings. May testify in court in regard to cases. Responsibility is included for assuring that assigned Assistant District Attorneys' case files are complete, that necessary service of legal process has been accomplished, and that witnesses and evidence are available as required. Work is reviewed through conferences and submission of reports.

Under direction, candidates in this position may conduct investigations of crimes and serious accidents or deaths which may have involved criminal conduct. The Police Detective interviews victims, witnesses, suspects; and assists in obtaining physical evidence. The Police Detective does, under normal circumstances, exercise supervision over other departmental employees, but may occasionally direct and coordinate investigative efforts of uniformed personnel. Police Detectives prepare all appropriate documentation to make arrests and work closely with the District Attorney's Office in prosecuting cases in court. Candidate is expected to perform related work, as assigned by a supervisor or Chief of Police.

TYPICAL WORK ACTIVITIES:
Responds to crime scenes to interview victims and witnesses and to assist in gathering physical evidence; conducts criminal investigations: interview victims, witnesses, suspects; prepares reports, takes statements, prepares legal documentation, information, search warrants, etc.; conducts searches for evidence and latent fingerprints; maintains evidence files and property room; assists prosecuting attorneys in the preparation of cases for Grand Jury and trial; maintains liaison with and assists other agencies such as courts, the District Attorney's Office, Social Services, Coroner's Office, as well as other law enforcement agencies; assists police officers, and other law enforcement personnel in investigating crimes and other incidents; testifies at all hearings, Grand Juries and trials regarding investigation results; conducts surveillances and undercover work; makes arrests; attends and conducts advanced training in specialized areas to include, but not limited to, homicide, child abuse, sex offences; performs background investigations and assists in other investigations as needed or assigned by a supervisor.

FULL PERFORMANCE, KNOWLEDGE, SKILLS, ABILITIES AND PERSONAL CHARACTERISTICS:
Good knowledge of the State Penal Law, Criminal Procedure Law and Vehicle and Traffic Law; good knowledge of the rights and protections provided individuals by the Constitution of the United States, as they relate to the State laws; good knowledge of the techniques of photography, latent fingerprints and other law enforcement I.D. techniques; good knowledge of investigative techniques; ability to develop sources of information using discretion in obtaining and releasing information; integrity; good language and writing skills; physical condition and skills commensurate with the demands of the job.

SUBJECTS OF EXAMINATION:
The written test is designed to evaluate knowledge, skills and /or abilities in the following areas:

1. **Evaluating information and evidence**: These questions test for the ability to evaluate and draw conclusions from information and evidence. Each question consists of a set of facts and a conclusion based on the facts. The candidate must decide if the conclusion is warranted by the facts.

2. **Investigative techniques and criminalistics**: These questions test for knowledge of criminal investigation techniques and criminalistics. The questions will deal with, but will not necessarily be restricted to, such concepts as: interviewing; interrogation; evidence gathering and preservation; and surveillance.

3. **State Laws**: These questions test for knowledge of law that law enforcement personnel may encounter in the course of their day-to-day work-related activities. The questions are a sampling of job-related sections of the Penal Law, Criminal Procedure Law, Vehicle and Traffic Law, Family Court Act and other laws relevant to law enforcement in the State.

4. **Understanding and interpreting written material**: These questions test how well you comprehend written material. You will be provided with brief reading selections and will be asked questions about the selections. All the information required to answer the questions will be presented in the selections; you will not be required to have any special knowledge relating to the subject areas of the selections.

5. **Preparing written material in a police setting**: These questions test for the ability to prepare the types of reports that police personnel write. Some questions test for the ability to present information clearly and accurately. They consist of restatements of information given in note form. You must choose the best version from each set of four choices. Other questions test for the ability to organize paragraphs. They consist of paragraphs with their sentences out of order. For each of the paragraphs you must choose, from four suggestions, the best order of the sentences.

HOW TO TAKE A TEST

I. YOU MUST PASS AN EXAMINATION

A. WHAT EVERY CANDIDATE SHOULD KNOW

Examination applicants often ask us for help in preparing for the written test. What can I study in advance? What kinds of questions will be asked? How will the test be given? How will the papers be graded?

As an applicant for a civil service examination, you may be wondering about some of these things. Our purpose here is to suggest effective methods of advance study and to describe civil service examinations.

Your chances for success on this examination can be increased if you know how to prepare. Those "pre-examination jitters" can be reduced if you know what to expect. You can even experience an adventure in good citizenship if you know why civil service exams are given.

B. WHY ARE CIVIL SERVICE EXAMINATIONS GIVEN?

Civil service examinations are important to you in two ways. As a citizen, you want public jobs filled by employees who know how to do their work. As a job seeker, you want a fair chance to compete for that job on an equal footing with other candidates. The best-known means of accomplishing this two-fold goal is the competitive examination.

Exams are widely publicized throughout the nation. They may be administered for jobs in federal, state, city, municipal, town or village governments or agencies.

Any citizen may apply, with some limitations, such as the age or residence of applicants. Your experience and education may be reviewed to see whether you meet the requirements for the particular examination. When these requirements exist, they are reasonable and applied consistently to all applicants. Thus, a competitive examination may cause you some uneasiness now, but it is your privilege and safeguard.

C. HOW ARE CIVIL SERVICE EXAMS DEVELOPED?

Examinations are carefully written by trained technicians who are specialists in the field known as "psychological measurement," in consultation with recognized authorities in the field of work that the test will cover. These experts recommend the subject matter areas or skills to be tested; only those knowledges or skills important to your success on the job are included. The most reliable books and source materials available are used as references. Together, the experts and technicians judge the difficulty level of the questions.

Test technicians know how to phrase questions so that the problem is clearly stated. Their ethics do not permit "trick" or "catch" questions. Questions may have been tried out on sample groups, or subjected to statistical analysis, to determine their usefulness.

Written tests are often used in combination with performance tests, ratings of training and experience, and oral interviews. All of these measures combine to form the best-known means of finding the right person for the right job.

II. HOW TO PASS THE WRITTEN TEST

A. NATURE OF THE EXAMINATION

To prepare intelligently for civil service examinations, you should know how they differ from school examinations you have taken. In school you were assigned certain definite pages to read or subjects to cover. The examination questions were quite detailed and usually emphasized memory. Civil service exams, on the other hand, try to discover your present ability to perform the duties of a position, plus your potentiality to learn these duties. In other words, a civil service exam attempts to predict how successful you will be. Questions cover such a broad area that they cannot be as minute and detailed as school exam questions.

In the public service similar kinds of work, or positions, are grouped together in one "class." This process is known as *position-classification*. All the positions in a class are paid according to the salary range for that class. One class title covers all of these positions, and they are all tested by the same examination.

B. FOUR BASIC STEPS

1) Study the announcement

How, then, can you know what subjects to study? Our best answer is: "Learn as much as possible about the class of positions for which you've applied." The exam will test the knowledge, skills and abilities needed to do the work.

Your most valuable source of information about the position you want is the official exam announcement. This announcement lists the training and experience qualifications. Check these standards and apply only if you come reasonably close to meeting them.

The brief description of the position in the examination announcement offers some clues to the subjects which will be tested. Think about the job itself. Review the duties in your mind. Can you perform them, or are there some in which you are rusty? Fill in the blank spots in your preparation.

Many jurisdictions preview the written test in the exam announcement by including a section called "Knowledge and Abilities Required," "Scope of the Examination," or some similar heading. Here you will find out specifically what fields will be tested.

2) Review your own background

Once you learn in general what the position is all about, and what you need to know to do the work, ask yourself which subjects you already know fairly well and which need improvement. You may wonder whether to concentrate on improving your strong areas or on building some background in your fields of weakness. When the announcement has specified "some knowledge" or "considerable knowledge," or has used adjectives like "beginning principles of…" or "advanced … methods," you can get a clue as to the number and difficulty of questions to be asked in any given field. More questions, and hence broader coverage, would be included for those subjects which are more important in the work. Now weigh your strengths and weaknesses against the job requirements and prepare accordingly.

3) Determine the level of the position

Another way to tell how intensively you should prepare is to understand the level of the job for which you are applying. Is it the entering level? In other words, is this the position in which beginners in a field of work are hired? Or is it an intermediate or advanced level? Sometimes this is indicated by such words as "Junior" or "Senior" in the class title. Other jurisdictions use Roman numerals to designate the level – Clerk I, Clerk II, for example. The word "Supervisor" sometimes appears in the title. If the level is not indicated by the title, check the description of duties. Will you be working under very close supervision, or will you have responsibility for independent decisions in this work?

4) Choose appropriate study materials

Now that you know the subjects to be examined and the relative amount of each subject to be covered, you can choose suitable study materials. For beginning level jobs, or even advanced ones, if you have a pronounced weakness in some aspect of your training, read a modern, standard textbook in that field. Be sure it is up to date and has general coverage. Such books are normally available at your library, and the librarian will be glad to help you locate one. For entry-level positions, questions of appropriate difficulty are chosen – neither highly advanced questions, nor those too simple. Such questions require careful thought but not advanced training.

If the position for which you are applying is technical or advanced, you will read more advanced, specialized material. If you are already familiar with the basic principles of your field, elementary textbooks would waste your time. Concentrate on advanced textbooks and technical periodicals. Think through the concepts and review difficult problems in your field.

These are all general sources. You can get more ideas on your own initiative, following these leads. For example, training manuals and publications of the government agency which employs workers in your field can be useful, particularly for technical and professional positions. A letter or visit to the government department involved may result in more specific study suggestions, and certainly will provide you with a more definite idea of the exact nature of the position you are seeking.

III. KINDS OF TESTS

Tests are used for purposes other than measuring knowledge and ability to perform specified duties. For some positions, it is equally important to test ability to make adjustments to new situations or to profit from training. In others, basic mental abilities not dependent on information are essential. Questions which test these things may not appear as pertinent to the duties of the position as those which test for knowledge and information. Yet they are often highly important parts of a fair examination. For very general questions, it is almost impossible to help you direct your study efforts. What we can do is to point out some of the more common of these general abilities needed in public service positions and describe some typical questions.

1) General information

Broad, general information has been found useful for predicting job success in some kinds of work. This is tested in a variety of ways, from vocabulary lists to questions about current events. Basic background in some field of work, such as sociology or economics, may be sampled in a group of questions. Often these are principles which have become familiar to most persons through exposure rather than through formal training. It is difficult to advise you how to study for these questions; being alert to the world around you is our best suggestion.

2) Verbal ability

An example of an ability needed in many positions is verbal or language ability. Verbal ability is, in brief, the ability to use and understand words. Vocabulary and grammar tests are typical measures of this ability. Reading comprehension or paragraph interpretation questions are common in many kinds of civil service tests. You are given a paragraph of written material and asked to find its central meaning.

3) Numerical ability
Number skills can be tested by the familiar arithmetic problem, by checking paired lists of numbers to see which are alike and which are different, or by interpreting charts and graphs. In the latter test, a graph may be printed in the test booklet which you are asked to use as the basis for answering questions.

4) Observation
A popular test for law-enforcement positions is the observation test. A picture is shown to you for several minutes, then taken away. Questions about the picture test your ability to observe both details and larger elements.

5) Following directions
In many positions in the public service, the employee must be able to carry out written instructions dependably and accurately. You may be given a chart with several columns, each column listing a variety of information. The questions require you to carry out directions involving the information given in the chart.

6) Skills and aptitudes
Performance tests effectively measure some manual skills and aptitudes. When the skill is one in which you are trained, such as typing or shorthand, you can practice. These tests are often very much like those given in business school or high school courses. For many of the other skills and aptitudes, however, no short-time preparation can be made. Skills and abilities natural to you or that you have developed throughout your lifetime are being tested.

Many of the general questions just described provide all the data needed to answer the questions and ask you to use your reasoning ability to find the answers. Your best preparation for these tests, as well as for tests of facts and ideas, is to be at your physical and mental best. You, no doubt, have your own methods of getting into an exam-taking mood and keeping "in shape." The next section lists some ideas on this subject.

IV. KINDS OF QUESTIONS

Only rarely is the "essay" question, which you answer in narrative form, used in civil service tests. Civil service tests are usually of the short-answer type. Full instructions for answering these questions will be given to you at the examination. But in case this is your first experience with short-answer questions and separate answer sheets, here is what you need to know:

1) Multiple-choice Questions
Most popular of the short-answer questions is the "multiple choice" or "best answer" question. It can be used, for example, to test for factual knowledge, ability to solve problems or judgment in meeting situations found at work.
A multiple-choice question is normally one of three types—
- It can begin with an incomplete statement followed by several possible endings. You are to find the one ending which *best* completes the statement, although some of the others may not be entirely wrong.
- It can also be a complete statement in the form of a question which is answered by choosing one of the statements listed.

- It can be in the form of a problem – again you select the best answer.

Here is an example of a multiple-choice question with a discussion which should give you some clues as to the method for choosing the right answer:

When an employee has a complaint about his assignment, the action which will *best* help him overcome his difficulty is to
- A. discuss his difficulty with his coworkers
- B. take the problem to the head of the organization
- C. take the problem to the person who gave him the assignment
- D. say nothing to anyone about his complaint

In answering this question, you should study each of the choices to find which is best. Consider choice "A" – Certainly an employee may discuss his complaint with fellow employees, but no change or improvement can result, and the complaint remains unresolved. Choice "B" is a poor choice since the head of the organization probably does not know what assignment you have been given, and taking your problem to him is known as "going over the head" of the supervisor. The supervisor, or person who made the assignment, is the person who can clarify it or correct any injustice. Choice "C" is, therefore, correct. To say nothing, as in choice "D," is unwise. Supervisors have and interest in knowing the problems employees are facing, and the employee is seeking a solution to his problem.

2) True/False Questions

The "true/false" or "right/wrong" form of question is sometimes used. Here a complete statement is given. Your job is to decide whether the statement is right or wrong.

SAMPLE: A roaming cell-phone call to a nearby city costs less than a non-roaming call to a distant city.

This statement is wrong, or false, since roaming calls are more expensive.

This is not a complete list of all possible question forms, although most of the others are variations of these common types. You will always get complete directions for answering questions. Be sure you understand *how* to mark your answers – ask questions until you do.

V. RECORDING YOUR ANSWERS

Computer terminals are used more and more today for many different kinds of exams.

For an examination with very few applicants, you may be told to record your answers in the test booklet itself. Separate answer sheets are much more common. If this separate answer sheet is to be scored by machine – and this is often the case – it is highly important that you mark your answers correctly in order to get credit.

An electronic scoring machine is often used in civil service offices because of the speed with which papers can be scored. Machine-scored answer sheets must be marked with a pencil, which will be given to you. This pencil has a high graphite content which responds to the electronic scoring machine. As a matter of fact, stray dots may register as answers, so do not let your pencil rest on the answer sheet while you are pondering the correct answer. Also, if your pencil lead breaks or is otherwise defective, ask for another.

Since the answer sheet will be dropped in a slot in the scoring machine, be careful not to bend the corners or get the paper crumpled.

The answer sheet normally has five vertical columns of numbers, with 30 numbers to a column. These numbers correspond to the question numbers in your test booklet. After each number, going across the page are four or five pairs of dotted lines. These short dotted lines have small letters or numbers above them. The first two pairs may also have a "T" or "F" above the letters. This indicates that the first two pairs only are to be used if the questions are of the true-false type. If the questions are multiple choice, disregard the "T" and "F" and pay attention only to the small letters or numbers.

Answer your questions in the manner of the sample that follows:

32. The largest city in the United States is
   A. Washington, D.C.
   B. New York City
   C. Chicago
   D. Detroit
   E. San Francisco

1) Choose the answer you think is best. (New York City is the largest, so "B" is correct.)
2) Find the row of dotted lines numbered the same as the question you are answering. (Find row number 32)
3) Find the pair of dotted lines corresponding to the answer. (Find the pair of lines under the mark "B.")
4) Make a solid black mark between the dotted lines.

VI. BEFORE THE TEST

Common sense will help you find procedures to follow to get ready for an examination. Too many of us, however, overlook these sensible measures. Indeed, nervousness and fatigue have been found to be the most serious reasons why applicants fail to do their best on civil service tests. Here is a list of reminders:

- Begin your preparation early – Don't wait until the last minute to go scurrying around for books and materials or to find out what the position is all about.
- Prepare continuously – An hour a night for a week is better than an all-night cram session. This has been definitely established. What is more, a night a week for a month will return better dividends than crowding your study into a shorter period of time.
- Locate the place of the exam – You have been sent a notice telling you when and where to report for the examination. If the location is in a different town or otherwise unfamiliar to you, it would be well to inquire the best route and learn something about the building.
- Relax the night before the test – Allow your mind to rest. Do not study at all that night. Plan some mild recreation or diversion; then go to bed early and get a good night's sleep.
- Get up early enough to make a leisurely trip to the place for the test – This way unforeseen events, traffic snarls, unfamiliar buildings, etc. will not upset you.
- Dress comfortably – A written test is not a fashion show. You will be known by number and not by name, so wear something comfortable.

- Leave excess paraphernalia at home – Shopping bags and odd bundles will get in your way. You need bring only the items mentioned in the official notice you received; usually everything you need is provided. Do not bring reference books to the exam. They will only confuse those last minutes and be taken away from you when in the test room.
- Arrive somewhat ahead of time – If because of transportation schedules you must get there very early, bring a newspaper or magazine to take your mind off yourself while waiting.
- Locate the examination room – When you have found the proper room, you will be directed to the seat or part of the room where you will sit. Sometimes you are given a sheet of instructions to read while you are waiting. Do not fill out any forms until you are told to do so; just read them and be prepared.
- Relax and prepare to listen to the instructions
- If you have any physical problem that may keep you from doing your best, be sure to tell the test administrator. If you are sick or in poor health, you really cannot do your best on the exam. You can come back and take the test some other time.

VII. AT THE TEST

The day of the test is here and you have the test booklet in your hand. The temptation to get going is very strong. Caution! There is more to success than knowing the right answers. You must know how to identify your papers and understand variations in the type of short-answer question used in this particular examination. Follow these suggestions for maximum results from your efforts:

1) Cooperate with the monitor

The test administrator has a duty to create a situation in which you can be as much at ease as possible. He will give instructions, tell you when to begin, check to see that you are marking your answer sheet correctly, and so on. He is not there to guard you, although he will see that your competitors do not take unfair advantage. He wants to help you do your best.

2) Listen to all instructions

Don't jump the gun! Wait until you understand all directions. In most civil service tests you get more time than you need to answer the questions. So don't be in a hurry. Read each word of instructions until you clearly understand the meaning. Study the examples, listen to all announcements and follow directions. Ask questions if you do not understand what to do.

3) Identify your papers

Civil service exams are usually identified by number only. You will be assigned a number; you must not put your name on your test papers. Be sure to copy your number correctly. Since more than one exam may be given, copy your exact examination title.

4) Plan your time

Unless you are told that a test is a "speed" or "rate of work" test, speed itself is usually not important. Time enough to answer all the questions will be provided, but this does not mean that you have all day. An overall time limit has been set. Divide the total time (in minutes) by the number of questions to determine the approximate time you have for each question.

5) Do not linger over difficult questions

If you come across a difficult question, mark it with a paper clip (useful to have along) and come back to it when you have been through the booklet. One caution if you do this – be sure to skip a number on your answer sheet as well. Check often to be sure that you have not lost your place and that you are marking in the row numbered the same as the question you are answering.

6) Read the questions

Be sure you know what the question asks! Many capable people are unsuccessful because they failed to *read* the questions correctly.

7) Answer all questions

Unless you have been instructed that a penalty will be deducted for incorrect answers, it is better to guess than to omit a question.

8) Speed tests

It is often better NOT to guess on speed tests. It has been found that on timed tests people are tempted to spend the last few seconds before time is called in marking answers at random – without even reading them – in the hope of picking up a few extra points. To discourage this practice, the instructions may warn you that your score will be "corrected" for guessing. That is, a penalty will be applied. The incorrect answers will be deducted from the correct ones, or some other penalty formula will be used.

9) Review your answers

If you finish before time is called, go back to the questions you guessed or omitted to give them further thought. Review other answers if you have time.

10) Return your test materials

If you are ready to leave before others have finished or time is called, take ALL your materials to the monitor and leave quietly. Never take any test material with you. The monitor can discover whose papers are not complete, and taking a test booklet may be grounds for disqualification.

VIII. EXAMINATION TECHNIQUES

1) Read the general instructions carefully. These are usually printed on the first page of the exam booklet. As a rule, these instructions refer to the timing of the examination; the fact that you should not start work until the signal and must stop work at a signal, etc. If there are any *special* instructions, such as a choice of questions to be answered, make sure that you note this instruction carefully.

2) When you are ready to start work on the examination, that is as soon as the signal has been given, read the instructions to each question booklet, underline any key words or phrases, such as *least, best, outline, describe* and the like. In this way you will tend to answer as requested rather than discover on reviewing your paper that you *listed without describing*, that you selected the *worst* choice rather than the *best* choice, etc.

3) If the examination is of the objective or multiple-choice type – that is, each question will also give a series of possible answers: A, B, C or D, and you are called upon to select the best answer and write the letter next to that answer on your answer paper – it is advisable to start answering each question in turn. There may be anywhere from 50 to 100 such questions in the three or four hours allotted and you can see how much time would be taken if you read through all the questions before beginning to answer any. Furthermore, if you come across a question or group of questions which you know would be difficult to answer, it would undoubtedly affect your handling of all the other questions.

4) If the examination is of the essay type and contains but a few questions, it is a moot point as to whether you should read all the questions before starting to answer any one. Of course, if you are given a choice – say five out of seven and the like – then it is essential to read all the questions so you can eliminate the two that are most difficult. If, however, you are asked to answer all the questions, there may be danger in trying to answer the easiest one first because you may find that you will spend too much time on it. The best technique is to answer the first question, then proceed to the second, etc.

5) Time your answers. Before the exam begins, write down the time it started, then add the time allowed for the examination and write down the time it must be completed, then divide the time available somewhat as follows:
    - If 3-1/2 hours are allowed, that would be 210 minutes. If you have 80 objective-type questions, that would be an average of 2-1/2 minutes per question. Allow yourself no more than 2 minutes per question, or a total of 160 minutes, which will permit about 50 minutes to review.
    - If for the time allotment of 210 minutes there are 7 essay questions to answer, that would average about 30 minutes a question. Give yourself only 25 minutes per question so that you have about 35 minutes to review.

6) The most important instruction is to *read each question* and make sure you know what is wanted. The second most important instruction is to *time yourself properly* so that you answer every question. The third most important instruction is to *answer every question*. Guess if you have to but include something for each question. Remember that you will receive no credit for a blank and will probably receive some credit if you write something in answer to an essay question. If you guess a letter – say "B" for a multiple-choice question – you may have guessed right. If you leave a blank as an answer to a multiple-choice question, the examiners may respect your feelings but it will not add a point to your score. Some exams may penalize you for wrong answers, so in such cases *only*, you may not want to guess unless you have some basis for your answer.

7) Suggestions
    a. Objective-type questions
        1. Examine the question booklet for proper sequence of pages and questions
        2. Read all instructions carefully
        3. Skip any question which seems too difficult; return to it after all other questions have been answered
        4. Apportion your time properly; do not spend too much time on any single question or group of questions

5. Note and underline key words – *all, most, fewest, least, best, worst, same, opposite,* etc.
6. Pay particular attention to negatives
7. Note unusual option, e.g., unduly long, short, complex, different or similar in content to the body of the question
8. Observe the use of "hedging" words – *probably, may, most likely,* etc.
9. Make sure that your answer is put next to the same number as the question
10. Do not second-guess unless you have good reason to believe the second answer is definitely more correct
11. Cross out original answer if you decide another answer is more accurate; do not erase until you are ready to hand your paper in
12. Answer all questions; guess unless instructed otherwise
13. Leave time for review

  b. Essay questions
1. Read each question carefully
2. Determine exactly what is wanted. Underline key words or phrases.
3. Decide on outline or paragraph answer
4. Include many different points and elements unless asked to develop any one or two points or elements
5. Show impartiality by giving pros and cons unless directed to select one side only
6. Make and write down any assumptions you find necessary to answer the questions
7. Watch your English, grammar, punctuation and choice of words
8. Time your answers; don't crowd material

8) Answering the essay question

Most essay questions can be answered by framing the specific response around several key words or ideas. Here are a few such key words or ideas:

M's: manpower, materials, methods, money, management
P's: purpose, program, policy, plan, procedure, practice, problems, pitfalls, personnel, public relations

  a. Six basic steps in handling problems:
1. Preliminary plan and background development
2. Collect information, data and facts
3. Analyze and interpret information, data and facts
4. Analyze and develop solutions as well as make recommendations
5. Prepare report and sell recommendations
6. Install recommendations and follow up effectiveness

  b. Pitfalls to avoid
1. *Taking things for granted* – A statement of the situation does not necessarily imply that each of the elements is necessarily true; for example, a complaint may be invalid and biased so that all that can be taken for granted is that a complaint has been registered

2. *Considering only one side of a situation* – Wherever possible, indicate several alternatives and then point out the reasons you selected the best one
3. *Failing to indicate follow up* – Whenever your answer indicates action on your part, make certain that you will take proper follow-up action to see how successful your recommendations, procedures or actions turn out to be
4. *Taking too long in answering any single question* – Remember to time your answers properly

IX. AFTER THE TEST

Scoring procedures differ in detail among civil service jurisdictions although the general principles are the same. Whether the papers are hand-scored or graded by machine we have described, they are nearly always graded by number. That is, the person who marks the paper knows only the number – never the name – of the applicant. Not until all the papers have been graded will they be matched with names. If other tests, such as training and experience or oral interview ratings have been given, scores will be combined. Different parts of the examination usually have different weights. For example, the written test might count 60 percent of the final grade, and a rating of training and experience 40 percent. In many jurisdictions, veterans will have a certain number of points added to their grades.

After the final grade has been determined, the names are placed in grade order and an eligible list is established. There are various methods for resolving ties between those who get the same final grade – probably the most common is to place first the name of the person whose application was received first. Job offers are made from the eligible list in the order the names appear on it. You will be notified of your grade and your rank as soon as all these computations have been made. This will be done as rapidly as possible.

People who are found to meet the requirements in the announcement are called "eligibles." Their names are put on a list of eligible candidates. An eligible's chances of getting a job depend on how high he stands on this list and how fast agencies are filling jobs from the list.

When a job is to be filled from a list of eligibles, the agency asks for the names of people on the list of eligibles for that job. When the civil service commission receives this request, it sends to the agency the names of the three people highest on this list. Or, if the job to be filled has specialized requirements, the office sends the agency the names of the top three persons who meet these requirements from the general list.

The appointing officer makes a choice from among the three people whose names were sent to him. If the selected person accepts the appointment, the names of the others are put back on the list to be considered for future openings.

That is the rule in hiring from all kinds of eligible lists, whether they are for typist, carpenter, chemist, or something else. For every vacancy, the appointing officer has his choice of any one of the top three eligibles on the list. This explains why the person whose name is on top of the list sometimes does not get an appointment when some of the persons lower on the list do. If the appointing officer chooses the second or third eligible, the No. 1 eligible does not get a job at once, but stays on the list until he is appointed or the list is terminated.

X. HOW TO PASS THE INTERVIEW TEST

The examination for which you applied requires an oral interview test. You have already taken the written test and you are now being called for the interview test – the final part of the formal examination.

You may think that it is not possible to prepare for an interview test and that there are no procedures to follow during an interview. Our purpose is to point out some things you can do in advance that will help you and some good rules to follow and pitfalls to avoid while you are being interviewed.

What is an interview supposed to test?

The written examination is designed to test the technical knowledge and competence of the candidate; the oral is designed to evaluate intangible qualities, not readily measured otherwise, and to establish a list showing the relative fitness of each candidate – as measured against his competitors – for the position sought. Scoring is not on the basis of "right" and "wrong," but on a sliding scale of values ranging from "not passable" to "outstanding." As a matter of fact, it is possible to achieve a relatively low score without a single "incorrect" answer because of evident weakness in the qualities being measured.

Occasionally, an examination may consist entirely of an oral test – either an individual or a group oral. In such cases, information is sought concerning the technical knowledges and abilities of the candidate, since there has been no written examination for this purpose. More commonly, however, an oral test is used to supplement a written examination.

Who conducts interviews?

The composition of oral boards varies among different jurisdictions. In nearly all, a representative of the personnel department serves as chairman. One of the members of the board may be a representative of the department in which the candidate would work. In some cases, "outside experts" are used, and, frequently, a businessman or some other representative of the general public is asked to serve. Labor and management or other special groups may be represented. The aim is to secure the services of experts in the appropriate field.

However the board is composed, it is a good idea (and not at all improper or unethical) to ascertain in advance of the interview who the members are and what groups they represent. When you are introduced to them, you will have some idea of their backgrounds and interests, and at least you will not stutter and stammer over their names.

What should be done before the interview?

While knowledge about the board members is useful and takes some of the surprise element out of the interview, there is other preparation which is more substantive. It *is* possible to prepare for an oral interview – in several ways:

1) Keep a copy of your application and review it carefully before the interview

This may be the only document before the oral board, and the starting point of the interview. Know what education and experience you have listed there, and the sequence and dates of all of it. Sometimes the board will ask you to review the highlights of your experience for them; you should not have to hem and haw doing it.

2) Study the class specification and the examination announcement

Usually, the oral board has one or both of these to guide them. The qualities, characteristics or knowledges required by the position sought are stated in these documents. They offer valuable clues as to the nature of the oral interview. For example, if the job involves supervisory responsibilities, the announcement will usually indicate that knowledge of modern supervisory methods and the qualifications of the candidate as a supervisor will be tested. If so, you can expect such questions, frequently in the form of a hypothetical situation which you are expected to solve. NEVER go into an oral without knowledge of the duties and responsibilities of the job you seek.

3) Think through each qualification required

Try to visualize the kind of questions you would ask if you were a board member. How well could you answer them? Try especially to appraise your own knowledge and background in each area, *measured against the job sought*, and identify any areas in which you are weak. Be critical and realistic – do not flatter yourself.

4) Do some general reading in areas in which you feel you may be weak

For example, if the job involves supervision and your past experience has NOT, some general reading in supervisory methods and practices, particularly in the field of human relations, might be useful. Do NOT study agency procedures or detailed manuals. The oral board will be testing your understanding and capacity, not your memory.

5) Get a good night's sleep and watch your general health and mental attitude

You will want a clear head at the interview. Take care of a cold or any other minor ailment, and of course, no hangovers.

What should be done on the day of the interview?

Now comes the day of the interview itself. Give yourself plenty of time to get there. Plan to arrive somewhat ahead of the scheduled time, particularly if your appointment is in the fore part of the day. If a previous candidate fails to appear, the board might be ready for you a bit early. By early afternoon an oral board is almost invariably behind schedule if there are many candidates, and you may have to wait. Take along a book or magazine to read, or your application to review, but leave any extraneous material in the waiting room when you go in for your interview. In any event, relax and compose yourself.

The matter of dress is important. The board is forming impressions about you – from your experience, your manners, your attitude, and your appearance. Give your personal appearance careful attention. Dress your best, but not your flashiest. Choose conservative, appropriate clothing, and be sure it is immaculate. This is a business interview, and your appearance should indicate that you regard it as such. Besides, being well groomed and properly dressed will help boost your confidence.

Sooner or later, someone will call your name and escort you into the interview room. *This is it.* From here on you are on your own. It is too late for any more preparation. But remember, you asked for this opportunity to prove your fitness, and you are here because your request was granted.

What happens when you go in?

The usual sequence of events will be as follows: The clerk (who is often the board stenographer) will introduce you to the chairman of the oral board, who will introduce you to the other members of the board. Acknowledge the introductions before you sit down. Do not be surprised if you find a microphone facing you or a stenotypist sitting by. Oral interviews are usually recorded in the event of an appeal or other review.

Usually the chairman of the board will open the interview by reviewing the highlights of your education and work experience from your application – primarily for the benefit of the other members of the board, as well as to get the material into the record. Do not interrupt or comment unless there is an error or significant misinterpretation; if that is the case, do not hesitate. But do not quibble about insignificant matters. Also, he will usually ask you some question about your education, experience or your present job – partly to get you to start talking and to establish the interviewing "rapport." He may start the actual questioning, or turn it over to one of the other members. Frequently, each member undertakes the questioning on a particular area, one in which he is perhaps most competent, so you can expect each member to participate in the examination. Because time is limited, you may also expect some rather abrupt switches in the direction the questioning takes, so do not be upset by it. Normally, a board member will not pursue a single line of questioning unless he discovers a particular strength or weakness.

After each member has participated, the chairman will usually ask whether any member has any further questions, then will ask you if you have anything you wish to add. Unless you are expecting this question, it may floor you. Worse, it may start you off on an extended, extemporaneous speech. The board is not usually seeking more information. The question is principally to offer you a last opportunity to present further qualifications or to indicate that you have nothing to add. So, if you feel that a significant qualification or characteristic has been overlooked, it is proper to point it out in a sentence or so. Do not compliment the board on the thoroughness of their examination – they have been sketchy, and you know it. If you wish, merely say, "No thank you, I have nothing further to add." This is a point where you can "talk yourself out" of a good impression or fail to present an important bit of information. Remember, *you close the interview yourself*.

The chairman will then say, "That is all, Mr. _____, thank you." Do not be startled; the interview is over, and quicker than you think. Thank him, gather your belongings and take your leave. Save your sigh of relief for the other side of the door.

How to put your best foot forward

Throughout this entire process, you may feel that the board individually and collectively is trying to pierce your defenses, seek out your hidden weaknesses and embarrass and confuse you. Actually, this is not true. They are obliged to make an appraisal of your qualifications for the job you are seeking, and they want to see you in your best light. Remember, they must interview all candidates and a non-cooperative candidate may become a failure in spite of their best efforts to bring out his qualifications. Here are 15 suggestions that will help you:

1) **Be natural – Keep your attitude confident, not cocky**

If you are not confident that you can do the job, do not expect the board to be. Do not apologize for your weaknesses, try to bring out your strong points. The board is interested in a positive, not negative, presentation. Cockiness will antagonize any board member and make him wonder if you are covering up a weakness by a false show of strength.

2) **Get comfortable, but don't lounge or sprawl**

Sit erectly but not stiffly. A careless posture may lead the board to conclude that you are careless in other things, or at least that you are not impressed by the importance of the occasion. Either conclusion is natural, even if incorrect. Do not fuss with your clothing, a pencil or an ashtray. Your hands may occasionally be useful to emphasize a point; do not let them become a point of distraction.

3) **Do not wisecrack or make small talk**

This is a serious situation, and your attitude should show that you consider it as such. Further, the time of the board is limited – they do not want to waste it, and neither should you.

4) Do not exaggerate your experience or abilities

In the first place, from information in the application or other interviews and sources, the board may know more about you than you think. Secondly, you probably will not get away with it. An experienced board is rather adept at spotting such a situation, so do not take the chance.

5) If you know a board member, do not make a point of it, yet do not hide it

Certainly you are not fooling him, and probably not the other members of the board. Do not try to take advantage of your acquaintanceship – it will probably do you little good.

6) Do not dominate the interview

Let the board do that. They will give you the clues – do not assume that you have to do all the talking. Realize that the board has a number of questions to ask you, and do not try to take up all the interview time by showing off your extensive knowledge of the answer to the first one.

7) Be attentive

You only have 20 minutes or so, and you should keep your attention at its sharpest throughout. When a member is addressing a problem or question to you, give him your undivided attention. Address your reply principally to him, but do not exclude the other board members.

8) Do not interrupt

A board member may be stating a problem for you to analyze. He will ask you a question when the time comes. Let him state the problem, and wait for the question.

9) Make sure you understand the question

Do not try to answer until you are sure what the question is. If it is not clear, restate it in your own words or ask the board member to clarify it for you. However, do not haggle about minor elements.

10) Reply promptly but not hastily

A common entry on oral board rating sheets is "candidate responded readily," or "candidate hesitated in replies." Respond as promptly and quickly as you can, but do not jump to a hasty, ill-considered answer.

11) Do not be peremptory in your answers

A brief answer is proper – but do not fire your answer back. That is a losing game from your point of view. The board member can probably ask questions much faster than you can answer them.

12) Do not try to create the answer you think the board member wants

He is interested in what kind of mind you have and how it works – not in playing games. Furthermore, he can usually spot this practice and will actually grade you down on it.

13) Do not switch sides in your reply merely to agree with a board member

Frequently, a member will take a contrary position merely to draw you out and to see if you are willing and able to defend your point of view. Do not start a debate, yet do not surrender a good position. If a position is worth taking, it is worth defending.

14) Do not be afraid to admit an error in judgment if you are shown to be wrong

The board knows that you are forced to reply without any opportunity for careful consideration. Your answer may be demonstrably wrong. If so, admit it and get on with the interview.

15) Do not dwell at length on your present job

The opening question may relate to your present assignment. Answer the question but do not go into an extended discussion. You are being examined for a *new* job, not your present one. As a matter of fact, try to phrase ALL your answers in terms of the job for which you are being examined.

Basis of Rating

Probably you will forget most of these "do's" and "don'ts" when you walk into the oral interview room. Even remembering them all will not ensure you a passing grade. Perhaps you did not have the qualifications in the first place. But remembering them will help you to put your best foot forward, without treading on the toes of the board members.

Rumor and popular opinion to the contrary notwithstanding, an oral board wants you to make the best appearance possible. They know you are under pressure – but they also want to see how you respond to it as a guide to what your reaction would be under the pressures of the job you seek. They will be influenced by the degree of poise you display, the personal traits you show and the manner in which you respond.

ABOUT THIS BOOK

This book contains tests divided into Examination Sections. Go through each test, answering every question in the margin. We have also attached a sample answer sheet at the back of the book that can be removed and used. At the end of each test look at the answer key and check your answers. On the ones you got wrong, look at the right answer choice and learn. Do not fill in the answers first. Do not memorize the questions and answers, but understand the answer and principles involved. On your test, the questions will likely be different from the samples. Questions are changed and new ones added. If you understand these past questions you should have success with any changes that arise. Tests may consist of several types of questions. We have additional books on each subject should more study be advisable or necessary for you. Finally, the more you study, the better prepared you will be. This book is intended to be the last thing you study before you walk into the examination room. Prior study of relevant texts is also recommended. NLC publishes some of these in our Fundamental Series. Knowledge and good sense are important factors in passing your exam. Good luck also helps. So now study this Passbook, absorb the material contained within and take that knowledge into the examination. Then do your best to pass that exam.

EXAMINATION SECTION

EXAMINATION SECTION
TEST 1

DIRECTIONS: Each question or incomplete statement is followed by several suggested answers or completions. Select the one that *BEST* answers the question or completes the statement. *PRINT THE LETTER OF THE CORRECT ANSWER IN THE SPACE AT THE RIGHT.*

1. Which one of the following is *most likely* to be the *BEST* place for a detective/investigator to interview a suspect in an important criminal case? In the

   A. suspect's home, in the presence of his family
   B. detective's/investigator's office with other suspects present
   C. suspect's home with the detective/investigator and the suspect as the only persons present
   D. detective's/investigator's office with no other persons present

2. *HOW* should *TWO* witnesses to the same event be interviewed?

   A. *Together; CHIEFLY* so that discrepancies in statements can be easily corrected
   B. *Together; CHIEFLY* so that the recollection of each can be refreshed by others
   C. *Separately; CHIEFLY* so that independent statements are obtained
   D. *Separately; CHIEFLY* because some people will not speak in the presence of others

3. You, a detective/investigator, are the first person to respond to the scene of a violent crime. *Which one* of the following actions would be the *LEAST* appropriate for you to try to take?

   A. Keep the person who notified the police of the crime at the scene so that person can be interviewed concerning the details related to the crime
   B. Physically isolate the area by excluding all unauthorized persons from the crime scene
   C. Arrange the possible evidence in such a way that the police photographer will be able to record it immediately
   D. Determine the perpetrator by direct inquiry or observation if possible

4. *Which one* of the following is the *LEAST* appropriate interrogation technique for a detective/investigator to use when questioning a suspect?

   A. Select a setting that will avoid outside interference
   B. Place recording devices where they will not distract the suspect
   C. Seat the suspect in a plain chair
   D. Continue the interrogation until the suspect shows signs of physical distress

5. A detective/investigator is the first person to arrive at the scene of a violent crime where one person is dead and another wounded. The *FIRST* thing that the detective/investigator should do is

   A. search for the perpetrator
   B. safeguard the crime scene
   C. aid the wounded person
   D. make a written record of the facts

6. Which one of the following is the MOST appropriate procedure for a team of detectives/ investigators to use when conducting a surveillance from a parked vehicle?

    A. Maintain the surveillance at the same location in the same vehicle for as long as necessary to obtain the desired evidence
    B. Keep the motor going so that a pursuit can be maintained in the event that the suspect leaves the site of the surveillance
    C. Keep the driver's seat vacant and make observations from the front passenger seat and the rear seat of the vehicle
    D. Park in an isolated position rather than between parked cars so that the observers' view of the scene is not blocked in any fashion

7. Which one of the following BEST describes the desirability of having persons witness a confession?

    A. Desirable; CHIEFLY because the witnesses can later testify that the detective/ investigator did not employ duress in the form of threats or promises when eliciting the confession
    B. Undesirable; CHIEFLY because the defendant may object strongly to the presence of witnesses when he dictates his confession
    C. Desirable; CHIEFLY because the witnesses may be able to suggest additional information required for the confession to stand up in court
    D. Undesirable; CHIEFLY because the defendant is less likely to implicate others if he knows that there are witnesses to the fact that he has confessed

8. Assume that you are a detective/investigator assigned to locate an important witness. You have reason to believe that a body in an advanced stage of decomposition that has just been fished out of the river may be that witness. Which one of the following possible sources of identification should be MOST accurate in determining the body's identity?

    A. Color of the hair on the head
    B. Facial features
    C. Fingerprints
    D. Dental work

9. A detective/investigator presents a suspect with a typed statement for the suspect's signature. He deliberately includes several obvious errors. He then instructs the suspect to read the statement carefully, to be sure that it is accurate and correct and initial any errors.
    Which one of the following BEST describes the desirability of this practice?

    A. Desirable; if the suspect fails to initial the obvious errors, the detective/investigator will know that the suspect was lying when giving the original statement
    B. Undesirable; the suspect will leave with a poor impression of the performance and ability of detectives/ investigators in that District Attorney's office
    C. Desirable; this method will enable the detective/investigator to prove that the suspect read and understood the statement before initialing it
    D. Undesirable; the statement as presented could become part of the official records of the case

10. An investigator is at the scene of a crime which occurred shortly before his arrival. The sales clerk who witnessed the crime starts telling the investigator, in a confused and excited manner, what happened.
    The investigator should INITIALLY

A. ask the clerk to write an account of what had happened
B. let the clerk tell his story without interruption
C. try to confine the clerk to answering relevent questions
D. wait until the clerk calms down before questioning him

11. *Which one* of the following is the *LEAST* appropriate technique for a team of detectives/investigators to use when conducting a surveillance of a suspect in a motor vehicle?

    A. Conduct the surveillance in a van which is large enough to conceal cameras and recording devices
    B. Travel at a rate of speed consistent with vehicular traffic in the surveillance area
    C. Obey all traffic laws unless it is absolutely necessary to break one in order to maintain contact with the suspect
    D. Avoid sudden movements of the surveillance vehicle which might attract the attention of the suspect you are following

12. A detective/investigator may appropriately conduct a surveillance for each of the following reasons *EXCEPT* to

    A. locate a suspect
    B. check on informants
    C. search for evidence
    D. protect a witness or a victim

13. *Which one* of the following objects would be *MOST* appropriate for a detective/investigator to carry when working undercover?

    A. Pictures of the detective's/investigator's family
    B. Membership cards in organizations of a non-police nature to which the detective/investigator belongs
    C. Identification stating that he is an employee of the District Attorney's Office
    D. Fictitious identification

14. A detective/investigator is maintaining a one-person surveillance of a suspect. The suspect boards a public bus.
    Which one of the following would be the *MOST* appropriate action for the detective/investigator to take in this situation?

    A. Board the same bus as the suspect at the same stop
    B. Attempt to board the same bus as the suspect but at a later stop
    C. Attempt to follow the bus in another vehicle
    D. Maintain visual contact with the bus while using a police phone to call for assistance

15. *Which one* of the following actions taken by a detective/investigator who is photographing the scene of a crime after the police department has finished the initial crime scene search is *LEAST* correct? The detective/investigator

    A. takes several photographs of the scene from different angles
    B. only photographs physical evidence in front of a dark screen so that it can be isolated from the background
    C. all areas contiguous to the scene of the crime
    D. takes a posed picture designed to simulate an actual description provided by a witness

16. A detective/investigator is tailing a subject. He observes the subject walk down a street, drop a piece of paper on the lid of a garbage can in front of a tenement building, and continue walking around the corner of the block.
    Which one of the following is the *MOST* appropriate action for the detective/investigator to take if he is working alone?

    A. Pick up the paper, examine it, and replace it on the lid of the garbage can
    B. Pick up the paper, put it in a pocket, and continue following the suspect
    C. Pick up the paper, copy its contents, and replace it inside the garbage can
    D. Place the paper inside the garbage can without examining its contents

17. Following are three techniques that may or may not be appropriate to determine the credibility of a witness:
    I. Asking the witness questions whose answers are not already known by the investigator
    II. Looking for nervousness, evasiveness, or embarrassment at certain questions
    III. Noting any unwarranted indignation or excessive protests to questions posed by the investigator

    Which one of the following *BEST* classifies the above techniques?

    A. I and II are generally appropriate but III is not
    B. I and III are generally appropriate but II is not
    C. II and III are generally appropriate but I is not
    D. I, II, and III are all generally appropriate

18. Assume that as a detective/investigator you receive an anonymous call at the office from an irate citizen complaining of a group of teenagers creating a disturbance in the next apartment. The caller tells you that he is certain that a "pot party" is in progress and demands that you take some action. You record the exact address of the alleged "pot party," but, before you can say anything, the caller hangs up.
    Which one of the following is the *MOST* appropriate course of action to take in this situation?

    A. Call in the information to the local police precinct, emphasizing that it came from an anonymous phone call
    B. Ignore the call since it came from an anonymous source
    C. Make preparations to raid the party quickly before the teenagers have a chance to disperse
    D. Attempt to attend the party to gather additional information before determining whether to make a narcotics arrest

19. As a detective/investigator you are assigned to conduct a line-up in a rape case where there are two witnesses due to appear to make identifications.
    Which one of the following would be the *MOST* appropriate action to take in this situation?

    A. Keep the witnesses separated before and during the line-up
    B. Suggest that the witnesses meet before the line-up to discuss the case and permit them to view the lineup together

C. Keep the witnesses separated before the line-up but request that they meet together at the line-up to agree on an identification
D. Suggest that the witnesses meet before the line-up to discuss the case but let only one witness view the line-up at a time

20. Which one of the following is the LEAST appropriate action to take when working undercover?   20._____

    A. Avoid drinking alcoholic beverages if at all possible
    B. Always claim to be a person with a lot of influence
    C. Provide persons in the background city who can vouch for the undercover identity
    D. Spend only as much money as the role requires

KEY (CORRECT ANSWERS)

1.	D	11.	A
2.	C	12.	C
3.	C	13.	D
4.	D	14.	A
5.	C	15.	B
6.	C	16.	A
7.	A	17.	C
8.	D	18.	A
9.	C	19.	A
10.	B	20.	B

TEST 2

DIRECTIONS: Each question or incomplete statement is followed by several suggested answers or completions. Select the one that *BEST* answers the question or completes the statement. *PRINT THE LETTER OF THE CORRECT ANSWER IN THE SPACE AT THE RIGHT.*

Questions 1-6.

DIRECTIONS: Answer Questions 1 through 6 based *SOLELY* on the information contained in the following passage.

On February 7, the defendant entered a liquor store in Prince County and, after asking the owner for change to use the pay phone across the street, drew a gun and demanded all the money in the cash register. After being given all the cash, the defendant left the store.

When the police arrived months later, the owner of the store described the robber to a detective and accompanied the detective to the police station where he subsequently identified photos of the defendant as the woman who held him up. The store owner indicated, however, he would have to see the defendant in person to be certain of a positive identification.

Nine weeks later, the defendant was being held in Prince County on charges unrelated to the liquor store holdup. The defendant was not under arrest at that time although a photo identification had been made. The defendant was placed in a line-up with four stand-ins and, because of a request for legal representation, a Legal Aid lawyer was present and assigned to represent the defendant. The owner identified the defendant as the robber and the defendant's attorney left. After the Legal Aid lawyer left, a police officer asked the detective if he wished to speak to the defendant. Despite his admitted knowledge that the defendant was now represented by counsel on the robbery charge, the detective indicated he would like to speak to the defendant. The detective had not told the lawyer he was going to speak to his client nor had he made any effort to contact the lawyer before talking to the defendant. At the police officer's request, the defendant signed an undescribed waiver (which the detective testified he had never seen) and agreed to talk to the detective. The defendant was then brought into an interview room.

The defendant was advised of her rights and indicated an understanding of them. The detective asked the defendant, "Do you wish to contact an attorney?" The defendant said, "No." The detective then asked, "Having these rights in mind, do you wish to talk to me now without a lawyer?" The defendant said, "Yes." The defendant asked the detective if the owner of the liquor store had identified her as the perpetrator and, when informed the owner had, expressed a desire to "clear up everything" and, in effect, confessed to the robbery.

1. The positive identification of the defendant as the perpetrator of the liquor store holdup was made by the

   A. cashier at the store
   B. owner of the store
   C. police officer conducting the line-up
   D. detective/investigator

1.____

2. Which of the following can *NOT* be deduced from the above passage? The defendant

   A. had been wanted for committing a robbery two weeks earlier when the liquor store was robbed
   B. possessed a gun at the time of the robbery

2.____

C. left the liquor store with all of the cash that had been in the cash register at the time of the robbery
D. was a woman

3. Which one of the following statements MOST accurately reflects the defendant's status at the time of the lineup? The

   A. defendant was not then represented by counsel
   B. witness had positively identified the defendant from a photograph
   C. detective had spoken to the defendant concerning the liquor store holdup
   D. defendant had not yet been arrested for committing the liquor store holdup

4. Of the following, it is MOST accurate to conclude that the defendant learned of the witness' identification of the defendant from the

   A. witness to the holdup
   B. defense attorney present at the line-up
   C. detective investigating the holdup
   D. police officer conducting the line-up

5. Based *solely* on the above passage it is MOST appropriate to conclude that the defendant confessed to the holdup because the

   A. defendant was already being held on a more serious charge at the time the confession to the crime was made
   B. detective's astute questioning produced a confession that the defendant had not wished to make
   C. defendant knew that the Legal Aid lawyer would advise a plea of guilty
   D. defendant knew that the witness had made a positive identification at the line-up

6. Which one of the following statements is MOST accurate concerning the role of the Legal Aid lawyer in this case? He

   A. was present at the line-up because the defendant had requested legal counsel
   B. advised the defendant to plead guilty to a holdup charge
   C. declined to represent the defendant after the defendant confessed to the crime
   D. was not present at the time of questioning because the defendant had told him that his presence was not desired at that time

7. Which one of the following is the MOST appropriate procedure to follow when communicating with an informant?

   A. Schedule as many meetings as possible at the detective's/investigator's office
   B. Address the informant by name when speaking to him on the telephone
   C. When meetings with the informant are necessary, vary the circumstances under which they are held
   D. When writing to the informant, use official letterhead stationery of the District Attorney's office

8. Following are two statements about Inducing witnesses to talk that may or may not be appropriate:
   I. Generally, neutral topics of conversation should be used to get a reticent witness to begin talking.
   II. If the witness seems reluctant to begin talking, he should be made to feel that he "owes" it to himself and others to testify.

   Which one of the following BEST classifies the above statements into those which are generally valid and those which are not?

   A. I is generally appropriate but II is not
   B. II is generally appropriate but I is not
   C. I and II are NOT generally appropriate
   D. I and II are generally appropriate

9. A detective/investigator has been assigned to the surveillance of a brokerage company employee suspected of the unauthorized removal of negotiable bonds from his company's offices. It is important that the subject not become aware that he is the object of a surveillance because the District Attorney's office is trying to discover who is receiving the bonds after they leave the brokerage house.
   Which one of the following is the MOST appropriate type of surveillance to use in this situation?

   A. Loose   B. Rough   C. Close   D. Progressive

10. After testifying in a case, a detective/investigator overhears the two defense lawyers criticizing one of the procedures in the District Attorney's office. The criticism appears to warrant consideration.
    Which one of the following is the MOST appropriate action for the detective/investigator to take in this situation?

    A. Tell the lawyers that he agrees with their criticism
    B. Ask the lawyers for further information to relay to his supervisor
    C. Defend the procedure in the District Attorney's office
    D. Ignore the lawyers' conversation since it neither includes him nor concerns him

11. Assume that you are a detective/investigator and that you and your partner have just arrested a suspect. Your partner is to drive the car.
    Which one of the following is the BEST procedure for you to follow in transporting the prisoner safely? Have the prisoner sit

    A. in the left rear seat of the car with his hands cuffed behind him while you sit next to the prisoner in the rear seat
    B. alone in the rear seat of the car with his hands cuffed in front of him while you sit in the front seat facing the prisoner
    C. in the left rear seat of the car with his hands cuffed in front of him while you sit next to the prisoner in the rear seat
    D. in the right front seat of the car with his hands cuffed behind him while you sit in the right rear seat

12. Assume that you are a detective/investigator working with a partner and that you and your partner wish to arrest the driver and sole occupant of a moving vehicle that you have been following in your car. Your partner has signaled the driver of the car to pull over and the driver has stopped his car.
Which one of the following is the MOST appropriate procedure to follow in effecting the arrest?

    A. Park to the rear of the suspect's vehicle. Both detectives/investigators approach the suspect's vehicle cautiously.
    B. Park in front of the suspect's vehicle. Both detectives/investigators approach the suspect's vehicle cautiously.
    C. Park to the rear of the suspect's vehicle. One detective/investigator approaches the suspect's vehicle cautiously while the other detective/investigator "covers" him from behind the right rear corner of the suspect's vehicle.
    D. Park directly alongside the suspect's vehicle. Both detectives/investigators get out of their vehicle and approach the suspect's vehicle cautiously.

13. An elderly man approaches you at the scene of a suspected arson you are investigating and tells you that he wants to confess to the arson.
Which one of the following is the BEST course of action for you, as a detective/investigator, to take in this situation?

    A. *Advise* him of his constitutional rights, *take* a written statement, and then *close* the case
    B. *Disregard* him and *continue* your investigation
    C. *Take* a sworn statement from him after advising him of his rights, then *require* him to take a polygraph test to verify the contents of his confession
    D. *Advise* him of his constitutional rights, *take* a written statement from him, and then *continue* to search for evidence that will support or disprove his statement

14. Which one of the following is the LEAST appropriate situation in which to use a phosphorescent ultra-violet medium? A

    A. retail store employee is suspected of pilfering store merchandise from the stockroom
    B. government official is suspected of accepting jewelry and cash bribes in exchange for political favors
    C. bookkeeper for a small company is suspected of committing fraud by making false entries in the company's books
    D. repair service is suspected of charging customers for new parts without actually replacing the old parts when making repairs at the customer's home

15. A detective/investigator is participating as a member of a team including City Police Department detectives and Federal narcotics agents. The team is about to raid a building for the purpose of executing a search warrant and making multiple arrests. Before entering the building, the detective/investigator pins his badge to his outer garment.
Which one of the following BEST describes the desirability of this action?

    A. *Desirable; CHIEFLY* because it will enable other members of the team to know that the detective/investigator is a law enforcement officer
    B. *Undesirable; CHIEFLY* because it will identify the detective/investigator to the suspects as being a law-enforcement officer

C. *Desirable; CHIEFLY* because it will eliminate the need for the detective/investigator to announce that he is a law enforcement officer each time he makes an arrest
D. *Undesirable; CHIEFLY* because it may serve as a visible target if the building is dark and any light reflects off it

16. In selecting the role to assume while working undercover, the detective/investigator should do each of the following EXCEPT:

    A. *Select* a personality which will make the detective/ investigator conspicuous
    B. *Select* shoes and clothing that fit the role to be assumed by the detective/investigator
    C. *Learn* the personal habits of persons in the role selected and adhere to them
    D. *Select* a background city which is familiar to the detective/investigator but not to the persons he will be investigating

17. Which one of the following is the *SAFEST* place for a detective/investigator to attempt to make an arrest? A

    A. quiet intersection
    B. crowded, narrow street
    C. quiet street with few people on it
    D. restaurant with many people in it

18. Which one of the following is *LEAST* likely to indicate that a fire is of suspicious origin?

    A. The pattern of the fire suggests more than one place of origin.
    B. There is an unexplained deviation from a fire pattern common to the structural characteristics of the building.
    C. There was a rapid buildup of a room fire in a location where highly combustible materials were stored.
    D. Several witnesses independently indicated that they had seen someone start the fire.

19. A detective/investigator takes a photograph of a lineup just before it is conducted. He includes all of the persons in the line-up in the same photograph.
    Which one of the following *BEST* describes the desirability of this procedure?

    A. *Desirable; CHIEFLY* because this photograph is required as evidence
    B. *Undesirable; CHIEFLY* because taking such a photograph is a violation of the suspect's rights
    C. *Desirable; CHIEFLY* because it will provide a visual record of the stand-ins who participated so that they won't be used too frequently
    D. *Undesirable; CHIEFLY* because only the suspect should appear in the photo

20. While enroute in your automobile to locate an important eye witness to a homicide, you see a uniformed police officer crouched behind a trash can with his revolver drawn, firing into a doorway.
    Which one of the following would be the *MOST* appropriate action for you to take in this situation?

A. Summon additional police assistance for the officer and continue on your assignment
B. Continue on to your assignment without delaying to summon additional help for the police officer because your case is very important
C. Stop your car, identify yourself, and ask the officer whether he needs help
D. Stop, draw your weapon, and assist the police officer

KEY (CORRECT ANSWERS)

1.	B	11.	A
2.	A	12.	C
3.	D	13.	D
4.	C	14.	C
5.	D	15.	A
6.	A	16.	A
7.	C	17.	C
8.	D	18.	C
9.	A	19.	A
10.	B	20.	C

EXAMINATION SECTION
TEST 1

DIRECTIONS: Each question or incomplete statement is followed by several suggested answers or completions. Select the one that *BEST* answers the question or completes the statement. *PRINT THE LETTER OF THE CORRECT ANSWER TN THE SPACE AT THE RIGHT.*

Questions 1-5.

DIRECTIONS: Answer Questions 1 through 5 based *SOLELY* on the contents of the following graph.

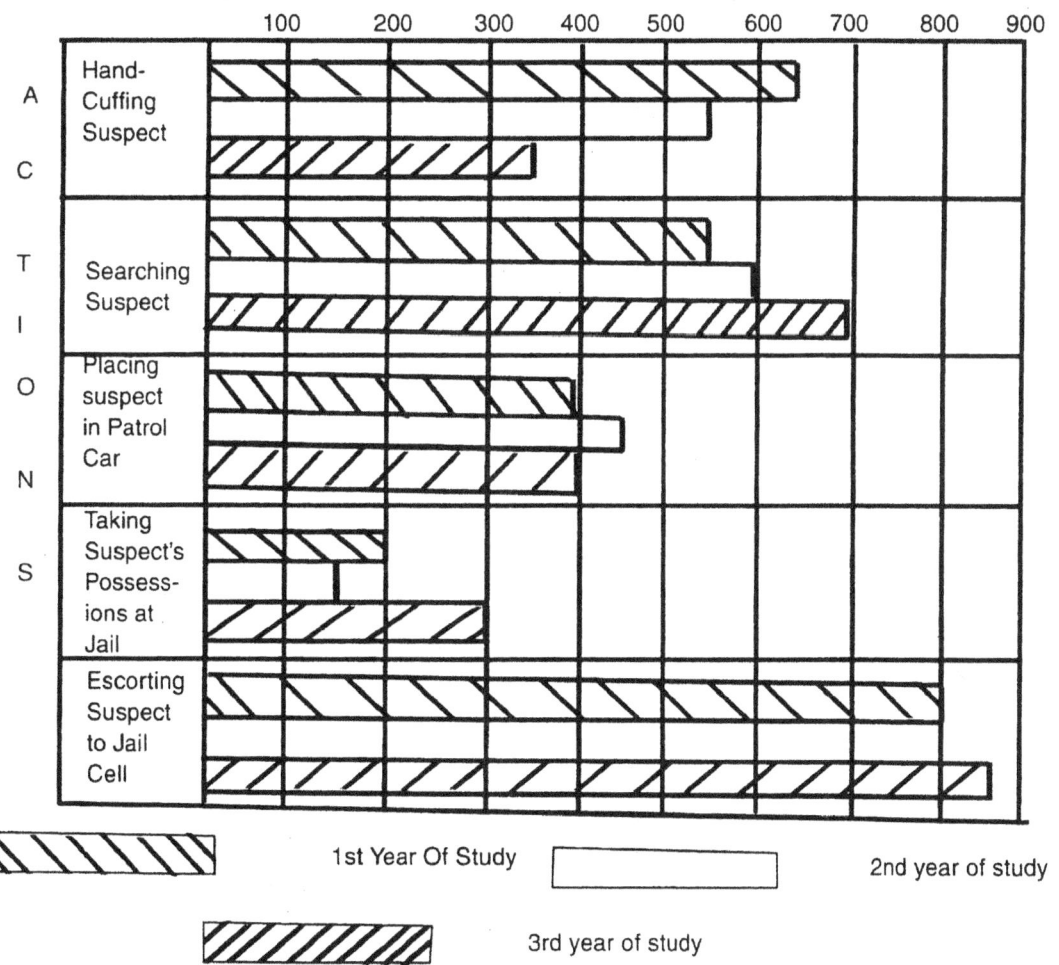

1. Which one of the following MOST closely approximates the number of assaults on Detectives/Investigators for all five actions during the second year of the study?

   A. 1850   B. 2450   C. 2500   D. 5050

2. Which one of the following conditions led to the GREATEST increase in number of assaults on Detectives/Investigators between the 2nd and 3rd years of the study?

   A. Handcuffing the suspect
   B. Searching the suspect
   C. Taking the suspect's possessions at the jail
   D. Escorting the suspect to the jail cell

3. Which one of the following MOST closely approximates the total number of Detective/Investigator injuries attributed to placing the suspect in patrol car for the three years of the study?

   A. 750   B. 1050   C. 1250   D. 1550

4. Which one of the following actions resulted in the GREATEST number of assaults on Detectives/Investigators throughout the three years of the study?

   A. Taking the suspect's possessions at the jail
   B. Handcuffing the suspect
   C. Placing the suspect in the patrol car
   D. Escorting the suspect to the jail cell

5. Compared to the first year, the number of assaults in the third year of the study attributable to all five situations was

   A. 300 more   B. 300 fewer   C. 600 more   D. the same

6. You have just arrested an individual who is charged with armed robbery.
   Which one of the following is the MOST appropriate sequence of action for you to take?

   A. Handcuff the suspect, advise him of his rights, then frisk him
   B. Frisk the suspect, handcuff him, then advise him of his rights
   C. Advise the suspect of his rights, handcuff him, then frisk him
   D. Frisk the suspect, advise him of his rights, then handcuff him

7. A detective/investigator finds some strands of human hair on a chair at the scene of a crime and decides to preserve the hair as physical evidence. The detective/investigator then takes each of the following actions:
   I. Lifts the hair off the chair with forceps.
   II. Wraps the hair loosely in filter paper.
   III. Folds the filter paper containing the hair and puts it in his pocket.
   Which one of the following BEST classifies the above actions?

   A. I and II are correct but III is not
   B. II and III are correct but I is not
   C. I is correct but II and III are not
   D. I, II, and III are all correct

8. Following are three statements which may or may not be valid concerning the maintenance of the chain of custody during and after an investigation:
    I. If the possession of the evidence is unaccountable even for a moment, that evidence can be rendered inadmissible as evidence for that trial of the suspect.
    II. Each person who has had possession of the evidence must be in a position to testify that the evidence did not leave his physical presence during the period for which he had custody of the evidence.
    III. A record must be kept of the time, date, and place of the transfer of evidence every time that transfer occurs.

   Which one of the following BEST classifies the above statements?

   A. I and II are generally valid but III is not
   B. I and III are generally valid but II is not
   C. II and III are generally valid but I is not
   D. I, II, and III are all generally valid

9. Assume that you are a detective/investigator searching the scene of a crime and you come across an object which you believe may be physical evidence of the crime. Which one of the following would be the MOST appropriate action for you to take FIRST?

   A. Pick up the object taking care not to damage it and try to determine whether it is physical evidence of the crime
   B. Make detailed notes to describe the object and the location in which it was found
   C. Photograph the object from several angles, being careful not to touch or otherwise disturb it in any way
   D. Properly mark and identify the evidence and place it in a safe container for transport to the lab for further analysis

10. A detective/investigator finds a document which appears to be physical evidence of a crime he is investigating. In handling the document prior to transferring it to an expert for detailed examination, the detective/investigator should do each of the following EXCEPT

    A. handle the document with wooden or plastic tongs
    B. determine whether a fingerprint processing is required before placing any identifying information on the document itself
    C. take care not to fold the document along any lines not already present
    D. make a tracing of the document to serve as a record while the original is being studied by the expert

11. A detective/investigator finds some hairs at the scene of a crime, collects them for evidence, and then obtains hairs from a suspect to determine whether they are similar. Which one of the following procedures followed by the detective/investigator is CORRECT? Hairs

    A. found on the victim's sweater are removed carefully and placed in a clearly labeled container
    B. found at different locations at the crime scene, believed to be from the same source, are placed together in a single clearly labeled container
    C. found at the crime scene are carefully cleaned and then placed in a clearly labeled container
    D. obtained from the suspect for comparison are pulled out at the root from different locations on the head and body

4 (#1)

12. When a detective/investigator feels that there is a possibility that the prisoner he is transporting might falsely accuse him of assault or other crime against the prisoner, the detective/investigator immediately contacts the dispatcher for a time check and gives the dispatcher the odometer reading of the transport vehicle. When the detective/investigator reaches the destination, the dispatcher is again contacted for a time check and the dispatcher is once again given the odometer reading of the vehicle.
Which one of the following BEST describes the desirability of this procedure?

   A. *Desirable;* it will eliminate any complaints that might otherwise be made by the prisoner
   B. *Undesirable;* it is a wasteful and unnecessary procedure
   C. *Desirable;* it will provide a good defense for any complaints if the shortest route is traveled in the least possible time
   D. *undesirable;* it will indicate the suspicions of the detective/ investigator

12.___

Questions 13-17.

DIRECTIONS: Answer Questions 13 through 17 based *SOLELY* on the contents of the crime scene sketch which follows.

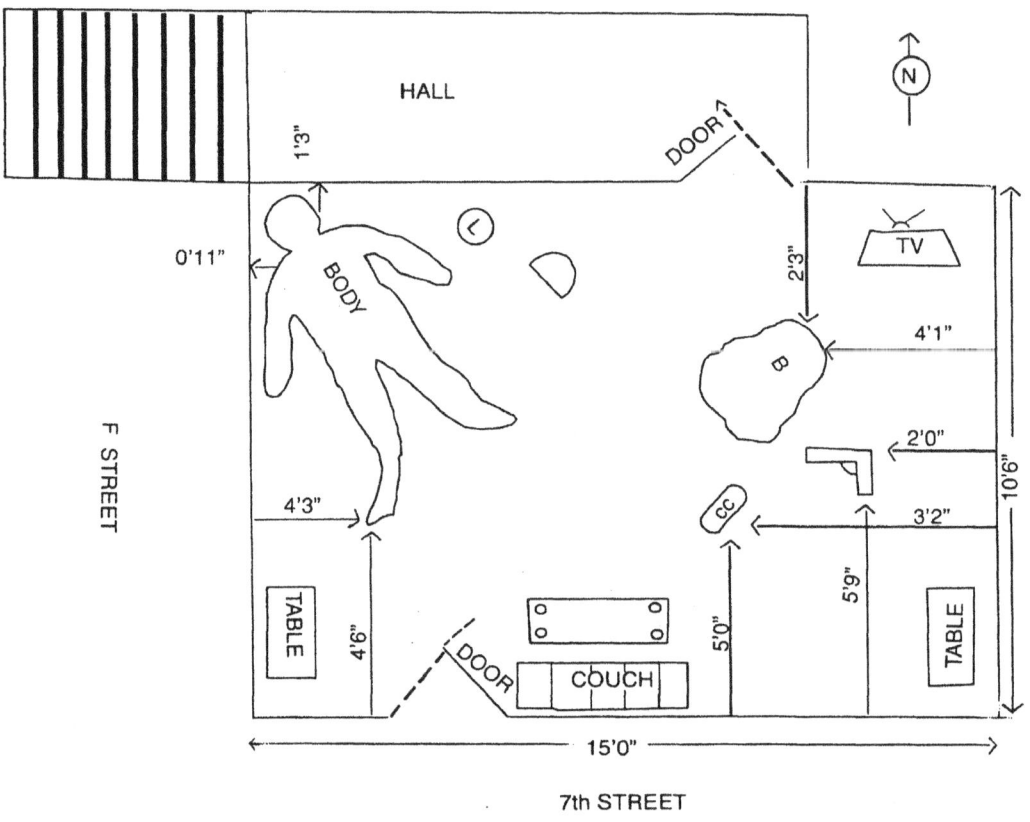

13. Based upon the above sketch, it is MOST accurate to conclude that the body was found   13.____

    A. in the chair
    B. on the couch
    C. on the floor near the lamp
    D. under the coffee table

14. Which one of the following BEST describes the compass location of the body? _____   14.____
    corner of the room.

    A. Northeast   B. Northwest
    C. Southeast   D. Southwest

15. Which one of the following BEST describes the location of the weapon? About   15.____

    A. 5 feet from the 7th Street wall
    B. 13 feet from the F Street wall
    C. 2 feet from the western wall
    D. 4 feet from the eastern wall

16. Which one of the following MOST closely approximates the distance of the body to the   16.____
    nearest wall?

    A. Eleven inches   B. Thirteen inches
    C. Fifteen inches   D. Fifty-one inches

17. Assuming the sketch were drawn to scale, which one of the following would the empty   17.____
    cartridge case be CLOSEST *to*?

    A. Coffee table   B. Chair   C. Body   D. Television

18. Under which one of the following circumstances would a confession be admissible in a   18.____
    court of law? The confession was

    A. made as a spontaneous statement by the accused rather than being obtained through questioning
    B. obtained through questioning during an official investigation after the accused was informed of the nature of the offense he was charged with, that any statement he might give would be used against him in a trial of law, and that a copy of his statement would be given to his attorney
    C. obtained without coercion during an official investigation and while the accused was in custody
    D. obtained during an official investigation after the accused had been informed of his right to remain silent

19. A detective/investigator made a lawful arrest of a suspect in the living room of the suspect's home. He then conducted a search which included the: 19.____
    I. part of the living room in which the prisoner was arrested, which was within his reach at the time the arrest was made
    II. remainder of the living room, including areas which were not within the prisoner's reach at the time of the arrest
    III. prisoner's bedroom which was on another floor of the house

Based *solely* on the information above, which one of the following BEST classifies the above searches?

- A. I was lawful but II and III were not
- B. I and II were lawful but III was not
- C. I, II, and III were *NOT* lawful
- D. I, II, and III were lawful

20. Assume that the following searches have been made by detectives/investigators. Each of these searches was made without a search warrant and, in each case, at least one arrest was made as a direct result of that search. A detective/investigator
    I. had the owner of a motel unlock the door of a motel room where one of the suspects in a case resided. The detective/investigator then conducted a search of the motel room.
    II. received written permission from the owner of a suspect's place of business to search the suspect's locker. The detective/investigator then conducted a search of the locker.
    III. received oral permission from one of the suspects in a case to search that suspect's garage. The detective/investigator then conducted a search of the garage.

    Which one of the following BEST classifies the above searches?

    - A. I was a lawful search but II and III were not
    - B. III was a lawful search but I and II were not
    - C. II and III were lawful searches but I was not
    - D. I, II, and III were not lawful searches

KEY (CORRECT ANSWERS)

1.	C	11.	D
2.	C	12.	C
3.	C	13.	C
4.	D	14.	B
5.	D	15.	B
6.	B	16.	A
7.	A	17.	A
8.	B	18.	A
9.	C	19.	A
10.	D	20.	C

TEST 2

DIRECTIONS: Each question or incomplete statement is followed by several suggested answers or completions. Select the one that *BEST* answers the question or completes the statement. *PRINT THE LETTER OF THE CORRECT ANSWER IN THE SPACE AT THE RIGHT.*

1. A detective/investigator has made a lawful arrest of a suspect and advised the suspect of his Miranda rights. The suspect has waived his right to an attorney and has consented to answer any questions the detective/investigator may ask.
Following are three situations in which it may or may not be appropriate for the detective/investigator to continue questioning the suspect at that time: During the questioning of the suspect,
    I. the suspect's attorney appears and asks to confer with his client concerning the crime in question even though the suspect has not requested his services in this matter
    II. the suspect states that he has changed his mind and now wishes to have an attorney present during any further questioning
    III. the suspect asks whether the court would appoint an attorney to defend him if he cannot afford to hire one

   Which one of the following BEST classifies the above situations into those in which it would be appropriate for the detective/investigator to continue questioning the suspect and those in which it would not? The detective/investigator should continue questioning the suspect in

   A. situations I and II but not in situation III
   B. situation III but not in situations I and II
   C. situation I but not in situations II and III
   D. situations II and III but not in situation I

1.____

2. A detective/investigator has arrested a suspect based solely on a witness' identification of the suspect from photographs shown to the witness by the detective/investigator. Based *solely* on the above information, which one of the following would be the MOST appropriate type of motion hearing for the suspect to request prior to being tried for the crime in question?

   A. Miranda   B. Huntley   C. Wade   D. Deno

2.____

3. A detective/investigator, upon arresting an individual, must inform that individual of the detective's/investigator's authority and the reason for the arrest in each of the following situations EXCEPT when

   A. *accompanied* by a uniformed police officer
   B. *encountering* physical resistance by the individual being arrested
   C. *executing* a felony warrant of arrest
   D. *accompanied* by a witness who identifies the individual being arrested as the person who committed the crime

3.____

4. Following are three statements concerning double jeopardy that may or may not be valid under State Law:
   I. Once a suspect has been arrested for a specific offense, that person cannot be arrested a second time for that offense, even if the second arrest results from new evidence which was not available when the first arrest was made.
   II. Once a suspect has been prosecuted for a specific offense and found not guilty, he cannot be tried again for that offense even if new evidence is later uncovered.
   III. Once a suspect has been found guilty of committing an offense, another person cannot be found guilty of committing the same offense if it was clearly established during the trial that there was only one perpetrator of the crime.

   Which one of the following BEST classifies the above statements?

   A. II is generally valid but I and III are not
   B. III is generally valid but I and II are not
   C. I and II are generally valid but III is not
   D. II and III are generally valid but I is not

5. As a detective/investigator, you have just executed an arrest warrant in the kitchen of the suspect's apartment. While searching and handcuffing the suspect, you observe a revolver on top of a television set in the living room. The revolver is approximately 30 feet from where the suspect was standing when the arrest occurred.
   Which one of the following is the MOST appropriate action for you to take FIRST in this situation?

   A. Arrange to have the premises placed under surveillance until you can obtain a search warrant
   B. Seize the revolver on the basis that it could be contraband
   C. Leave the revolver alone because you can only search in the immediate vicinity of the arrest
   D. Ask the suspect for permission to seize the revolver as evidence

6. Assume that you are a detective/investigator. A woman has come to see you at the office to register a complaint that her husband raped her two hours earlier.
   Which one of the following is the MOST appropriate action for you to take FIRST in this case?

   A. Refer her to the Family Court
   B. Advise her that her husband has not committed any crime
   C. Ask her for additional information about the circumstances surrounding her allegation
   D. Have her sign a criminal information in the court

7. You are working with the victim of an embezzlement case and you want to obtain corroborative evidence. You decide to place a concealable tape recorder on the victim's person and have him meet with and have a conversation with the suspect.
   Which one of the following is the MOST important permission to receive?

   A. Permission from the suspect authorizing you to record the conversation
   B. A court order from a judge authorizing you to record the conversation
   C. Permission from your superior to record the conversation
   D. A statement by the victim read onto the tape authorizing you to record the conversation

8. Assume that, in executing a search warrant, a detective/ investigator does each of the following:
      I.   Executes the warrant 12 days after the date of issuance
      II. Upon being denied entry, breaks down an outer door after giving notice of his authority and the purpose for which he is seeking entrance
      III. Gives the occupant a copy of the search warrant

   Which one of the following BEST classifies the above actions?

   A. I and II are generally correct but III is not
   B. I and III are generally correct but II is not
   C. II and III are generally correct but I is not
   D. I, II, and III are not generally correct

9. A detective/investigator observes two known burglars engaged in conversation. He then observes them entering a house with a key. The detective/investigator maintains surveillance of the house. He observes the two known burglars leave and enter the house several times. Then he observes them stand near a front bedroom window, look in his direction, step away from the window, and turn out the lights in the room.
   Based *solely* on the above information, which one of the following BEST describes the most appropriate action for the detective/investigator to take at this point in the surveillance?

   A. Obtain a search warrant to enter and search the premises and question the two known burglars
   B. Forcibly enter the premises now, if the burglars won't admit him peacefully, without a search warrant since he has sufficient reason to believe that a crime is in progress
   C. Notify your supervisor of the circumstances, including the date, time, exact address, and identity of the known burglars
   D. Continue the surveillance from outside the house, but stop and frisk both known burglars as soon as they leave the house

10. A detective/investigator observes a subject suspected of being a drug addict leaving a building in a suspicious manner. The subject is apprehended by the detective/investigator, who proceeds to "frisk" him and, in so doing, discovers a soft package in the subjects pocket. The detective/investigator then confiscates the package and places the subject under arrest.
    Which one of the following BEST describes the desirability of the detective's/investigator's action:

    A. *Desirable;* chiefly because the detective/investigator has reason to believe the subject is armed and dangerous
    B. *Undesirable;* chiefly because the detective/investigator did not have sufficient probable cause to believe that a crime had been committed
    C. *Desirable;* chiefly because the detective/investigator could reasonably suspect under the circumstances that a crime was about to be committed
    D. *Undesirable;* chiefly because the detective/investigator did not arrest the subject before conducting the "frisk"

11. A detective/investigator meets with the prosecuting attorney in a pretrial conference just before the detective/investigator is scheduled to testify at a jury trial. During the course of this conference, the prosecuting attorney attempts to determine the extent of the detective's/investigator's knowledge concerning the case about to be tried.
Which one of the following BEST describes the desirability of the detective's/investigator's participating in such a pre-trial conference?

   A. *Desirable;* chiefly because it will enable the detective/investigator to change his testimony in such a way as to provide the kind of testimony the prosecuting attorney wants in the presentation of the case
   B. *Undesirable;* chiefly because the detective's/investigator's testimony may sound rehearsed and he may have to admit under oath that he discussed his testimony with the prosecuting attorney prior to the trial
   C. *Desirable;* chiefly because it will enable the prosecuting attorney to ask meaningful questions of the detective/investigator during the trial which can lead to a more effective presentation of the detective's/investigator's testimony
   D. *Undesirable;* chiefly because the case could be thrown out of court if the judge learned that the detective/Investigator and the prosecuting attorney had discussed the extent of the detective's/investigator's knowledge of the case just before the trial

12. Which one of the following is the *best* example of a privileged communication which is NOT admissible as evidence in a court of, law without the consent of the communicator?

   A. Client to his accountant
   B. Informant to a law enforcement officer
   C. Defendant to his spouse
   D. Parent to his child

13. Following are two statements concerning the Miranda admonition that may or may not be valid:
   I. It must be given when a suspect is in custody.
   II. It must be given when a suspect is deprived of freedom of action in a significant way.
   Which one of the following BEST classifies the above statements?

   A. I is generally valid but II is not
   B. II is generally valid but I is not
   C. Neither I nor II is generally valid
   D. Both I and II are generally valid

14. Following are two statements concerning the admissibility of evidence that may or may not be valid:
   I. For evidence to be admissible, it must be material to the case.
   II. For evidence to be admissible, it must be relevant to the case.
   Which one of the following BEST classifies the above statements?

   A. I is generally valid but II is not
   B. II is generally valid but I is not
   C. Neither I nor II is generally valid
   D. Both I and II are generally valid

15. Which one of the following is the LEAST appropriate action for a detective/investigator to take when testifying in a court of law?

    A. Consider each question carefully before answering
    B. Answer all questions as concisely as possible
    C. Supply additional important information not specifically asked for by the prosecuting attorney
    D. Answer all questions in an unemotional manner

16. A defense attorney demands that he be present in the viewing room when his client appears in a line-up. He also makes each of the following demands: That he be
    I. able to participate in the selection of the stand-ins
    II. permitted to discuss the case with the witness prior to the line-up
    III. able to select the positioning of the stand-ins in the line-up

    Which one of the following BEST classifies the above demands?

    A. I and II should be granted but III should not
    B. I and III should granted but II should not
    C. I, II, and III should all be granted
    D. I, II, and III should not be granted

17. Following are three situations in which a detective/investigator may prepare a closing report:
    I. The case is being turned over to another detective/ investigator
    II. All leads in the case are being exhausted and there appears to be no further steps to take
    III. A supervisor orders the detective/investigator to prepare a closing report

    Which one of the following BEST classifies the above situations? A detective/investigator should prepare a closing report in

    A. situation III but not in situations I and II
    B. situations I and II but not in situation III
    C. situations II and III but not in situation I
    D. situations I, II, and III

18. Following are three types of notations which were made by a detective/investigator while searching a crime scene and which may or may not be appropriate:
    I. The types of special equipment used in conducting the search
    II. Damage to objects found at the scene of the search
    III. Any unusual or foreign object present at the scene of the search

    Which one of the following BEST classifies the above notations into those which should generally be included in field notes and those which should not?

    A. I and II should generally be included in field notes but III should not
    B. I and III should generally be included in field notes but II should not
    C. II and III should generally be included in field notes but I should not
    D. I, II, and III should all generally be included in field notes

19. A detective/investigator disposes of his notes on a particular crime five years after the date of the trial.
    Which one of the following BEST describes the desirability of this action?

    A. *Desirable;* chiefly because the statute of limitations will have expired after five years
    B. *Undesirable;* chiefly because an appeal or other civil action may require the detective's/investigator's reappearance in court after the five years are up
    C. *Desirable;* chiefly because all of the vital information concerning the case will have been incorporated in the case records by this time
    D. *Undesirable;* chiefly because the detective/investigator will find himself retaining notes indefinitely on cases that never come to trial

20. A detective/investigator makes detailed and accurate notes in his field notebook and fills out all other required report forms as completely as possible.
    Which one of the following BEST describes the desirability of this action?

    A. *Desirable;* chiefly because the contents of the notebook and other written reports may become the basis for his testimony when the case comes to court
    B. *Undesirable;* chiefly because it takes time away from the more important activities of gathering evidence and determining the identity of the perpetrator
    C. *Desirable;* chiefly because the detective/investigator is developing good, methodical work habits which will carry over to a methodical approach to his investigation duties
    D. *Undesirable;* chiefly because his notes may be made available to the defense attorney once the detective/investigator has testified at the trial

KEY (CORRECT ANSWERS)

1.	B	11.	C
2.	C	12.	C
3.	B	13.	D
4.	A	14.	D
5.	B	15.	C
6.	C	16.	B
7.	D	17.	C
8.	C	18.	D
9.	C	19.	B
10.	B	20.	A

EXAMINATION SECTION
TEST 1

DIRECTIONS: Each question or incomplete statement is followed by several suggested answers or completions. Select the one that BEST answers the question or completes the statement. PRINT THE LETTER OF THE CORRECT ANSWER IN THE SPACE AT THE RIGHT

1. A detective/investigator has just arrested a suspect who is believed to be wearing the same clothing that he wore earlier in the day when he allegedly committed a crime. The detective/investigator, therefore, wishes to collect the suspect's clothing to examine the trace evidence.
   Which one of the following procedures followed by the detective/investigator in collecting and preparing the clothing for transport to the crime lab is LEAST appropriate?

   A. The suspect is instructed to stand on a clean piece of wrapping paper while undressing
   B. All items of clothing removed from the suspect are carefully folded
   C. Each item is placed in a clean plastic bag with care taken to package each item separately
   D. The suspect is watched carefully to make sure that the pockets of the clothing are not turned inside out in an attempt to destroy evidence

1._____

2. Following are three statements which may or may not be valid concerning the value of tool marks as evidence:
   I. Tool marks can frequently be proven to have a unique relationship with the item that made them
   II. Impressions made by objects in metal are generally of poor quality
   III. It is usually desirable to remove an item containing tool marks to the crime laboratory for further examination
   Which one of the following BEST classifies the above statements?

   A. I and II are generally valid but III is not
   B. I and III are generally valid but II is not
   C. II and III are generally valid but I is not
   D. I, II, and III are all generally valid

2._____

3. In preserving a fingerprint found in an ink stain on a cardboard blotter, the detective/investigator should do each of the following EXCEPT:

   A. Sprinkle dusting powder on the ink stain to develop the fingerprint
   B. Photograph the portion of the ink stain containing the fingerprint
   C. Cover the fingerprint area with protective tape
   D. Have the blotter transported to the crime laboratory for further analysis

3._____

4. A person who falsely uses a credit card to obtain property is thereby guilty of

   A. burglary   B. forgery   C. larceny   D. robbery

4._____

25

5. A detective/investigator is assigned to administer a financial status questionnaire to all employees in a city agency and then analyze its results in an attempt to discover whether any of the employees are receiving money from organized crime.
   Which one of the following is the *BEST* reason for using a financial status questionnaire for this purpose?

   A. It is likely to clear every employee of the agency since none of them will admit to being on the take.
   B. Any outside money claimed by the employees can be easily traced to see whether it is coming from organized crime sources.
   C. The dates of additional income receipt can be checked against the dates on which leaks are thought to have occurred to see whether there is a discernible pattern.
   D. Employees showing an income lower than that required to support their current life style can be watched to see whether they are contacted by known organized crime figures.

6. *Which one* of the following is generally the *best* procedure to follow when *FIRST* interrogating a witness to a crime?

   A. *Help* the witness to remember what happened by giving him information concerning the crime which was supplied by other witnesses
   B. *Tell* the witness that he will be held in custody as a material witness until he agrees to answer all questions concerning the crime
   C. *Interrupt* the witness every time he strays from the specific response required in order to keep the discussion on relevant matters
   D. *Ask* the witness to describe the crime as he saw it and wait until the witness clearly appears to have finished talking, then ask follow-up questions for additional clarification

7. Each one of the following persons would be guilty of patronizing a prostitute *EXCEPT* a

   A. *man* who, pursuant to prior understanding, pays a fee to another man as compensation for that man having engaged in sexual conduct with him
   B. *woman* who offers to engage in sexual conduct with a man in return for a fee
   C. *woman* who agrees to pay a fee to a man pursuant to an agreement that, in return for the fee, he will engage in sexual conduct with her
   D. *man* who requests a woman to engage in sexual conduct with him in return for paying her a fee

8. A detective/investigator frequently uses police slang in official reports in describing specific incidents that relate to the case under investigation.
   Which one of the following *BEST* describes the desirability of this practice?

   A. *Desirable, CHIEFLY* because the police slang will be readily understood by other persons in the District Attorney's office who refer to the report
   B. *Undesirable; CHIEFLY* because the detective/investigator who uses police slang n such reports will appear uneducated
   C. *Desirable; CHIEFLY* because it will take less time to use police slang than the long descriptions that this slang may replace
   D. *Undesirable; CHIEFLY* because such slang may be ambiguous

9. A detective/investigator in preparing a written report of a surveillance should prepare it in such a way that it will provide each of the following EXCEPT a

   A. permanent official record of the relevant information obtained in the course of the investigation
   B. source of reference to provide other investigators with information necessary to further advance the investigation
   C. statement of the facts on which designated authorities may base a criminal, corrective, or disciplinary action if warranted
   D. record of the detective's/investigator's opinions concerning important aspects of the case

10. In order to determine whether a specific individual was a passenger on a foreign vessel which arrived in New York harbor on a given day, the detective/investigator should arrange to contact *which one* of the following agencies?

    A. Interstate Commerce Commission
    B. Immigration and Naturalization Service
    C. New York Port Authority
    D. United States Maritime Commission

11. Each one of the following suspects should be charged with forgery EXCEPT one who

    A. *has attempted* to cash a series of checks to be drawn on a bank where he does not have an account
    B. *has altered* the contents of a close relative's will in order to receive a larger sum of money than he would otherwise have received
    C. *has altered* a pari-mutuel ticket so that it now bears the number of the winning horse in the race for which it was purchased
    D. *is not* a licensed medical doctor who prepares a prescription for an opiate and presents it to a pharmacist for filling

12. *Which one* of the following is the MOST appropriate method for a detective/investigator to use when handling a gun that is to be used as evidence in a court case?

    A. Pick up the gun by grasping the checkered wooden handle with the fingers
    B. Pick up the gun by inserting a wooden pencil in the gun barrel and lifting
    C. Pick up the gun by the trigger guard
    D. Dismantle the gun so that it may be transported more safely

13. *Which* one of the following actions taken by a detective/investigator in gathering and presenting expert testimony is MOST generally correct? A detective/investigator

    A. arranges to have persons in no way connected with any police agency available to help conduct an experiment in the field designed to verify that the character and audibility of sound at a given location matches that stated by a witness testifying in court
    B. who is highly knowledgeable in a given field as a result of many years of handling investigations of a nature requiring some knowledge in this field, testifies in court as an expert witness in his own case

C. accepts the content and conclusions that an expert witness will present in court without further trying to independently verify them
D. decides not to submit a sample of dirt found at the scene of a crime to a chemist for analysis

Questions 14-20.

DIRECTIONS: Answer Questions 14 through 20 based *SOLELY* on the contents of the following passage and a knowledge of good report writing procedures and techniques.

1 On July 21, at approximately 10 p.m., Harold Gray, the informant, met with two suspects in room 502 of the Midway Hotel. *2* The informant had been fitted with a small recording device by Detective Santora and myself at 9:30 p.m. that day and had been driven by us to the scene of the stake-out. *3* Detective Santora and I escorted Mr. Gray to room 504 of the Midway Hotel, where Detective Santora and I set up a listening post. *4* As soon as our preparations were complete, we instructed Mr. Gray to knock on the door of room 742 and engage the suspects, Jose Candelaria and Pepe Mangual, in conversation. *5* A discussion got underway in which Mr. Gray attempted to negotiate the price he would pay for a large shipment of cocaine. *6* He was told by Mr. Santora that the cocaine would be arriving by air the following week at the date, time, and place they had agreed to in their previous conversation. *7* The discussion then became heated when Mr. Gray demanded that a change in the plans be made. *8* Mr. Candelaria stated that no change was possible and demanded $1,500,000 for the shipment. *9* There was a short silence while Mr. Gray lit a cigarette for Mr. Mangual. *10* Then Mr. Santora started screaming abuse at Mr. Gray and accused him of being a police spy. *11* The next words I heard were those of Mr. Candelaria, accusing Mr. Gray of being bugged. *12* I immediately left my listening post, handing the earphones to Detective/Investigator Santora, and rushed next door to room 744. *13* The door to the room was open and the room was empty. *14* The window in the bathroom of room 742 was open and I could see two men climbing quickly down the fire escape. *15* My eye caught a shadow on the shower curtain strung across the bathtub. *16* I pulled the shower curtain aside and found Mr. Gray's body slumped inside. *17* There was a bullet hole in Mr. Gray's head located in the center of his forehead. *18* A quick check of his pulse revealed that Mr. Gray was dead. *19* I secured the area of the murder and picked up the telephone in the room to tell my partner that the suspects were fleeing down the fire escape. *20* On my instruction, Detective/Investigator Santora called our office to alert them to the facts of the encounter and Mr. Gray's demise. *21* Then Santora joined me in the room where the shooting occurred, where we both waited until the police arrived.

14. *Which one* of the following sentences includes information that *COULD NOT* have been known to the Detective/ Investigator who prepared this report?

   A. 2   B. 9   C. 14   D. 18

15. *Which one* of the following sentences contains material which is out *of sequence?*

   A. 1   B. 10   C. 16   D. 19

16. *Which one* of the following sentences contains a conclusion on the part of the Detective Investigator which is *unwarranted* based upon the contents of this report?

   A. 4   B. 6   C. 16   D. 19

17. Which one of the following sentences contains a statement which is *contradicted* elsewhere in this report?　　17.____

    A. 5　　　　B. 11　　　　C. 12　　　　D. 17

18. Which one of the following sentences contains material for which *further clarification* is needed?　　18.____

    A. 2　　　　B. 4　　　　C. 5　　　　D. 20

19. Which one of the following sentences contains information which is *NOT* consistent with the rest of this report?　　19.____

    A. 7　　　　B. 8　　　　C. 10　　　　D. 15

20. Which one of the following sentences requires *further clarification*?　　20.____

    A. 3　　　　B. 8　　　　C. 18　　　　D. 21

KEY (CORRECT ANSWERS)

1. D	11. A
2. B	12. A
3. C	13. A
4. C	14. B
5. D	15. A
6. D	16. D
7. B	17. C
8. D	18. C
9. D	19. C
10. B	20. D

EXAMINATION SECTION
TEST 1

DIRECTIONS: Each question or incomplete statement is followed by several suggested answers or completions. Select the one that BEST answers the question or completes the statement. *PRINT THE LETTER OF THE CORRECT ANSWER IN THE SPACE AT THE RIGHT.*

1. If S, the subject that investigator H is tailing, enters a large department store, H should
    A. wait outside the store in a concealed place until S comes out
    B. follow S into the store
    C. enter the store, but wait by the door
    D. wait outside the store but in a position near the door S entered

    1.____

2. Which of the following is MOST likely to indicate an attempt at falsification of a particular document?
    A. Change in style of handwriting within the document
    B. Illegible writing
    C. Erasures or alterations
    D. Folds or creases in the document

    2.____

3. A subject being tailed during a foot surveillance quickly turns and confronts the shadower and states, *Say, Bud, are you tailing me?*
    Of the following, the MOST appropriate action for the shadower to take is to
    A. ignore the question and keep on walking
    B. admit that he is shadowing the subject but refuse to tell him why
    C. deny the accusation but give no explanations
    D. give some excuse for his presence in the form of a cover-up

    3.____

4. K, an investigator, has been given the assignment of tailing S, a suspect, who will be traveling by car at night in the city.
    Of the following, the SIMPLEST way for K to carry out this surveillance would be to
    A. mark S's car beforehand so it is identifiable at night
    B. memorize the model, color, and style of S's car
    C. memorize the license plate of S's car
    D. mechanically disable S's car so it will be unusable

    4.____

5. The United States Treasury Department may prove to be a valuable source of information in specialized instances.
    Which of the following types of information usually would NOT be in the custody of that Federal agency?
    A. Immigration records
    B. Records of licensed manufacturers of narcotics
    C. Importers and exporters records
    D. Records of persons or firms manufacturing alcohol

    5.____

6. Which of the following is a writ directing that documents or records be produced in court?
   A. Writ of habeas corpus
   B. Subpoena habeas corpus
   C. Order, pro hoc vice
   D. Subpoena duces tecum

7. *Modus Operandi* is a phrase frequently used in investigative work to refer to a
   A. specific type of investigation
   B. particular policy in tracing missing persons
   C. manner in which a criminal operates
   D. series of crimes committed by more than one person

8. P, an investigator, has been assigned to interview W, a witness, concerning a minor automobile accident. Although P has made no breach of the basic rules of contact and approach, he nevertheless recognizes that he and W have a personality clash and that a natural animosity has resulted.
   Of the following, P MOST appropriately should
   A. discuss the personality problem with W and attempt to resolve the difference
   B. stop the interview on some pretext and leave in a calm and pleasant manner, allowing an associate to continue the interview
   C. ignore the personality problem and continue as though nothing had happened
   D. change the subject matter being discussed since the facts sought may be the source of the animosity

9. Assume that an investigator desires to interview W, a reluctant witness to a bribery attempt that took place several weeks previously. Assume further that the interview can take place at a location to be designated by the interviewer.
   Of the following, the place of interview should PREFERABLY be the
   A. office of the interviewer
   B. home of W
   C. office of W
   D. scene where the event took place

10. Assume that T, an investigator, is testifying in court. He does not clearly remember the details of the incident about which he is testifying.
    Of the following, the MOST appropriate action for T to take is to
    A. admit he does not remember the details and go on to the next question
    B. look at his statement previously given to the attorney interviewing him before trial
    C. refresh his memory by referring to his notebook
    D. testify to only those items he can recall

11. Assume that as an investigator you are interviewing W, a witness. During the interview, it becomes apparent that W's statements are inaccurate and at variance with the facts previously established.
    In these circumstances, it would be BEST for you to
    A. tell W that his statements are inaccurate and point out how they conflict with previously established facts

B. reword your questions and ask additional questions about the facts being discussed
C. warn W that he may be required to testify under oath at a later date
D. ignore W's statements if you have other information that support the facts

12. Assume that W, a witness being interviewed by you, an investigator, shows a tendency to ramble. His answers to your questions are lengthy and not responsive.
In this situation, the BEST action for you to take is to
A. permit W to continue because at some point he will tell you the information sought
B. tell W that he is rambling and unresponsive and that more will be accomplished if he is brief and to the point
C. control the interview so that complete and accurate information is obtained
D. patiently listen to W since rambling is W's style and it cannot be changed

12.____

13. Assume that an investigator is to interview a witness.
Of the following, the BEST procedure for the investigator to follow in regard to the use of his notebook is to
A. take out his notebook at the start of the interview and immediately begin taking notes
B. memorize the important facts related during the interview and enter them after the interview has been completed
C. advise the witness that all his answers are being taken down to insure that he will tell the truth
D. establish rapport with the witness and ask permission to jot down various data in his notebook

13.____

14. The first duty of the investigator who has in his possession a document which may be used in evidence is to preserve it in its original condition.
Following are three actions which might constitute rules for the handling of a document:
I. Pick up the document with tweezers or a pin
II. Staple the document to a folder so that it is protected
III. Photograph or photocopy the document
Which one of the following choices MOST accurately classifies the above statements into those which are APPROPRIATE and those which are NOT APPROPRIATE as procedures for handling such documents?
A. I and III are appropriate, but II is not appropriate
B. I and II are appropriate, but III is not appropriate
C. II is appropriate, but I and III are not appropriate
D. III is appropriate, but I and II are not appropriate

14.____

15. Of the following, which one would be the CLEAREST indication that a suspicious check is a forgery?
A. There are smudges from carbon paper at the edges of the back of the check.

15.____

B. The signature on the check is an exact duplicate of an authentic signature.
C. The amount of the check has been crossed out and a new amount written in.
D. Two different color inks were used in making out the check.

16. Assume an investigator is making an inspection of a desk and finds a writing pad on which a suspect may have written. The top page of the pad has indentations which were formed when the previous page was written on. Following are three procedures which might be appropriate in order to read the indentation:
   I. Hold the paper in such a manner that a single light source falls along the sheet at a parallel or oblique angle.
   II. Soak the pad in water and thoroughly dry it in the sun.
   III. Rub a piece of carbon paper lightly across the underside of the paper in question.
   Which one of the following choices classifies the above statements into those which are APPROPRIATE procedures and those which are NOT APPROPRIATE?
   A. I and II are appropriate, but III is not appropriate
   B. II and III are appropriate, but I is not appropriate
   C. I and III are appropriate, but II is not appropriate
   D. II is appropriate, but I and III are not appropriate

17. In order to conduct an effective interview, an interviewer's attention must be continuously directed in two ways, toward himself as well as toward the interviewee.
   Of the following, the PRIMARY danger in this division of attention is that the
   A. interviewer's behavior may become less natural and thus alienate the interviewee
   B. interviewee's span of attention will be shortened
   C. interviewer's response may be interpreted by the interviewee as being antagonistic
   D. interviewee's more or less concealed prejudices will come to the surface

18. X and Y go into a vault together and close the door. A shot is heard, and Y rushes out with a smoking gun in his hand.
   A witness to his event who said *Y shot X* would be offering _____ evidence.
   A. direct   B. real
   C. circumstantial   D. hearsay

19. Assume that an investigator is attempting to get a suspect to agree to take a lie detector or polygraph test.
   Which of the following actions on the part of the investigator would be LEAST appropriate?
   A. Describe the test to the suspect in simple language so that he understands the procedure
   B. Suggest that the test is a means for the suspect to indicate his innocence

C. Discuss the test's capability of indicating whether a person is telling the truth
D. Suggest that a refusal to take the test indicates guilt

20. The term *corpus delicti* is MOST appropriately used to refer to
    A. a body of criminal law
    B. the body of a person
    C. a body of civil law
    D. the body of a crime

21. Which of the following is considered the BEST type of permanent ink to use in preparing documents?
    A. Ballpoint
    B. Nigrosine
    C. Log wood
    D. Iron gallotannate

22. An important aspect of investigative work is the preservation of materials which may be used as evidence.
    Following are three statements which might constitute rules for the proper handling of blood in a fluid condition found at a crime scene:
    I. The blood should be removed with an eye dropper and placed in a test tube.
    II. Saline solution should be added to the blood sample in a ratio of 1 to 4.
    III. The sample blood should be frozen and delivered to the laboratory as soon as possible.
    Which of the following choices classifies the above actions into those which are APPROPRIATE and those which are INAPPROPRIATE?
    A. I and II are appropriate, but III is inappropriate.
    B. I and III are appropriate, but II is inappropriate.
    C. I is appropriate, but II and III are inappropriate.
    D. III is appropriate, but I and II are inappropriate.

23. The term *entrapment* refers to the act of
    A. peace officers or agents of the government in inducing a person to commit a crime not contemplated by him for the purpose of instituting a criminal prosecution against him
    B. private individuals inducing a person to commit an act not contemplated by him for the purpose of bringing a civil against him
    C. peace officers or agents of the government in observing a person engaged in the commission of a criminal act and, therefore, obtaining direct evidence against the person
    D. private individuals or investigators in interrupting a person engaged in committing a criminal act

24. Assume you are investigating a person who is alleged to be an officer in a manufacturing corporation doing business in New York City.
    Which of the following sources of information is the LEAST appropriate source to consult in checking whether this is true?
    A. Poor's Register of Directors and Executives
    B. Polk's Banker's Encyclopedia
    C. Moody's Manual of Investments, American and Foreign
    D. Polk's Copartnership and Corporation Directory

25. If an investigator is assigned to the surveillance of a suspect which requires the use of an automobile, it would generally be LEAST advisable for him to use a car
   A. rented from a rental agency
   B. personally owned by the investigator
   C. bearing special unregistered plates
   D. borrowed by someone who is trustworthy but has no official associations

KEY (CORRECT ANSWERS)

1.	B		11.	B
2.	C		12.	C
3.	D		13.	D
4.	A		14.	A
5.	A		15.	B
6.	D		16.	C
7.	C		17.	A
8.	B		18.	C
9.	A		19.	D
10.	C		20.	D

21.	D
22.	A
23.	A
24.	B
25.	B

TEST 2

DIRECTIONS: Each question or incomplete statement is followed by several suggested answers or completions. Select the one that BEST answers the question or completes the statement. *PRINT THE LETTER OF THE CORRECT ANSWER IN THE SPACE AT THE RIGHT.*

1. Following are three statements regarding writing instruments:
   I. The hardness of the lead and the sharpness of the point affect the appearance of pencil writing.
   II. The ballpoint pen obscures the writer's ability to exhibit his characteristic habits of quality, rhythm, and shading.
   III. An examination of writing performed with a ballpoint pen easily reveals the angle at which the pen was held with relation to the writer's body and the paper.
   Which of the following choices classifies the above statements into those which are generally CORRECT and those which are generally INCORRECT?
   A. I is correct, but II and III are incorrect.
   B. II is correct, but I and III are incorrect.
   C. I and II are correct, but III is incorrect.
   D. I and III are correct, but II is incorrect.

   1.____

2. Following are three statements regarding procedures to be followed in obtaining exemplars from a suspect which may or may not be appropriate.
   I. After the suspect is seated and provided with writing materials, the investigator should dictate the comparison text, always indicating punctuation and paragraphing.
   II. The material should be dictated several times, the speed of the dictation being increased each time so that the suspect will be inclined to lapse into his normal handwriting habits.
   III. As each sheet is completed, it should be removed from the suspect so that he will not be able to imitate the first exemplars he has prepared.
   Which of the following choices classifies the above procedures into those which are APPROPRIATE and those which are INAPPROPRIATE?
   A. I and II are appropriate, but III is inappropriate.
   B. I and III are appropriate, but II is inappropriate.
   C. I is appropriate, but II and III are inappropriate.
   D. III is appropriate, but I and II are inappropriate.

   2.____

3. During an investigation, it may be necessary to take a *deposition*.
   The one of the following which BEST describe a *deposition* is
   A. a record made of the case progress
   B. a statement made by a witness in which he agrees to give testimony in court without resort to subpoena
   C. testimony of a witness reduced to writing under oath or affirmation, in answer to interrogatories
   D. another name for an *affidavit*

   3.____

4. Examination of handwriting on the basis of comparing the outer shapes of letters is known as the _____ method.
   A. holographic   B. penographic   C. calligraphic   D. pedographic

5. An investor who receives a lead from an anonymous phone caller would generally be BEST advised to
   A. ignore the information as unfounded
   B. tell the informant to call back when he is ready to divulge his identity
   C. determine from the informant the motivation behind his making the call
   D. get all relevant information possible on the assumption he will not hear from the caller again

6. In order to demonstrate his findings to the court, a document examiner must use enlarged, mounted photographs.
   Which of the following should ALSO be submitted to the court?
   A. Color enlargements, as well as black and white
   B. Normal-size photographs of the enlarged documents
   C. Negatives of the enlarged photographs
   D. Duplicates of the enlarged photographs

7. X, an investigator, has come upon a few documents belonging to Y, a person whom X is investigating. The documents cannot be taken or moved.
   Of the following, the MOST appropriate action for X to take is to
   A. make a record of the documents, making certain to include any names, addresses, and numbers mentioned even though they may appear meaningless at the time of discovery
   B. make a record only of those documents deemed relevant by him at the time of discover, including names, addresses, and numbers mentioned
   C. leave the documents without making any notes because documents that cannot be moved may not be copied
   D. make a record only of those names, addresses, or numbers mentioned which are clearly relevant to the case

8. Assume that you are interviewing W, a neighbor of N, whom you are investigating. It is important to establish whether or not N uses alcoholic beverages excessively.
   Which of the following questions is MOST appropriate for obtaining the information you seek?
   A. Have you ever seen N intoxicated?
   B. Can you tell me something about N's habits?
   C. Do you know whether or not N is a patron of nearby bars?
   D. What is N's reputation in the neighborhood?

9. A check may be altered to change the amount, the name, or some other element. The one of the following which can BEST be used to discover any changes is
   A. a magnetometer   B. an ultra-violet lamp
   C. a tensimeter   D. polarography

10. Z, an investigator, is attempting to interview W concerning an accident witnessed by W. However, W is disinterested and indifferent.
    In order to encourage W's cooperation, Z should
    A. stimulate W's interest by stressing the importance of the information that he possesses
    B. impress upon W that Z is an investigator performing an official function
    C. warn W that the withholding of information may be considered as an obstruction of justice
    D. gain W's sympathy for Z, who is merely trying to do his job

11. Of the following, the three types of ink MOST commonly used in the United States today are:
    A. gallotannic, logwood, and nigrosine
    B. gallotannic, vanadium, and wolfram
    C. wolfram, logwood, and nigrosine
    D. vanadium, logwood, and nigrosine

12. Which of the following BEST describes the science of poroscopy?
    Identification
    A. by the casting of footprints
    B. by the tracing of tools used in a crime
    C. by means of sweat pores indicated on a fingerprint
    D. through the examination of human hairs

13. Which of the following statements concerning the folding of paper is ACCURATE:
    A. When uncut paper has been folded, the fibers remain unbroken.
    B. If an ink line is first drawn and the paper is subsequently folded, the line over the fold will not be even and uniform.
    C. If an ink line is written over an already existing fold, the ink will spread over the fold but protruding fibers will not become stained.
    D. It is almost impossible to determine whether a lead pencil line was drawn on a paper before or after it was folded.

14. All of the following are generally good methods of making erased lead-pencil writing visible EXCEPT
    A. examination in non-polarized light   B. use of iodine fumes
    C. contrast photography   D. photography in oblique light

15. Following are four statements concerning crime-scene photography that may or may not be valid:
    I. The general procedure of crime-scene photography aims at obtaining views of broad areas of the crime locale, supplemented by closer views of sections containing important detail.
    II. The crime scene should be first photographed in its original, undisturbed state.
    III. Crime-scene photographs are of great value to the investigator because they accurately show the distances between objects.

IV. If a room is to be photographed, a set of at least four views will be required to show the room adequately.

Which of the following choices MOST accurately classifies the above into those which are VALID procedures and those which are NOT VALID?
A. I and II are valid, but III and IV are not valid.
B. I, II, and IV are valid, but III is not valid.
C. III and IV are valid, but I and II are not valid.
D. I, II, and III are valid, but IV is not valid.

16. Following are four statements concerning the erasing of ink which may or may not be valid:
   I. It may be difficult to detect an erasure made with an eradicator, especially after a considerable length of time has elapsed.
   II. When an erasure has been made with a knife or rubber, it is general easy to detect the area involved, as it is translucent.
   III. The sulfocyanic acid method is inappropriate for the detection of residue of iron-containing inks.
   IV. Examination with ultra-violet rays should not be strongly relied upon because clever forgers have been known to wash away all residue of eradication with distilled water.

   Which of the following choices MOST accurately classifies the above statements into those which are generally VALID and those which are not generally valid?
   A. I and II are generally valid, but III and IV are not generally valid.
   B. IV is generally valid, but I, II, and III are not generally valid.
   C. I, II, and IV are generally valid, but III is not generally valid.
   D. III and IV are generally valid, but I and II are not generally valid.

17. Following are four statements concerning fingerprints which may or may not be true:
   I. Plastic fingerprints are found on such objects as a bar of soap or ball of melted wax.
   II. Visible fingerprints are left by fingers covered with a colored material such as blood or grease.
   III. The majority of latent fingerprints are relatively invisible and must be developed.
   IV. Dirty surfaces and absorbent materials readily bear prints.

   Which of the following choices MOST accurately classifies the above statements into those which are TRUE and those which are NOT TRUE?
   A. I and II are true; III and IV are not true.
   B. I and III are true; II and IV are not true.
   C. I, II, and III are true, and IV is not true.
   D. I, II, and IV are true, and III is not true.

18. Of the following, the method of fingerprint classification MOST commonly used in the United States is the _____ system.
   A. Henry   B. Vucetich   C. Bertillon   D. Pottecher

19. Of the following, the term *curtilage* is MOST appropriately used to refer to
    A. the enclosed space of ground and buildings immediately surrounding a dwelling
    B. a surgical procedure used to induce an abortion
    C. the illegal detention of suspects by law enforcement personnel
    D. a legal action taken by a judge to curtail the irrelevant testimony of witnesses in court

20. Which of the following statements is MOST valid as a guide to investigators in their dealings with informants?
    A. Whether they are agreeable or not, informants should be made available for questioning by other agencies since they may have good information in areas other than those which directly concern you.
    B. Many informants work out of revenge, while some others do it only for money. Therefore, you should evaluate the information they give you with regard to their motivation.
    C. Informants tend to use their connections with law enforcement agencies. From time to time, they must be put in their place by letting them know they are *stool pigeons*.
    D. To cultivate informants, it is a good practice to give them some money in advance so they will be assured of a reward when they have good information.

21. The more meager the evidence against a suspect, the later the suspect should be allowed to know of it.
    As a practical rule to guide the investigator during an interrogation, the advice contained in this statement is GENERALLY
    A. *bad*, chiefly because suspects have a right to know the details of the offense being investigated
    B. *good*, chiefly because the interrogator will not look foolish due to his lack of information
    C. *bad*, chiefly because the investigator will be unable to develop the proper rapport with the suspect during the interrogation
    D. *good*, chiefly because the suspect, not sensing the direction of the interrogation, is more likely to reveal information

22. Following are three statements concerning fingerprinting which may or may not be valid:
    I. The best paper for fingerprinting purposes has a rough surface which will absorb ink.
    II. The subject should roll his fingers on the paper from right to left exercising as much pressure as possible on the paper to make a print.
    III. Fingerprints taken with stamp-pad ink are not usually legible or permanent.
    Which of the following classifies the above statements into those which are VALID and those which are NOT VALID?
    A. I is valid, but II and III are not valid.
    B. I and II are valid, but III is not valid.
    C. II is valid, but I and III are not valid
    D. III is valid, but I and II are not valid.

23. All of the following statements concerning fingerprints are true EXCEPT:
    A. There are no two identical fingerprints.
    B. Fingerprint patterns are not generally changed by illness.
    C. A modern procedure called dactylmogrification has been developed to change the fingerprints of individuals relatively easily.
    D. If the skin on the fingertips is wounded, the whole fingerprint pattern will reappear when the wound heals.

24. Mechanical erasures on a document produce an abrasion of the paper. Assume that a forger makes an ink writing which crosses an area which has been previously erased.
    Following are three conditions which might result in the erased area from such an action:
    I. The ink line is brighter.
    II. The ink line is wider.
    III. The ink line tends to run or feather out sideways.
    Which one of the following choices MOST accurately classifies the above statements into those which would result from writing over the erased area and those which would not?
    A. I and II would result, but III would not result.
    B. I and III would result, but I would not result.
    C. II would result, but I and III would not result.
    D. II and III would result, but I would not result.

25. In the investigation of the periodic theft of equipment from stockrooms, the detection of the thieves is USUALLY accomplished by
    A. the use of strict inventory controls
    B. careful background investigation of applicants for the stockroom jobs
    C. issuing photo identification cards to all employees of the agency
    D. the use of intelligent surveillance

KEY (CORRECT ANSWERS)

1.	C	11.	A
2.	D	12.	C
3.	C	13.	D
4.	C	14.	A
5.	D	15.	B
6.	B	16.	C
7.	A	17.	C
8.	A	18.	A
9.	B	19.	A
10.	A	20.	B

21. D
22. D
23. C
24. D
25. D

EXAMINATION SECTION
TEST 1

DIRECTIONS: Each question or incomplete statement is followed by several suggested answers or completions. Select the one that BEST answers the question or completes the statement. *PRINT THE LETTER OF THE CORRECT ANSWER IN THE SPACE AT THE RIGHT.*

Questions 1-4.

DIRECTIONS: Questions 1 through 4 consist of sentences concerning criminal law. Some of the sentences contain errors in English grammar or usage, punctuation, spelling or capitalization. A sentence does not contain an error simply because it could be written in a different manner. Choose answer
- A. if the sentence contains an error in English grammar or usage
- B. if the sentence contains an error in punctuation
- C. if the sentence contains an error in spelling or capitalization
- D. if the sentence does not contain any errors

1. The severity of the sentence prescribed by contemporary statutes - including both the former and the revised New York Penal Laws - do not depend on what crime was intended by the offender. 1.____

2. It is generally recognized that two defects in the early law of attempt played a part in the birth of burglary: (1) immunity from prosecution for conduct short of the last act before completion of the crime, and (2) the relatively minor penalty imposed for an attempt (it being a common law misdemeanor) vis-a-vis the completed offense. 2.____

3. The first sentence of the statute is applicable to employees who enter their place of employment, invited guests, and all other persons who have an express or implied license or privilege to enter the premises. 3.____

4. Contemporary criminal codes in the United States generally divide burglary into various degrees, differentiating the categories according to place, time and other attentent circumstances. 4.____

Questions 5-8.

DIRECTIONS: Questions 5 through 8 are to be answered SOLELY on the basis of the following passage.

The difficulty experienced in determining which party has the burden of proving payment or non-payment is due largely to a tack of consistency between the rules of pleading and the rules of proof. In some cases, a plaintiff is obligated by a rule of pleading to allege non-payment on his complaint, yet is not obligated to prove non-payment on the trial. An action upon a contract for the payment of money will serve as an illustration. In such a case, the plaintiff must allege non-payment in his complaint, but the burden of proving payment on the trial is upon the defendant. An important and frequently cited case on this problem is Conkling v. Weatherwax. In that case, the action was brought to establish and enforce a legacy as a lien upon real property. The defendant alleged in her answer that the legacy had been paid. There was no witness competent to testify for the plaintiff to show that the legacy had not been paid. Therefore, the question of the burden of proof became of primary importance since, if the plaintiff had the burden of proving non-payment, she must fail in her action; whereas, if the burden of proof was on the defendant to prove payment, the plaintiff might win. The Court of Appeals held that the burden of proof was on the plaintiff. In the course of his opinion, Judge Vann attempted to harmonize the conflicting cases on this subject, and for that purpose formulated three rules. These rules have been construed and applied to numerous subsequent cases. As so construed and applied, these may be summarized as follows:

Rule 1: In an action upon a contract for the payment of money only, where the complaint does not allege a balance due over and above all payments made, the plaintiff must allege nonpayment in his complaint, but the burden of proving payment is upon the defendant. In such a case, payment is an affirmative defense which the defendant must plead in his answer. If the defendant fails to plead payment, but pleads a general denial instead, he will not be permitted to introduce evidence of payment.

Rule 2: Where the complaint sets forth a balance in excess of all payments, owing to the structure of the pleading, burden is upon the plaintiff to prove his allegation. In this case, the defendant is not required to plead payment as a defense in his answer but may introduce evidence of payment under a general denial.

Rule 3: When the action is not upon contract for the payment of money, but is upon an obligation created by operation of law, or is for the enforcement of a lien where non-payment of the amount secured is part of the cause of action, it is necessary both to allege and prove the fact of nonpayment.

5. In the above passage, the case of Conkling v. Weatherwax was cited PRIMARILY to illustrate

   A. a case where the burden of proof was on the defendant to prove payment
   B. how the question of the burden of proof can affect the outcome of a case
   C. the effect of a legacy as a lien upon real property
   D. how conflicting cases concerning the burden of proof were harmonized

6. According to the above passage, the pleading of payment is a defense in

   A. Rule 1, but not Rules 2 and 3
   B. Rule 2, but not Rules 1 and 3
   C. Rules 1 and 3, but not Rule 2
   D. Rules 2 and 3, but not Rule 1

7. The facts in Conkling v. Weatherwax closely resemble the conditions described in Rule

   A. 1
   B. 2
   C. 3
   D. none of the rules

8. The major topic of the above passage may BEST be described as

   A. determining the ownership of property
   B. providing a legal definition
   C. placing the burden of proof
   D. formulating rules for deciding cases

Questions 9-12.

DIRECTIONS: Questions 9 through 12 consist of six sentences which can be arranged in a logical sequence. For each question, select the choice which places the numbered sentences in the MOST logical sequence.

9. I. The burden of proof as to each issue is determined before trial and remains upon the same party throughout the trial.
    II. The jury is at liberty to believe one witness testimony as against a number of contradictory witnesses.
    III. In a civil case, the party bearing the burden of proof is required to prove his contention by a fair preponderance of the evidence.
    IV. However, it must be noted that a fair preponderance of evidence does not necessarily mean a greater number of witnesses.
    V. The burden of proof is the burden which rests upon one of the parties to an action to persuade the trier of the facts, generally the jury, that a proposition he asserts is true.
    VI. If the evidence is equally balanced, or if it leaves the jury in such doubt as to be unable to decide the controversy either way, judgment must be given against the party upon whom the burden of proof rests.

    The CORRECT sequence is:

    A. III, II, V, IV, I, VI
    B. I, II, VI, V, III, IV
    C. III, IV, V, I, II, VI
    D. V, I, III, VI, IV, II

10. I. If a parent is without assets and is unemployed, he cannot be convicted of the crime of non-support of a child.
    II. The term *sufficient ability* has been held to mean sufficient financial ability.
    III. It does not matter if his unemployment is by choice or unavoidable circumstances.
    IV. If he fails to take any steps at all, he may be liable to prosecution for endangering the welfare of a child.
    V. Under the penal law, a parent is responsible for the support of his minor child only if the parent is of sufficient ability.
    VI. An indigent parent may meet his obligation by borrowing money or by seeking aid under the provisions of the Social Welfare Law.

    The CORRECT sequence is:

    A. VI, I, V, III, II, IV
    B. I, III, V, II, IV, VI
    C. V, II, I, III, VI, IV
    D. I, VI, IV, V, II, III

11.
   I. Consider, for example, the case of a rabble rouser who urges a group of twenty people to go out and break the windows of a nearby factory.
   II. Therefore, the law fills the indicated gap with the crime of *inciting to riot*.
   III. A person is considered guilty of inciting to riot when he urges ten or more persons to engage in tumultuous and violent conduct of a kind likely to create public alarm.
   IV. However, if he has not obtained the cooperation of at least four people, he cannot be charged with unlawful assembly.
   V. The charge of inciting to riot was added to the law to cover types of conduct which cannot be classified as either the crime of *riot* or the crime of *unlawful* assembly.
   VI. If he acquires the acquiescence of at least four of them, he is guilty of unlawful assembly even if the project does not materialize.

   The CORRECT sequence is:
   A. III, V, I, VI, IV, II
   B. V, I, IV, VI, II, III
   C. III, IV, I, V, II, VI
   D. V, I, IV, VI, III, II

12.
   I. If, however, the rebuttal evidence presents an issue of credibility, it is for the jury to determine whether the presumption has, in fact, been destroyed.
   II. Once sufficient evidence to the contrary is introduced, the presumption disappears from the trial.
   III. The effect of a presumption is to place the burden upon the adversary to come forward with evidence to rebut the presumption.
   IV. When a presumption is overcome and ceases to exist in the case, the fact or facts which gave rise to the presumption still remain.
   V. Whether a presumption has been overcome is ordinarily a question for the court.
   VI. Such information may furnish a basis for a logical inference.

   The CORRECT sequence is:
   A. IV, VI, II, V, I, III
   B. III, II, V, I, IV, VI
   C. V, III, VI, IV, II, I
   D. V, IV, I, II, VI, III

13. In order to obtain an accurate statement from a person who has witnessed a crime, it is BEST to question the witness

   A. as soon as possible after the crime was committed
   B. after the witness has discussed the crime with other witnesses
   C. after the witness has had sufficient time to reflect on events and formulate a logical statement
   D. after the witness has been advised that he is obligated to tell the whole truth

14. A young woman was stabbed in the hand in her home by her estranged boyfriend. Her mother and two sisters were at home at the time.
   Of the following, it would generally be BEST to interview the young woman in the presence of

   A. her mother only
   B. all members of her immediate family
   C. members of the family who actually observed the crime
   D. the official authorities

15. The one of the following which is NOT effective in obtaining complete testimony from a 15._____
    witness during an interview is to
    A. ask questions in chronological order
    B. permit the witness to structure the interview
    C. make sure you fully understand the response to each question
    D. review questions to be asked beforehand

KEY (CORRECT ANSWERS)

1. A
2. D
3. D
4. C
5. B

6. A
7. C
8. C
9. D
10. C

11. A
12. B
13. A
14. D
15. B

TEST 2

DIRECTIONS: Each question or incomplete statement is followed by several suggested answers or completions. Select the one that BEST answers the question or completes the statement. *PRINT THE LETTER OF THE CORRECT ANSWER IN THE SPACE AT THE RIGHT.*

1. You are conducting an initial interview with a witness who expresses reluctance, even hostility, to being questioned. You feel it would be helpful to take some notes during the interview.
   In this situation, it would be BEST to

   A. put off note-taking until a follow-up interview and concentrate on establishing rapport with the witness
   B. explain the necessity of note-taking and proceed to take notes during the interview
   C. make notes from memory after the witness has left
   D. take notes, but as unobtrusively as possible

2. An assistant is starting an interview with an elderly man who was the victim of a robbery. The man begins by mentioning his minor aches and pains. The aide immediately changes the subject to the robbery.
   This action by the aide should GENERALLY be considered

   A. *proper* chiefly because it speeds up the interviewing process
   B. *improper* chiefly because the man is likely to become confused as to what information is really important
   C. *proper* chiefly because the man is likely to be impressed with the aide's interest in the crime
   D. *improper* chiefly because an opportunity for gaining pertinent information may be lost

3. You are interviewing the owner of a stolen car about facts relating to the robbery. After completing his statement, the car owner suddenly states that some of the details he has just related are not correct. You realize that this change might be significant.
   Of the following, it would be BEST for you to

   A. ask the owner what other details he may have given incorrectly
   B. make a note of the discrepancy for discussion at a later date
   C. repeat your questioning on the details that were misstated until you have covered that area completely
   D. explain to the owner that because of his change of testimony, you will have to repeat the entire interview

4. You are interviewing a client who has just been assaulted. He has trouble collecting his thoughts and telling his story coherently.
   Which of the following represents the MOST effective method of questioning under these circumstances?

   A. Ask questions which structure the client's story chronologically into units, each with a beginning, middle, and end.
   B. Ask several questions at a time to structure the interview.

C. Ask open-ended questions which allow the client to respond in a variety of ways.
D. Begin the interview with several detailed questions in order to focus the client's attention on the situation.

5. Following are two statements that might be correct concerning the relationship with clients:
    I. When practical the client should be encouraged to take some steps on his own behalf to aid the office in handling his case
    II. The client should be told what steps the office proposes to take on his behalf

    Which of the following CORRECTLY classifies the above statements?

    A. Statement I is generally correct, but Statement II is not.
    B. Statement II is generally correct, but Statement I is not.
    C. Both statements are generally correct.
    D. Neither statement is generally correct.

6. You are in the District Attorney's office interviewing an elderly female victim of an assault in order to prepare a list of charges.
    The one of the following which would be MOST important in determining all the facts is

    A. creating a close, cooperative working relationship with the victim
    B. establishing your authority at the beginning of the interview
    C. maintaining a relaxed atmosphere during the interview
    D. having access to the particular statutes which might apply to this case

7. A client is critical of the way he has been treated by government agencies in the past. A paralegal aide interviewing him defends the overall performance of government employees.
    This reaction by the aide is GENERALLY

    A. *appropriate;* the aide has an obligation to defend fellow workers in government service when such defense is justified
    B. *inappropriate;* the aide should remain neutral rather than volunteer his personal opinions
    C. *appropriate;* the aide should honestly express his personal opinions in such circumstances unless it is likely to provoke antagonism
    D. *inappropriate;* the aide should agree with the client's comments to help establish a greater rapport with him

Questions 8-11.

DIRECTIONS: Questions 8 through 11 are to be answered SOLELY on the basis of the following passage.

A person may use physical force upon another person when and to the extent he reasonably believes such to be necessary to defend himself or a third person from what he reasonably believes to be the use or imminent use of unlawful physical force by such other person, unless (a) the latter's conduct was provoked by the actor himself with intent to cause physical injury to another person, or (b) the actor was the initial aggressor; or (c) the physical force involved is the product of a combat by agreement not specifically authorized by law.

A person may not use deadly physical force upon another person under the circumstances specified above unless: (a) he reasonably believes that such other person is using or is about to use deadly physical force. Even in such case, however, the actor may not use deadly physical force if he knows he can with complete safety as to himself and others avoid the necessity of doing so by retreating, except that he is under no duty to retreat if he is in his dwelling and is not the initial aggressor; or (b) he reasonably believes that such other person is committing or attempting to commit a kidnapping, forcible rape, or forcible sodomy.

8. Jones and Smith, who have not met before, get into an argument in a tavern. Smith takes a punch at Jones but misses. Jones then hits Smith on the chin with his fist. Smith falls to the floor and suffers minor injuries. According to the above passage, it would be CORRECT to state that

    A. *only* Smith was justified in using physical force
    B. *only* Jones was justified in using physical force
    C. both Smith and Jones were justified in using physical force
    D. neither Smith nor Jones was justified in using physical force

9. While walking down the street, Brady observes Miller striking Mrs. Adams on the head with his fist in an attempt to steal her purse.
   According to the above passage, it would be CORRECT to state that Brady would

    A. not be justified in using deadly physical force against Miller since Brady can safety retreat
    B. be justified in using physical force against Miller, but not deadly physical force
    C. not be justified in using physical force against Miller since Brady himself is not being attacked
    D. be justified in using deadly physical force

10. Winters is attacked from behind by Sharp, who attempts to beat up Winters with a blackjack. Winters disarms Sharp and succeeds in subduing him with a series of blows to the head. Sharp stops fighting and explains that he thought Winters was the person who had robbed his apartment a few minutes before, but now realizes his mistake. According to the above passage, it would be CORRECT to state that

    A. Winters was justified in using physical force on Sharp only to the extent necessary to defend himself
    B. Winters was not justified in using physical force on Sharp since Sharp's attack was provoked by what he believed to be Winters' behavior
    C. Sharp was justified in using physical force on Winters since he reasonably believed that Winters had unlawfully robbed him
    D. Winters was justified in using physical force on Sharp only because Sharp was acting mistakenly in attacking him

11. Roberts hears a noise in the cellar of his home and, upon investigation, discovers an intruder, Welch. Welch moves towards Roberts in a threatening manner, thrusts his hand into a bulging pocket, and withdraws what appears to be a gun. Roberts thereupon strikes Welch over the head with a golf club. He then sees that the *gun* is a toy. Welch later dies of head injuries.
    According to the above passage, it would be CORRECT to state that Roberts

A. *was justified* in using deadly physical force because he reasonably believed Welch was about to use deadly physical force
B. *was not justified* in using deadly physical force
C. *was justified* in using deadly physical force only because he did not provoke Welch's conduct
D. *was justified* in using deadly physical force only because he was not the initial aggressor

Questions 12-15.

DIRECTIONS: Questions 12 through 15 are to be answered SOLELY on the basis of the following passage.

From the beginning, the Supreme Court has supervised the fairness of trials conducted by the Federal government. But the Constitution, as originally drafted, gave the court no such general authority in state oases. The court's power to deal with state cases comes from the Fourteenth Amendment, which became part of the Constitution in 1868. The crucial provision forbids any state to "deprive any person of life, liberty or property without due process of law."

The guarantee of "due process" would seem, at the least, to require fair procedure in criminal trials. But curiously, the Supreme Court did not speak on the question for many decades. During that time, however, the due process clause was interpreted to bar "unreasonable" state economic regulations, such as minimum wage laws.

In 1915, there came the case of Leo M. Frank, a Georgian convicted of murder in a trial that he contended was dominated by mob hysteria. Historians now agree that there was such hysteria, with overtones of anti-semitism.

The Supreme Court held that it could not look past the findings of the Georgia courts that there had been no mob atmosphere at the trial. Justices Oliver Wendell Holmes and Charles Evans Hughes dissented, arguing that the constitutional guarantee would be "a barren one" if the Federal courts could not make their own inferences from the facts.

In 1923, the case of Moore v. Dempsey involved five Arkansas blacks convicted of murder and sentenced to death in a community so aroused against them that at one point they were saved from lynching only by Federal troops. Witnesses against them were said to have been beaten into testifying.

The court, though not actually setting aside the convictions, directed a lower Federal court to hold a habeas corpus hearing to find out whether the trial had been fair, or whether the whole proceeding had been "a mask — that counsel, jury, and judge were swept to the fatal end by an irresistible wave of public opinion."

12. According to the above passage, the Supreme Court's INITIAL interpretation of the Fourteenth Amendment

    A. protected state supremacy in economic matters
    B. increased the scope of Federal jurisdiction
    C. required fair procedures in criminal trials
    D. prohibited the enactment of minimum wage laws

12.____

13. According to the above passage, the Supreme Court in the Frank case

    A. denied that there had been mob hysteria at the trial
    B. decided that the guilty verdict was supported by the evidence
    C. declined to question the state court's determination of the facts
    D. found that Leo Frank had not received *due process*

14. According to the above passage, the dissenting judges in the Frank case maintained that

    A. due process was an empty promise in the circumstances of that case
    B. the Federal courts could not guarantee certain provisions of the Constitution
    C. the Federal courts should not make their own inferences from the facts in state cases
    D. the Supreme Court had rendered the Constitution *barren*

15. Of the following, the MOST appropriate title for the above passage is:

    A. THE CONDUCT OF FEDERAL TRIALS
    B. THE DEVELOPMENT OF STATES' RIGHTS: 1868-1923
    C. MOORE V. DEMPSEY: A CASE STUDY IN CRIMINAL JUSTICE
    D. DUE PROCESS - THE EVOLUTION OF A CONSTITUTIONAL CORNERSTONE

KEY (CORRECT ANSWERS)

1.	B	6.	A
2.	D	7.	B
3.	C	8.	B
4.	A	9.	B
5.	C	10.	A

11.	A
12.	D
13.	C
14.	A
15.	D

EVALUATING INFORMATION AND EVIDENCE
EXAMINATION SECTION
TEST 1

DIRECTIONS: Each question or incomplete statement is followed by several suggested answers or completions. Select the one that BEST answers the question or completes the statement. *PRINT THE LETTER OF THE CORRECT ANSWER IN THE SPACE AT THE RIGHT.*

Questions 1-9.

DIRECTIONS: Questions 1 through 9 measure your ability to (1) determine whether statements from witnesses say essentially the same thing and (2) determine the evidence needed to make it reasonably certain that a particular conclusion is true.

1. Which of the following pairs of statements say essentially the same thing in two different ways?
   I. Some employees at the water department have fully vested pensions.
      At least one employee at the water department has a pension that is not fully vested.
   II. All swans are white birds.
       A bird that is not white is not a swan.
   The CORRECT answer is:
   A. I only   B. I and II   C. II only   D. Neither I nor II

   1.____

2. Which of the following pairs of statements say essentially the same thing in two different ways?
   I. If you live in Humboldt County, your property taxes are high.
      If your property taxes are high, you live in Humboldt County.
   II. All the Hutchinsons live in Lindsborg.
       At least some Hutchinsons do not live in Lindsborg.
   The CORRECT answer is;
   A. I only   B. I and II   C. II only   D. Neither I nor II

   2.____

3. Which of the following pairs of statements say essentially the same thing in two different ways?
   I. Although Spike is a friendly dog, he is also one of the most unpopular dogs on the block.
      Although Spike is one of the most unpopular dogs on the block, he is a friendly dog.
   II. Everyone in Precinct 19 is taller than Officer Banks.
       Nobody in Precinct 19 is shorter than Officer Banks.
   The CORRECT answer is:
   A. I only   B. I and II   C. II only   D. Neither I nor II

   3.____

55

4. Which of the following pairs of statements say essentially the same thing in two different ways?
   I. On Friday, every officer in Precinct 1 is assigned parking duty or crowd control, or both.
      If a Precinct 1 officer has been assigned neither parking duty nor crowd control, it is not Friday.
   II. Because the farmer mowed the hay fields today, his house will have mice tomorrow.
      Whenever the farmer mows his hay fields, his house has mice the next day.
   The CORRECT answer is:
   A. I only   B. I and II   C. II only   D. Neither I nor II

4._____

5. Summary of Evidence Collected to Date:
   I. Fishing in the Little Pony River is against the law.
      Captain Rick caught an 8-inch trout and ate it for dinner.
   Prematurely Drawn Conclusion: Captain Rick broke the law.
   Which of the following pieces of evidence, if any, would make it reasonably certain that the conclusion drawn is true?
   A. Captain Rick caught his trout in the Little Pony River.
   B. There is no size limit on trout mentioned in the law.
   C. A trout is a species of fish.
   D. None of the above

5._____

6. Summary of Evidence Collected to Date:
   I. Some of the doctors in the ICU have been sued for malpractice.
   II. Some of the doctors in the ICU are pediatricians.
   Prematurely Drawn Conclusion: Some of the pediatricians in the ICU have never been sued for malpractice.
   Which of the following pieces of evidence, if any, would make it reasonably certain that the conclusion drawn is true?
   A. The number of pediatricians in the ICU is the same as the number of doctors who have been sued for malpractice.
   B. The number of pediatricians in the ICU is smaller than the number of doctors who have been sued for malpractice.
   C. The number of ICU doctors who have been sued for malpractice is smaller than the number who are pediatricians.
   D. None of the above

6._____

7. Summary of Evidence Collected to Date:
   I. Along Paseo Boulevard, there are five convenience stores.
   II. EZ-GO is east of Pop-a-Shop.
   III. Kwik-E-Mart is west of Bob's Market.
   IV. The Nightwatch is between EZ-GO and Kwik-E-Mart.
   Prematurely Drawn Conclusion: Pop-a-Shop is the westernmost convenience store on Paseo Boulevard.

7._____

Which of the following pieces of evidence, if any, would make it reasonably certain that the conclusion drawn is true?
   A. Bob's Market is the easternmost convenience store on Paseo.
   B. Kwik-E-Mart is the second store from the west.
   C. The Nightwatch is west of the EZ-GO.
   D. None of the above

8. Summary of Evidence Collected to Date:
   Stark drove home from work at 70 miles an hour and wasn't breaking the law.
   Prematurely Drawn Conclusion: Stark was either on an interstate highway or in the state of Montana.
   Which of the following pieces of evidence, if any, would make it reasonably certain that the conclusion drawn is true?
   A. There are no interstate highways in Montana.
   B. Montana is the only state that allows a speed of 70 miles an hour on roads other than interstate highways.
   C. Most states don't allow speed of 70 miles an hour on state highways.
   D. None of the above

9. Summary of Evidence Collected to Date:
   I. Margaret, owner of MetroWoman magazine, signed a contract with each of her salespeople promising an automatic $200 bonus to any employee who sells more than 60 subscriptions in a calendar month.
   II. Lynn sold 82 subscriptions to MetroWoman in the month of December.
   Prematurely Drawn Conclusion: Lynn received a $20 bonus.
   Which of the following pieces of evidence, if any, would make it reasonably certain that the conclusion is true?
   A. Lynn is a salesperson.
   B. Lynn works for Margaret.
   C. Margaret offered only $200 regardless of the number of subscriptions sold.
   D. None of the above

Questions 10-14.

DIRECTIONS: Questions 10 through 14 refer to Map #3 and measure your ability to orient yourself within a given section of town, neighborhood or particular area. Each of the questions describes a starting point and a destination. Assume that you are driving a car in the area shown on the map accompanying the questions. Use the map as a basis for the shortest way to get from one point to another without breaking the law.
On the map, a street marked by arrows, or by arrows and the words "One Way," indicates one-way travel and should be assumed to be one-way for the entire length, even when there are breaks or jogs in the street. EXCEPTION: A street that does not have the same name over the full length.

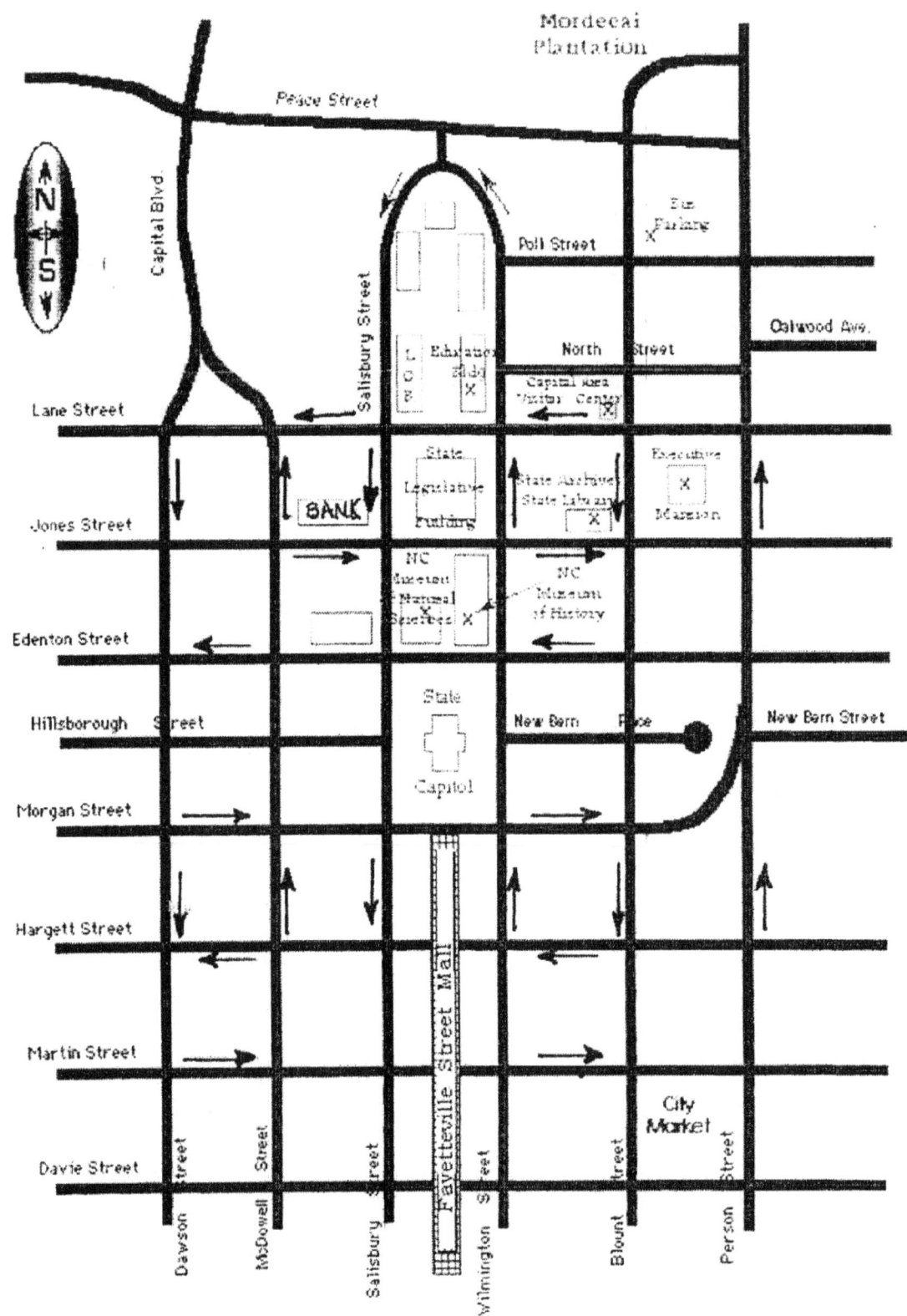

10. The SHORTEST legal way from the south end of the Fayetteville Street Mall, at Davie Street, to the city of Raleigh Municipal Building is
    A. west on Davie, north on McDowell
    B. west on Davie, north on Dawson
    C. east on Davie, north on Wilmington, west on Morgan
    D. east on Davie, north on Wilmington, west on Hargett

11. The SHORTEST legal way from the City Market to the Education Building is
    A. north on Blount, west on North
    B. north on Person, west on Lane
    C. north on Blount, west on Lane
    D. west on Martin, north on Wilmington

12. The SHORTEST legal way from the Education Building to the State Capitol is
    A. south on Wilmington
    B. north on Wilmington, west on Peace, south on Capitol, bear west to go south on Dawson, and east on Morgan
    C. west on Lane, south on Salisbury
    D. each on North, south on Blount, west on Edenton

13. The SHORTEST legal way from the State Capitol to Peace College is
    A. north on Wilmington, jog north, east on Peace
    B. east on Morgan, north on Person, west on Peace
    C. west on Edenton, north on McDowell, north on Capitol Blvd., east on Peace
    D. east on Morgan, north on Blount, west on Peace

14. The SHORTEST legal way from the State Legislative Building to the City Market is
    A. south on Wilmington, east on Martin
    B. east on Jones, south on Blount
    C. south on Salisbury, east on Davie
    D. east on Lane, south on Blount

Questions 15-19.

DIRECTIONS: Questions 15 through 19 refer to Figure #3, on the following page, and measure your ability to understand written descriptions of events. Each question presents a description of an accident or event and asks you which of the following five drawings in Figure #3 BEST represents it.
In the drawings, the following symbols are used:
Moving vehicle ◊   Non-moving vehicle ▲
Pedestrian or bicyclist •
The path and direction of travel of a vehicle or pedestrian is indicated by a solid line.
The path and direction of travel of each vehicle or pedestrian directly involved in a collision from the point of impact is indicated by a dotted line.

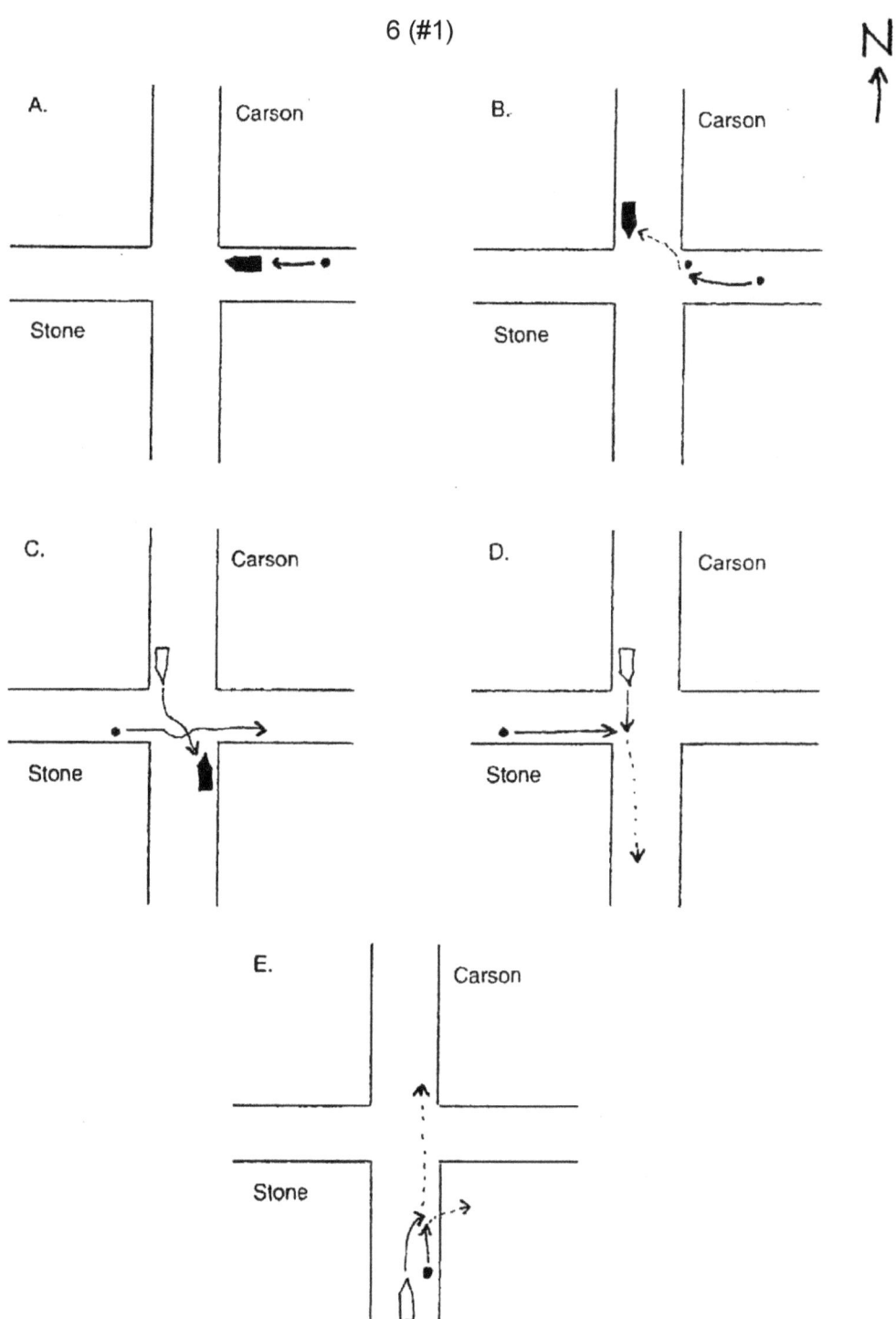

In the space at the right, print the letter of the drawing that BEST fit the descriptions written below.

15. A driver headed north on Carson veers to the right and strikes a bicyclist who is also headed north. The bicyclist is thrown from the road. The driver flees north on Carson.

15.____

16. A driver heading south on Carson runs the stop sign and barely misses colliding with an eastbound cyclist. The cyclist swerves to avoid the collision and continues traveling east. The driver swerves to avoid the collision and strikes a car parked in the northbound lane on Carson.

16.____

17. A bicyclist heading west on Stone collides with a pedestrian in the crosswalk, then veers through the intersection and collides with the front of a car parked in the southbound lane on Carson.

17.____

18. A driver traveling south on Carson runs over a bicyclist who has run the stop sign, and then flees south on Carson.

18.____

19. A bicyclist heading west on Stone collides with the rear of a car parked in the westbound lane.

19.____

Questions 20-22.

DIRECTIONS: In Questions 20 through 22, choose the word or phrase CLOSEST in meaning to the word or phrase printed in capital letters.

20. INSOLVENT
    A. bankrupt   B. vagrant   C. hazardous   D. illegal

20.____

21. TENANT
    A. laborer   B. occupant   C. owner   D. creditor

21.____

22. INFRACTION
    A. portion   B. violation   C. remark   D. detour

22.____

Questions 23-25.

DIRECTIONS: Questions 23 through 25 measure your ability to do fieldwork-related arithmetic. Each question presents a separate arithmetic problem for you to solve.

23. Officer Jones has served on the police force longer than Smith. Smith has served longer than Moore. Moore has served less time than Jones, and Park has served longer than Jones.
    Which officer has served the LONGEST on the police force?
    A. Jones   B. Smith   C. Moore   D. Park

23.____

24. A car wash has raised the price of an outside-only wash from $4 to $5. The car wash applies the same percentage increase to its inside-and-out wash, which was $10.
    What is the new cost of the inside-and-out wash?
    A. $8   B. $11   C. $12.50   D. $15

24.____

25. Ron and James, college students, make $10 an hour working at the restaurant.　　25.____
　　Ron works 13 hours a week and James works 20 hours a week.
　　To make the same amount that Ron earns in a year, James would work about
　　_____ weeks.
　　A. 18　　　　　B. 27　　　　　C. 34　　　　　D. 45

KEY (CORRECT ANSWERS)

1.	C	11.	B
2.	D	12.	C
3.	B	13.	A
4.	B	14.	B
5.	A	15.	E
6.	D	16.	C
7.	B	17.	B
8.	B	18.	D
9.	B	19.	A
10.	A	20.	A

21. B
22. B
23. D
24. C
25. C

SOLUTIONS TO QUESTIONS 1-9

P implies Q = original statement

Not Q implies not P = contrapositive of the original statement. A statement and its contrapositive are logically equivalent.

Q implies P = converse of the original statement

Not P implies not Q = inverse of the original statement. The converse and inverse of an original statement are logically equivalent.

P implies Q = Not P or Q.

1. The CORRECT answer is C.
   Item I is wrong because "some employees" means "at least one employee" and possibly "all employees." If it is true that all employees have fully vested pensions, then the second statement is false. Item II is correct because the second statement is the contrapositive of the first statement.

2. The CORRECT answer is D.
   Item I is wrong because the converse of a statement does not necessarily follow from the original statement. Item II is wrong because statement I implies that there are no Hutchinson family members who live outside Lindsborg.

3. The CORRECT answer is B. Item I is correct because it is composed of the same two compound statements that are simply mentioned in a different order. Item II is correct because if each person is taller than Officer Banks, then there is no person in that precinct who can possibly be shorter than Officer Banks.

4. The CORRECT answer is B.
   Item I is correct because the second statement is the contrapositive of the first statement. Item II is correct because each statement indicates that mowing the hay fields on a particular day leads to the presence of mice the next day.

5. The CORRECT answer is A.
   If Captain Rick caught his trout in the Little Pony River, then we can conclude that he was fishing there. Since statement I says that fishing in the Little Pony Rive is against the law, we conclude that Captain Rick broke the law.

6. The CORRECT answer is D.
   The number of doctors in each group, whether the same or not, has no bearing on the conclusion. There is nothing in evidence to suggest that the group of doctors sued for malpractice overlaps with the group of doctors that are pediatricians.

7. The CORRECT answer is B.
   If we are given that Kwik-E-Mart is the second store from the west, then the order of stores from west to east, is Pop-a-Shop, Kwik-E-Mart, Nightwatch, EZ-GO, and Bob's Market.

8. The CORRECT answer is B.
We are given that Stark drove at 70 miles per hour and didn't break the law. If we also know that Montana is the only state that allows a speed of 70 miles per hour, then we can conclude that Stark must have been driving in Montana or else was driving on some interstate.

9. The CORRECT answer is B.
The only additional piece of information needed is that Lynn works for Margaret. This will guarantee that Lynn receives the promised $200 bonus.

TEST 2

DIRECTIONS: Each question or incomplete statement is followed by several suggested answers or completions. Select the one that BEST answers the question or completes the statement. *PRINT THE LETTER OF THE CORRECT ANSWER IN THE SPACE AT THE RIGHT.*

Questions 1-9.

DIRECTIONS: Questions 1 through 9 measure your ability to (1) determine whether statements from witnesses say essentially the same thing and (2) determine the evidence needed to make it reasonably certain that a particular conclusion is true.
To do well on this part of the test, you do NOT have to have a working knowledge of police procedures and techniques. Nor do you have to have any more familiarity with criminals and criminal behavior than that acquired from reading newspapers, listening to radio or watching TV. To do well in this part, you must read and reason carefully.

1. Which of the following pairs of statements say essentially the same thing in two different ways? 1.____
   I. All of the teachers at Slater Middle School are intelligent, but some are irrational thinkers.
      Although some teachers at Slater Middle School are irrational thinkers, all of them are intelligent.
   II. Nobody has no friends.
      Everybody has at least one friend.
   The CORRECT answer is:
   A. I only B. I and II C. II only D. Neither I nor II

2. Which of the following pairs of statements say essentially the same thing in two different ways? 2.____
   I. Although bananas taste good to most people, they are also a healthy food.
      Bananas are a healthy food, but most people eat them because they taste good.
   II. If Dr. Jones is in, we should call at the office.
      Either Dr. Jones is in, or we should not call at the office.
   The CORRECT answer is:
   A. I only B. I and II C. II only D. Neither I nor II

3. Which of the following pairs of statements say essentially the same thing in two different ways? 3.____
   I. Some millworker work two shifts.
      If someone works only one shift, he is probably not a millworker.
   II. If a letter carrier clocks in at nine, he can finish his route by the end of the day.
      If a letter carrier does not clock in at nine, he cannot finish his route by the end of the day.
   The CORRECT answer is:
   A. I only B. I and II C. II only D. Neither I nor II

65

4. Which of the following pairs of statements say essentially the same thing in two different ways?
   I. If a member of the swim team attends every practice, he will compete in the next meet.
      Either a swim team member will compete in the next meet, or he did not attend every practice.
   II. All the engineers in the drafting department who wear glasses know how to use AutoCAD.
       If an engineer wears glasses, he will know how to use AutoCAD.
   The CORRECT answer is:
   A. I only   B. I and II   C. II only   D. Neither I nor II

5. Summary of Evidence Collected to Date:
   All of the parents who attend the weekly parenting seminars are high school graduates.
   Prematurely Drawn Conclusion: Some parents who attend the weekly parenting seminars have been convicted of child abuse.
   Which of the following pieces of evidence, if any, would make it reasonably certain that the conclusion drawn is true?
   A. Those convicted of child abuse are often high school graduates.
   B. Some high school graduates have been convicted of child abuse.
   C. There is no correlation between education level and the incidence of child abuse.
   D. None of the above

6. Summary of Evidence Collected to Date:
   I. Mr. Cantwell promised to vote for new school buses if he was reelected to the board.
   II. If the new school buses are approved by the school board, then Mr. Cantwell was not reelected to the board.
   Prematurely Drawn Conclusion: Approval of the new school buses was defeated in spite of Mr. Cantwell's vote.
   Which of the following pieces of evidence, if any, would make it reasonably certain that the conclusion drawn is true?
   A. Mr. Cantwell decided not to run for reelection.
   B. Mr. Cantwell was reelected to the board.
   C. Mr. Cantwell changed his mind and voted against the new buses.
   D. None of the above

7. Summary of Evidence Collected to Date:
   I. The station employs three detectives: Francis, Jackson, and Stern. One of the detectives is a lieutenant, one is a sergeant, and one is a major.
   II. Francis is not a lieutenant.
   Prematurely Drawn Conclusion: Jackson is a lieutenant.
   Which of the following pieces of evidence, if any, would make it reasonably certain that the conclusion drawn is true?
   A. Stern is not a sergeant.   B. Stern is a major.
   C. Francis is a major.   E. None of the above

8. Summary of Evidence Collected to Date: 8.____
   I. In the office building, every survival kit that contains a gas mask also contains anthrax vaccine.
   II. Some of the kits containing water purification tablets also contain anthrax vaccine.
   Prematurely Drawn Conclusion: If the survival kit near the typists' pool contains a gas mask, it does not contain water purification tablets.
   Which of the following pieces of evidence, if any, would make it reasonably certain that the conclusion drawn is true?
   A. Some survival kits contain all three items.
   B. The survival kit near the typists' pool contains anthrax vaccine.
   C. The survival kit near the typists' pool contains only two of these items.
   D. None of the above

9. Summary of Evidence Collected to Date: 9.____
   The shrink-wrap mechanism is designed to shut itself off if the heating coil temperature drops below 400 during the twin cycle.
   Prematurely Drawn Conclusion: If the machine was operating the twin cycle on Monday, it was not operating properly.
   Which of the following pieces of evidence, if any, would make it reasonably certain that the conclusion drawn is true?
   A. On Monday, the heating coil temperature reached 450.
   B. When the machine performs functions other than the twin cycle, the heating coil temperature sometimes drops below 400.
   C. The shrink-wrap mechanism did not shut itself off on Monday.
   D. None of the above

Questions 10-14.

DIRECTIONS: Questions 10 through 14 refer to Map #3 and measure your ability to orient yourself within a given section of town, neighborhood or particular area. Each of the questions describes a starting point and a destination. Assume that you are driving a car in the area shown on the map accompanying the questions. Use the map as a basis for the shortest way to get from one point to another without breaking the law.
On the map, a street marked by arrows, or by arrows and the words "One Way," indicates one-way travel and should be assumed to be one-way for the entire length, even when there are breaks or jogs in the street. EXCEPTION: A street that does not have the same name over the full length.

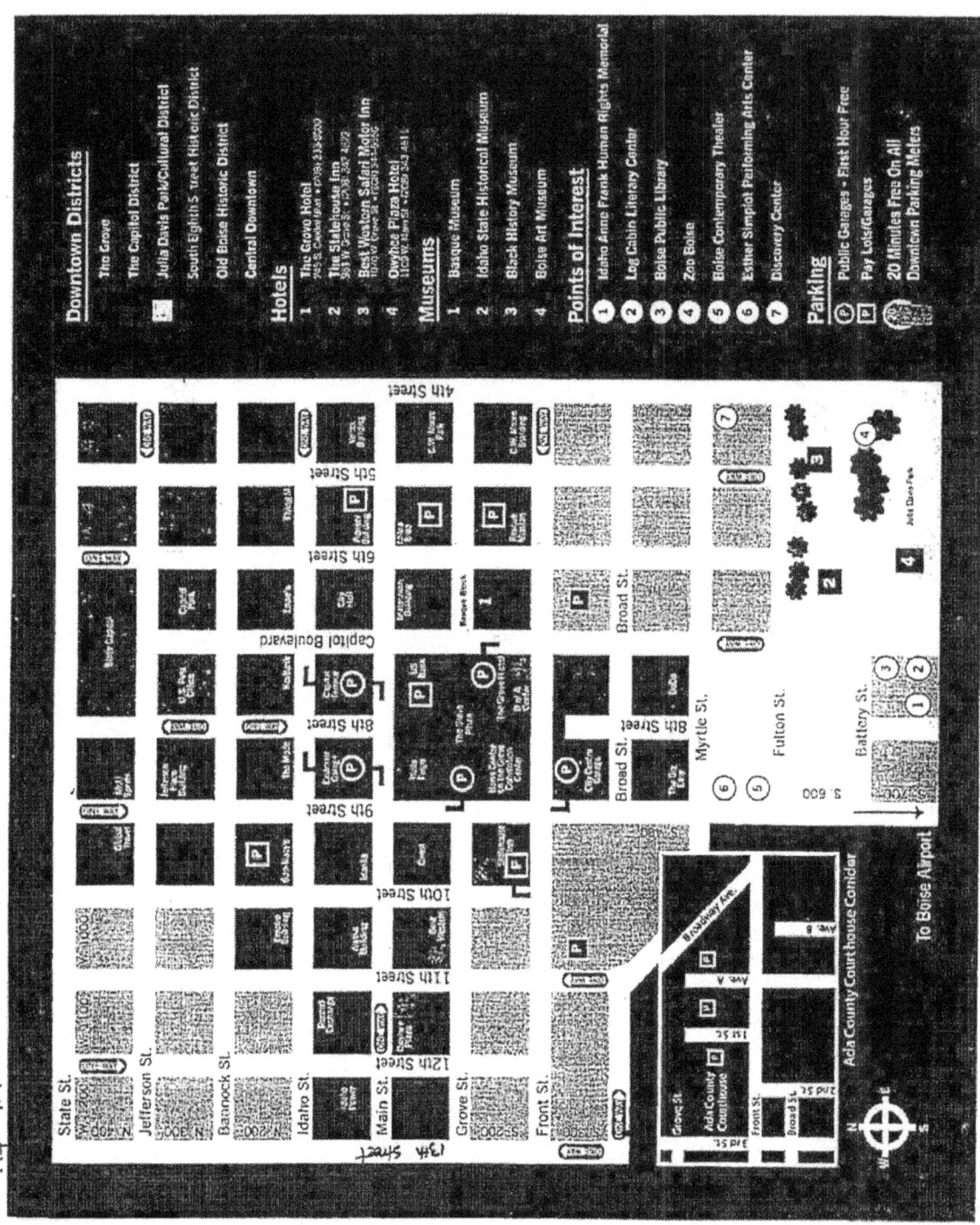

10. The SHORTEST legal way from the State Capitol to Idaho Power is 10.____
    A. south on Capitol Blvd., west on Main, north on 12th
    B. south on 8th, west on Main
    C. west on Jefferson, south on 12th
    D. south on Capitol Blvd., west on Front, north on 12th

11. The SHORTEST legal way from the Jefferson Place Building to the Statesman Building is   11._____
    A. east on Jefferson, south on Capitol Blvd.
    B. south on 8th, east on Main
    C. east on Jefferson, south on 4th, west on Main
    D. south on 9th, east on Main

12. The SHORTEST legal way from Julia Davis Park to Owyhee Plaza Hotel is   12._____
    A. north on 5th, west on Front, north on 11th
    B. north on 6th, west on Main
    C. west on Battery, north on 9th, west on Front, north on Main
    D. north on 5th, west on Front, north on 13th, east on Main

13. The SHORTEST legal way from the Big Easy to City Hall is   13._____
    A. north on 9th, east on Main
    B. east on Myrtle, north on Capitol Blvd.
    C. north on 9th, east on Idaho
    D. east on Myrtle, north on 6th

14. The SHORTEST legal way from the Boise Contemporary Theater to the Pioneer Building is   14._____
    A. north on 9th, east on Main
    B. north on 9th, east on Myrtle, north on 6th
    C. east on Fulton, north on Capitol Blvd., east on Main
    D. east on Fulton, north on 6th

Questions 15-19.

DIRECTIONS: Questions 15 through 19 refer to Figure #3, on the following page, and measure your ability to understand written descriptions of events. Each question presents a description of an accident or event and asks you which of the following five drawings in Figure #3 BEST represents it.
In the drawings, the following symbols are used:
Moving vehicle ◊   Non-moving vehicle ▮
Pedestrian or bicyclist •
The path and direction of travel of a vehicle or pedestrian is indicated by a solid line.
The path and direction of travel of each vehicle or pedestrian directly involved in a collision from the point of impact is indicated by a dotted line.

In the space at the right, print the letter of the drawing that BEST fit the descriptions written below.

6 (#2)

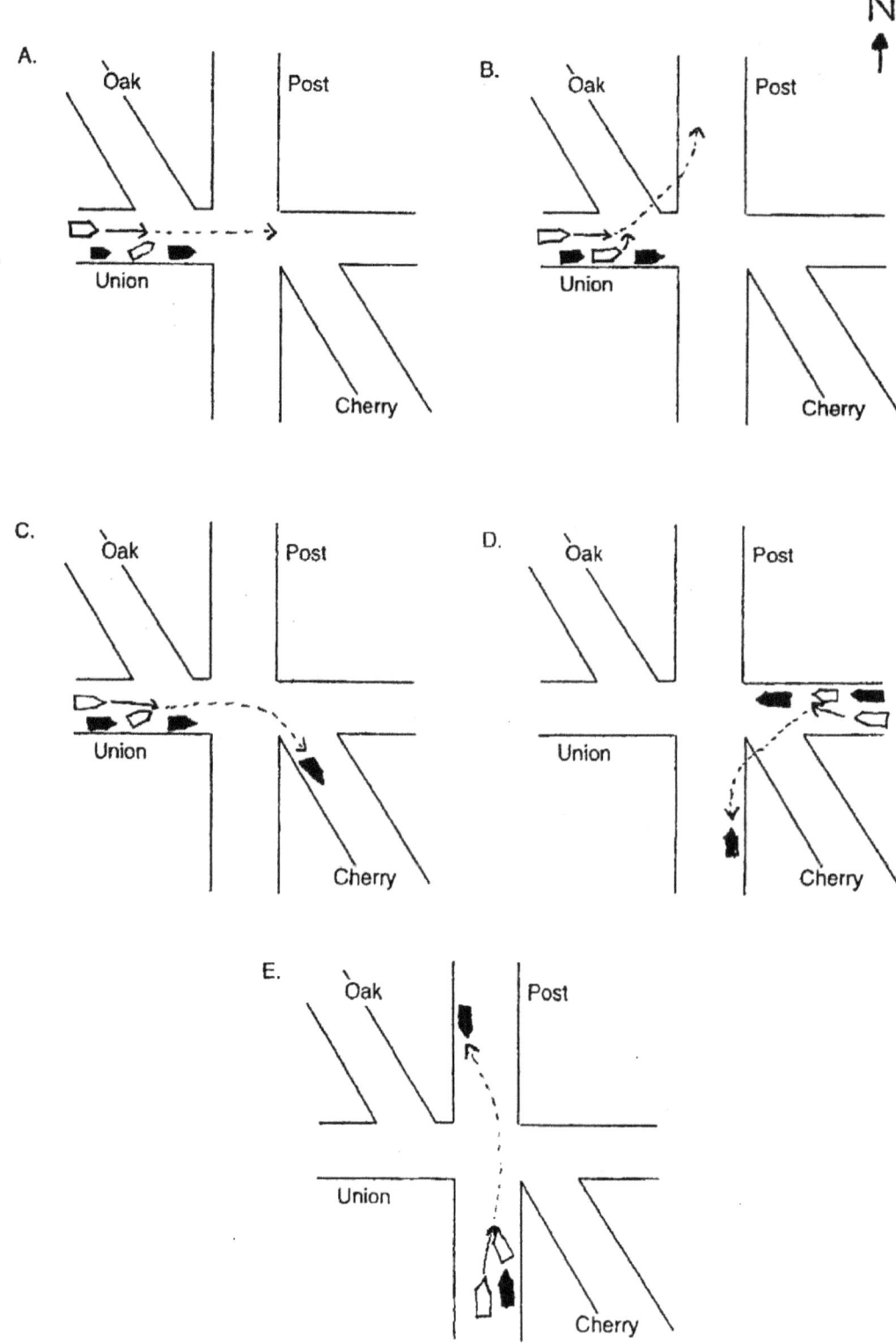

15. A driver headed east on Union strikes a car that is pulling out from between two parked cars, and then continues east. 15.____

16. A driver headed north on Post strikes a car that is pulling out from in front of a parked car, then veers into the oncoming lane and collides head-on with a car that is parked in the southbound lane of Post. 16.____

17. A driver headed east on Union strikes a car that is pulling out from two parked cars, travels through the intersection, and makes a sudden right turn onto Cherry, where he strikes a parked car in the rear. 17.____

18. A driver headed west on Union strikes a car that is pulling out from between two parked cars, and then swerves to the left. He cuts the corner and travels over the sidewalk at the intersection of Cherry and Post, and then strikes a car that is parked in the northbound lane on Post. 18.____

19. A driver headed east on Union strikes a car that is pulling out from between two parked cars, and then swerves to the left. He cuts the corner and travels over the sidewalk at the intersection of Oak and Post, and then flees north on Post. 19.____

Questions 20-22.

DIRECTIONS: In Questions 20 through 22, choose the word or phrase CLOSEST in meaning to the word or phrase printed in capital letters.

20. TITLE 20.____
 A. danger   B. ownership   C. description   D. treatise

21. REVOKE 21.____
 A. cancel   B. imagine   C. solicit   D. cause

22. BRIEF 22.____
 A. summary   B. ruling   C. plea   D. motion

Questions 23-25.

DIRECTIONS: Questions 23 through 25 measure your ability to do fieldwork-related arithmetic. Each question presents a separate arithmetic problem for you to solve.

23. An investigator plans to drive from his home to Los Angeles, a trip of 2,800 miles. His car has a 24-gallon tank and gets 18 miles to the gallon. If he starts out with a full tank of gasoline, what is the FEWEST number of stops he will have to make for gasoline to complete his trip to Los Angeles? 23.____
 A. 4   B. 5   C. 6   D. 7

24. A caseworker has 24 home visits to schedule for a week. She will visit three homes on Sunday, and on every day that follows she will visit one more home than she visited on the previous day.
At the end of the day on _____, the caseworker will have completed all of her home visits.
   A. Wednesday   B. Thursday   C. Friday   D. Saturday

25. Ms. Langhorn takes a cab from her house to the airport. The cab company charges $3.00 to start the meter and $.50 per mile after that. It's 15 miles from Ms. Langhorn's house to the airport.
How much will she have to pay for a cab?
   A. $10.50   B. $11.50   C. $14.00   D. $15.50

KEY (CORRECT ANSWERS)

1.	B		11.	D
2.	A		12.	A
3.	D		13.	B
4.	B		14.	C
5.	D		15.	A
6.	B		16.	E
7.	B		17.	C
8.	C		18.	D
9.	C		19.	B
10.	C		20.	B

21. A
22. A
23. C
24. B
25. A

SOLUTIONS TO QUESTIONS 1-9

P implies Q = original statement

Not Q implies not P = contrapositive of the original statement. A statement and its contrapositive are logically equivalent.

Q implies P = converse of the original statement

Not P implies not Q = inverse of the original statement. The converse and inverse of an original statement are logically equivalent.

P implies Q = Not P or Q.

1. The CORRECT answer is B.
   For Item I, the irrational thinking teachers at the Middle School belong the group of all Middle School teachers. Since all teachers at the Middle School are intelligent, this includes the subset of irrational thinkers. For item II, if no one person has no friends, this implies that each person must have at least one friend.

2. The CORRECT answer is A.
   In item I, both statements state that (a) bananas are healthy and (b) bananas are eaten mainly because they taste good. In item II, the second statement is not equivalent to the first statement. An equivalent statement to the first statement would be "Either Dr. Jones is not in or we should call at the office."

3. The CORRECT answer is D.
   In item I, given that a person works one shift, we cannot draw any conclusion about whether he/she is a millworker. It is possible that a millworker works one, two, or a number more than two shifts. In item II, the second statement is the inverse of the first statement; they are not logically equivalent.

4. The CORRECT answer is B.
   In item I, any statement in the form "P implies Q" is equivalent to "Not P or Q." In this case, P = A member of the swim team attends practice, and Q = He will compete in the next meet. In item II, "P implies Q" is equivalent to "all P belongs to Q." In this case, P = Engineer wears glasses, and Q = He will know how to use AutoCAD.

5. The CORRECT answer is D. Because the number of high school graduates is so much larger than the number of convicted child abusers, none of the additional pieces of evidence make it reasonably certain that there are convicted abusers within this group of parents.

6. The CORRECT answer is B.
   Statement II is equivalent to "If Mr. Cantwell is reelected to the school board, then school buses are not approved. Statement I assures us that Mr. Cantwell will vote for new school buses. The only logical conclusion is that in spite of Mr. Cantwell's reelection to the board and subsequent vote, approval of the buses was still defeated.

7. The CORRECT answer is B. From Statement II, we conclude that Francis is either a sergeant or a major. If we also know that Stern is a major, we can deduce that Francis is a sergeant. This means that the third person, Jackson, must be a lieutenant.

8. The CORRECT answer is C.
Given that a survival kit contains a gas mask, Statement I assures us that it also contains the anthrax vaccine. If the survival kit near the typist pool only contains two items, than we can conclude that the gas mask in this location cannot contain a third item, namely the anthrax vaccine.

9. The CORRECT answer is C.
The original statement can be written in "P implies Q" form, where P = the heating coil temperature drops below 400 during the twin cycle, and Q = the mechanism shuts itself off. The contrapositive (which must be true) would be "If the mechanism did not shut itself off then the heating coil temperature did not drop below 400." We would then conclude that the temperature was too high and, therefore, the machine did not operate properly.

EXAMINATION SECTION
TEST 1

DIRECTIONS: Each question or incomplete statement is followed by several suggested answers or completions. Select the one that BEST answers the question or completes the statement. *PRINT THE LETTER OF THE CORRECT ANSWER IN THE SPACE AT THE RIGHT.*

1. R forcibly stole property from Z.
   Which one of the following additional elements, if present, would MOST properly justify charging R with robbery in the first degree, rather than robbery in the third degree?
   R

   A. punched Z during the robbery, giving Z a black eye
   B. used a motor vehicle to escape from the robbery scene
   C. was aided by an accomplice when committing the robbery
   D. produced a knife and threatened to use it, but did not stab Z, when committing the robbery
   E. produced a gun and threatened to use it during the robbery. The gun was unloaded but Z did not know this.

   1._____

2. Patrolman P, having received information from a reliable third party that Z had committed a misdemeanor, arrests Z without a warrant and drives him to the lockup. As Z is being transferred from the patrol car to the lockup, he breaks away from P and runs into a crowd of persons. After a ten-minute foot chase, P reapprehends Z.
   Which one of the following BEST states the offense or offenses, if any, for which P may now properly arrest Z without a warrant?

   A. Only escape in the third degree
   B. Only escape in the second degree
   C. Only the misdemeanor for which he was originally arrested
   D. P may not properly arrest Z for any of the above offenses
   E. The misdemeanor for which he was originally arrested, and escape in the third degree

   2._____

3. A stolen car with three occupants is stopped after a high speed chase and the occupants are arrested. P, one of the occupants, has an unloaded, but operable, .32 caliber pistol tucked in his belt, and six .32 caliber rounds in his pocket. U, the second occupant, has an unloaded, but operable, .45 caliber pistol in his pants' pocket and has no bullets on his person. L, the driver, has neither a pistol nor any ammunition on his person. When the vehicle is searched, a loaded .38 caliber pistol is found under the right front seat. None of the occupants of the car has ever been convicted of a crime and none has a valid license for any of the weapons.
   Which one of the following BEST states which weapon or weapons each man may properly be charged with felonious possession of?

   A. P, U, and L may each properly be charged with felonious possession of only the .32 and the .38.
   B. P, U, and L may each properly be charged with felonious possession of the .32, the .38, and the .45.

   3._____

C. P may properly be charged only with felonious possession of the .32, and both U and L may not be properly charged with the felonious possession of any of the weapons.
D. P may properly be charged with felonious possession of only the .32, U may properly be charged only with the felonious possession of the .45, and L may not be properly charged with the felonious possession of any of the weapons.
E. P may properly be charged with felonious possession only of the .32 and the .38, U may properly be charged with felonious possession only of the .45 and the .38, and L may properly be charged with felonious possession only of the .38.

4. Following are three situations in which a police officer might possibly be justified in using deadly physical force upon another person:
   I. To prevent the escape of an unarmed person who was seen by the officer snatching a woman's purse
   II. To arrest an unarmed person observed by the officer committing arson
   III. To arrest an unarmed person when the officer reasonably believes that the person is likely to inflict serious physical injury to a third party unless apprehended without delay, under conditions that do not amount to imminent use of deadly physical force

   Which one of the following choices lists ALL of the above cases in which a police officer is actually justified in using deadly physical force and NONE in which he is not?
   He is

   A. justified in I, II, and III
   B. not justified in I, II, or III
   C. justified in I and III, but not in II
   D. justified in II but not in I and III
   E. justified in II and III, but not in I

5. L lends R a pistol, believing that R intends to use the pistol to rob V. During the robbery, with which L had no further part, R kills V.
   Which one of the following, if any, is the MOST serious crime with which L may properly be charged?

   A. Conspiracy in the fourth degree
   B. Criminal facilitation in the first degree
   C. Criminal facilitation in the second degree
   D. Criminal solicitation in the second degree
   E. None of the above, since he may not properly be charged with any crime

6. Which one of the following is LEAST likely to be a degree-raising factor for the crime of assault?
   That

   A. a dangerous instrument was used
   B. the assailant was over 18 years of age when the assault occurred
   C. serious physical injury rather than ordinary physical injury was caused
   D. physical injury was caused intentionally rather than recklessly
   E. physical injury was inflicted in the course of the commission of an independent felony

7. R and S, while planning an armed robbery of an armored truck, study the route taken by the truck from a bank to a factory where payroll money is delivered every Thursday. A bartender hears their conversation and informs the police. Part of the plan involves staging an automobile accident along the route taken by the truck, and robbing the truck when the driver stops. On the day of the intended robbery, the route taken by the truck is altered so that it will not pass by the location where R and S have staged the accident; and R and S, both heavily armed, are arrested by police at the scene.
Which one of the following is the MOST serious crime with which R and S may properly be charged?

   A. Robbery in the first degree
   B. Conspiracy in the third degree
   C. Conspiracy in the second degree
   D. Attempted robbery in the first degree
   E. Attempted robbery in the second degree

8. The section of the State Penal Law dealing with murder has been modified in several respects. One such modification concerned an aspect of the *felony murder* doctrine of the law.
Which one of the following is both the MOST accurate statement as to how the felony murder doctrine was modified and also the APPARENT legislative intent therefor?

   A. Listing certain specific felonies, to clarify the meaning of the term *any felony* in the former statute
   B. Including all felonies under the felony murder doctrine, so that a fatality which occurs during the commission of any felony is punishable as murder
   C. Including all felonies in which a motor vehicle is used, either in committing the felony or in escaping from the scene, so that fatalities which occur in these cases are punishable as murder
   D. Excluding certain non-violent felonies from the felony murder doctrine, so that a fatality which is either accidental or which the perpetrator cannot reasonably foresee is not punishable as murder
   E. Adding the necessity of proving intent as an element of murder in non-violent felonies, so that a fatality in connection with a non-violent felony is not punishable as murder when intent cannot be proved

9. While on duty, P, a police officer, received from his superior a description of Z, who was involved in a robbery, and believed to be in P's area. The superior officer's information concerning Z's involvement in the robbery came from a reliable third party. P observes a person closely matching Z's description. When P approaches, the person starts to run, but is quickly apprehended and placed under arrest for robbery. While searching this person for weapons, P discovers a quantity of narcotics in his inside coat pocket and forthwith seizes the narcotics.
Which one of the following MOST properly evaluates both whether or not the seizure of the narcotics was proper in this case and also the BEST reason therefor?
The seizure was

   A. *proper,* but only because narcotics are contraband
   B. *proper,* since it was made incident to a lawful arrest
   C. *improper,* since P did not have an arrest warrant for Z
   D. *improper,* since P did not have probable cause for arrest
   E. *improper,* since the narcotics were unrelated to the crime for which the arrest was made

10. Following are three situations in which *Miranda* warnings were not given when the confessions made by the persons involved might possibly be admissible as evidence:
A person
   I. walks into a police station and volunteers a statement to the desk sergeant implicating himself in a robbery
   II. in prison for committing a certain crime, being questioned concerning his involvement in a second crime, confesses to the second crime
   III. arrested at the scene of a robbery attempt, being questioned concerning the crime, confesses to the crime

Which one of the following choices lists all of the above situations in which the confession is ADMISSIBLE and none in which it is NOT?
The confession is admissible in

   A. I, but not in II and III
   B. I and II, but not in III
   C. I, II, and III
   D. I and III, but not in II
   E. III, but not in I and II

KEY (CORRECT ANSWERS)

1.	D	6.	B
2.	D	7.	D
3.	A	8.	D
4.	D	9.	B
5.	C	10.	A

TEST 2

DIRECTIONS: Each question or incomplete statement is followed by several suggested answers or completions. Select the one that BEST answers the question or completes the statement. *PRINT THE LETTER OF THE CORRECT ANSWER IN THE SPACE AT THE RIGHT.*

1. According to the Criminal Procedure Law, the decision of the judge presiding in the court in which the crime is triable is final with respect to bail. An order denying bail is non-appealable and so any attack on such a denial of bail must be by other means.
The *other means* is by resort to the prisoner's separate and different right to test the legality of his detention by a

   A. writ of coram nobis
   B. writ of habeas corpus
   C. writ of certiorari
   D. certificate of reasonable doubt

   1.____

2. X, intending to rob Y, points an unloaded revolver at him.
The element which makes the assault involved here assault, second degree, is the fact that

   A. there is no intent to kill
   B. the revolver is unloaded
   C. the injury, if any were sustained, would be relatively light
   D. the intent is thus shown to be to secure property and not to inflict grave bodily harm

   2.____

3. One of the defenses available to one accused of crime is that of entrapment.
The defense of entrapment is LEAST likely to be met with in _____ cases.

   A. narcotics   B. prostitution
   C. gambling   D. rape

   3.____

4. With respect to the review of convictions in state courts by the Supreme Court of the United States, the latter has stated that, so far as due process affects admissions before trial of the defendant, the accepted test of the admissibility of such admissions is their

   A. voluntariness   B. timeliness
   C. materiality   D. motivation

   4.____

5. A very important rule in the law of evidence is that known as the *best evidence rule*.
This rule applies to

   A. documents   B. judicial notice
   C. eyewitness testimony   D. oral testimony

   5.____

6. The one of the following statements which is LEAST correct, according to the Criminal Procedure Law, is that a peace officer may arrest a person

   A. without warrant for a felony when he has reasonable cause for believing that a felony has been committed and that the person arrested committed it
   B. with a warrant at any hour of the day or night for any crime provided the arrest is made in the same county where the warrant was issued

   6.____

C. without a warrant when a felony has in fact been committed and he has reasonable cause for believing the person to be arrested to have committed it
D. at night with a warrant for a misdemeanor when directed by the issuing judge's endorsement upon the warrant

7. The one of the following statements concerning arrests by private persons which is INCORRECT is:

   A. A private person who has arrested another for the commission of a crime must deliver him to a peace officer
   B. A private person may arrest another for a crime committed or attempted in his presence
   C. A private person makes an arrest for a felony at his peril if he arrests the wrong person
   D. Except when making an arrest during the actual commission of a crime or on pursuit immediately after its commission, a private person before making an arrest, must inform the person to be arrested of the cause thereof, and require him to submit

8. A change in the Criminal Procedures Law in relation to filing complaints against a youthful offender so that he may be adjudged a wayward minor provides that a new class of individuals who may lay such an information before the judge is that of

   A. peace officers
   B. other persons standing in parental relation as being the next of kin
   C. principals or teachers of any school where such person is registered for attendance
   D. representatives of an incorporated society doing charitable or philanthropic work

9. Persons apprehended by Federal agents in conjunction with city police in many narcotics arrests are frequently tried under the State law in a State court.
   Of the following, the PRINCIPAL reason for this procedure is that

   A. more expeditious handling of the case is assured due to the unusually heavy caseload in the Federal courts in the city
   B. it is then not necessary to reveal the identity of the Federal agents involved in an arrest
   C. the penalties in the state courts are more certain and usually more drastic
   D. state courts are less severe with respect to the admissibility of certain kinds of evidence

10. It has been suggested that in reducing a confession to writing it is desirable to include several errors and to have the person making the confession make the corrections and sign or initial them.
    The one of the following which MOST supports this suggestion is that such corrections by the person making the confession

    A. helps to minimize the credibility of possible later denials concerning the material set forth in the confession
    B. is likely to encourage the investigator to continue his investigation on the corrected matter and thereby discourages a complete reliance on the confession itself

C. provides additional and new evidence which links the person making the confession to the crime charged
D. provides additional corroboration of facts which only the person making the confession would know about

KEY (CORRECT ANSWERS)

1. B
2. B
3. D
4. A
5. A

6. B
7. A
8. C
9. D
10. A

EXAMINATION SECTION
TEST 1

DIRECTIONS: Each question or incomplete statement is followed by several suggested answers or completions. Select the one that BEST answers the question or completes the statement. *PRINT THE LETTER OF THE CORRECT ANSWER IN THE SPACE AT THE RIGHT.*

Questions 1-3.

DIRECTIONS: Questions 1 through 3 are to be answered on the basis of the following fact pattern.

Dave asks his son, Junior, to drop off a package to their neighbor. Dave knows there are drugs in the package. Dave's neighbor, Tom, is expecting the package. However, Junior is intercepted by a police officer who happened to be driving by at the time of the delivery.

1. When charged, what will Dave MOST likely be accused of committing? 1.____
    A. Drug trafficking violation
    B. Drug offense
    C. Drug trafficking felony
    D. Misdemeanor

2. Which of the following scenarios also falls under the same category as described above? 2.____
    A. Criminal sale of a controlled substance in or near schools
    B. Sexual assault of a minor
    C. Burglary of a senior citizen or assisted living facility
    D. Burglary of a school

3. At trial, Dave argues that he did not possess any drugs at the time of his arrest. Which of the following is the BEST argument that Dave was in possession of the drugs? 3.____
    A. Possession requires only physical custody.
    B. Possession can be physical custody, dominion or control which he had until the time of delivery
    C. Possession is not necessary to charge Dave with a crime.
    D. Possession is a requirement to prove all crimes.

4. If John is sentenced to a term of imprisonment of more than six months, he has been convicted of a 4.____
    A. misdemeanor
    B. violation
    C. serious offense
    D. felony

Questions 5-7.

DIRECTIONS: Questions 5 through 7 are to be answered on the basis of the following fact pattern.

Amy ran a stop sign in her suburban neighborhood as she was driving to visit her boyfriend in Manhattan. While driving in Manhattan, Amy also runs a red light. In running the red light, she hit a bicyclist. The bicyclist did not want to file a report, although he suffered minor injuries. Amy drove away and a week later received a ticket in the mail for running the red light.

5. Amy's running of a red light is a
   A. violation
   B. traffic infraction
   C. misdemeanor
   D. not a crime

6. What is the BEST argument that Amy's collision with the bicyclist is a crime?
   A. No crime was committed because the accident was not fatal.
   B. No crime was committed because the bicyclist was uninsured.
   C. A crime is a misdemeanor or a felony; Amy may have committed a misdemeanor.
   D. A crime is a misdemeanor or a felony; Amy most likely committed a felony.

7. Amy's running of the stop sign in her own neighborhood is
   A. not a crime because she was in her own neighborhood
   B. not a crime because no one reported her and she did not report herself
   C. a traffic infraction
   D. a more serious violation, which is punishable by a term of imprisonment

8. Which of the following is classified as a "deadly weapon"?
   A. Metal knuckles
   B. Switchblade knife
   C. Plastic knuckles
   D. All of the above

9. Physical force which, under the circumstances in which it is used, is readily capable of causing death or other serious physical injury is deemed
   A. deadly physical force
   B. force that is sustainable
   C. serious force
   D. tangle force

10. Anthony, Carl, and Dave are called for jury duty at the federal courthouse. Anthony is impaneled to serve on a grand jury. Carl and Dave are still waiting to be called. Who is considered a juror?
    A. Anthony, Carl, and Dave
    B. Anthony only
    C. Carl and Dave only
    D. None of them are jurors

11. If Jackie is charged as a juvenile offender, what is the MAXIMUM age Jackie can be?
    A. Fifteen   B. Fourteen   C. Thirteen   D. Twelve

12. Which designation includes a "Class D" category?   12.____
    A. Felony   B. Misdemeanor
    C. Violation   D. Offense

13. Forcible touching is classified as a   13.____
    A. misdemeanor   B. Class A felony
    B. Class B felony   D. Class C felony

Questions 14-17.

DIRECTIONS: Questions 1through 17 are to be answered on the basis of the following fact
              pattern.

Bill, nineteen, is on trial for conspiracy to commit murder. During Bill's trial, his best friend Alex testifies for the defense. Under oath, Alex states that Bill was with him the night of the murder and the two of them never left Alex's house. In fact, Alex and Bill had not seen one another for months before the murder. After the trial ended, but before deliberations concluded, Alex garnered the name of the jury foreperson and attempted to pay him in exchange for swinging the jury in Bill's favor.

14. Bill is being charged with a   14.____
    A. felony, because the intent was to commit a felonious crime
    B. felony, because all conspiracy charges are felonies
    C. misdemeanor, because all conspiracy charges are misdemeanors
    D. misdemeanor, because the murder did not take place

15. Where can Bill be tried for conspiracy?   15.____
    A. The county where the conspiracy was entered into
    B. The county where an overt act in furtherance of the conspiracy was
       committed

16. At the conclusion of the trial, Alex will be charged with _____, which in the   16.____
    first degree is a _____.
    A. perjury; Class D felony   B. perjury; Class A felony
    C. negligence; Class C felony   D. tortious act; Class C felony

17. Alex's attempted involvement with a juror is deemed   17.____
    A. tampering with a juror   B. influencing a juror
    C. improper juror gifting   D. forcible tampering

18. May a fine be imposed as a sentence for a felony conviction?   18.____
    A. No, only imprisonment can be a sentence for a felony
    B. No, unless the convicted felon consents to the alternate sentence
    C. Yes, and it may not exceed $50,000
    D. Yes

19. Suppose Damien is convicted of armed robbery and assault, stemming from a single act, both of which are felonies. After conviction, assume the judge imposes a sentence of $5,000 for the armed robbery conviction. What will be the sentence for the assault?
    A. An additional fine
    B. There will be no sentence for the assault conviction
    C. There will be a reduced sentence for the assault conviction
    D. A fine cannot be imposed for the assault conviction

20. If a person has gained money or property through the commission of any misdemeanor or violation, the court may sentence the defendant to pay an amount not exceeding _____ the amount of the defendant's gain from the commission of the offense.
    A. double   B. triple   C. half   D. four times

21. Assume the same facts as Question 20. The imposition of this sentence, as opposed to the sentence prescribed by the penal code is known as a(n)
    A. sustainable charge   B. alternate sentence
    C. alternative imposition   D. resistant change

22. Fines for corporations will generally not exceed _____ for a misdemeanor.
    A. $100,000   B. $50,000   C. $5,000   D. $1,000

23. The fine for a Class B misdemeanor shall not exceed
    A. $1,000   B. $750   C. $500   D. $250

24. Menacing in the second degree and hazing in the first degree are both considered
    A. serious violations   B. misdemeanors
    C. felonies   D. minor violations

25. Promoting a suicide attempt and stalking in the first degree are both considered
    A. minor violations   B. minor felonies
    C. major felonies   D. felonies

KEY (CORRECT ANSWERS)

1.	C		11.	C
2.	A		12.	A
3.	B		13.	A
4.	D		14.	A
5.	B		15.	A
6.	C		16.	A
7.	C		17.	A
8.	D		18.	D
9.	A		19.	D
10.	A		20.	A

21. B
22. C
23. C
24. B
25. D

TEST 2

DIRECTIONS: Each question or incomplete statement is followed by several suggested answers or completions. Select the one that BEST answers the question or completes the statement. *PRINT THE LETTER OF THE CORRECT ANSWER IN THE SPACE AT THE RIGHT.*

Questions 1-3.

DIRECTIONS: Questions 1 through 3 are to be answered on the basis of the following fact pattern.

Olivia and Amy, both nineteen, have conspired to assault one of their classmates. They enlist the help of Amy's sister, Jane, to help them carry out the assault. Amy does not tell Jane what her and Olivia are attempting to do, but instead instructs Jane to pretend that she is lost and lure the classmate to the parking lot where Olivia and Amy will be waiting.

1. The scenario described involves the implication of which two crimes? 1.____
   A. Solicitation and conspiracy
   B. Perjury and conspiracy
   C. Negligence and conspiracy
   D. Conspiracy only

2. Assuming that assault is a felony, which is Amy MOST likely to be guilty of? 2.____
   A. A misdemeanor
   B. A serious violation
   C. A felony
   D. An infraction

3. At trial, Amy and Olivia claim that they are not guilty of any crime because they did not know conspiracy was a crime. Is this a defense? 3.____
   A. No
   B. Not unless they can prove they did not know the law
   C. Yes, ignorance is always a defense
   D. Yes

4. Matt stole a garden gnome, worth $700, from his stepdad's neighbor's lawn. He is charged with a misdemeanor. The court can charge Matt with which of the following? 4.____
   A. $5,500
   B. $1,000
   C. $1,400, equal to double the amount of the stolen good
   D. Any of the above

5. The MAXIMUM fine for a Class B misdemeanor is 5.____
   A. $100   B. $150   C. $200   D. $500

6. Criminally negligent homicide is classified as a 6.____
   A. Class E felony
   B. Class B felony
   C. Class A felony
   D. misdemeanor

7. A person is guilty of issuing abortion articles when he manufactures, sells, or delivers any instrument, article, medicine, drug or substance with intent that the same be used in unlawfully procuring the miscarriage of a female, which is a
    A. Class A misdemeanor
    B. Class B misdemeanor
    C. Class A felony
    D. Class B felony

7.____

8. Issuing a bad check and false personation are both deemed Class _____ misdemeanors.
    A. A
    B. B
    C. C
    D. D

8.____

9. James writes a check for $75 at the grocery store, knowing that he does not have the funds in his account to cover the check. He realizes he has his credit card in his wallet and decides, instead, to pay with his credit card. What crime has James committed?
    A. Issuing a bad check
    B. Conspiracy to defraud
    C. Attempting to issue a bad check
    D. No crime was committed

9.____

10. Criminal sale of a police uniform is
    A. not a crime
    B. a minor violation
    C. a felony in New York City only
    D. a misdemeanor

10.____

11. Susan and James's father suddenly passed away. As Susan was cleaning out their father's home, she discovered his last will which left all of his possessions to James only. Susan does not tell anyone that she discovered her father's will and takes it home with an intent to destroy it. What crime is Susan guilty of?
    A. Unlawfully concealing a will
    B. Tampering with evidence
    C. Conspiracy to impersonate
    D. Fraud

11.____

12. Assume the same facts as in Question 11. Susan's crime is deemed a
    A. Class A misdemeanor
    B. Class C misdemeanor
    C. Class E felony
    D. Unclassified misdemeanor

12.____

13. Which one of the following individuals qualifies as a corporate official for the purposes of the crime of misconduct by a corporate official?
    A. Director of a stock corporation
    B. Receptionist of a stock corporation
    C. Consultant at a private company
    D. Part-time employee of a bank

13.____

14. A person is guilty of _____ when, not being authorized or permitted by law to do so, he knowingly charges, takes, or receives any money or other property as interest on the loan or forbearance of any money or other property, at a rate exceeding twenty-five perc centum per annum or the equivalent rate for a longer or shorter period.
    A. Criminal trespass
    B. Criminal usury in the second degree
    C. Criminal negligence
    D. Civil tort

14.____

15. Unlawful collection practices are always classified as
    A. violations
    B. infractions
    C. misdemeanors
    D. felonies

16. Making a false statement of credit terms violates which law?
    A. Truth in Lending Act
    B. Dodd Frank
    C. Bank Secrecy Act
    D. Humanitarian Relief Act

17. Identity theft can be charged as a misdemeanor or a felony. A person who obtains goods, money, property, or services or uses credit in the name of such other person in an aggregate amount that exceeds five hundred dollars has committed a
    A. petty misdemeanor
    B. misdemeanor
    C. minor felony
    D. felony

18. A person is guilty of _____ when he or she knowingly and with intent to defraud assumes the identity of another person by presenting himself as that other person, or by acting as that other person or by using personal identifying information of that other person, and knows that such person is a member of the armed forces.
    A. Armed theft
    B. Minor identify theft
    C. Aggravated identity theft
    D. Unlawful impersonation

19. Dave, seventeen, used a stolen drivers license to buy alcohol. The store owner called the police, suspecting that Dave was underage, and Dave was charged with identity theft. What is Dave's BEST defense?
    A. Dave was under 21 and only used the ID to purchase alcohol
    B. Dave found the ID on the ground and thought it was abandoned
    C. Dave was under 18 at the time of the offense
    D. There is no affirmative defense for the alleged crime

20. Daniel has filed for bankruptcy. After the commencement of the bankruptcy petitions, Daniel is prohibited from moving or concealing any assets that may be available to his creditors. Daniel decides to withdraw $5,000 out of his checking account and hide the money in his home so that creditors cannot get to it. What crime has Daniel committed?
    A. Banking fraud
    B. Truth in Lending violation
    C. Fraud in Insolvency
    D. Negligent fraud

21. Assume the same facts as in Question 20. What is the category of crime Daniel has committed?
    A. Class A felony
    B. Class B felony
    C. Class A misdemeanor
    D. Violation

22. A person is guilty of _____ when he renders criminal assistance to a person who has committed a Class B or Class C felony.
    A. hindering prosecution in the second degree
    B. tampering with evidence
    C. harboring a fugitive
    D. criminal solicitation

22.____

23. A person is guilty of _____ when he intentionally prevents or attempts to prevent a police office or peace officer from effecting an authorized arrest of himself or another person.
    A. fraud
    B. negligence
    C. resisting arrest
    D. trespass

23.____

24. After Dalia is arrested, she escapes from the cop car. She is guilty of _____, which is a _____.
    A. escape; misdemeanor
    B. escape; violation
    C. escape; infraction
    D. absconding; misdemeanor

24.____

25. Marlene performs a marriage ceremony for Bob and Danielle. Marlene charges a fee of $125 for the ceremony and performs the ceremony in front of the courthouse. Marlene is not authorized by the state to perform marriage ceremonies. Marlene has committed what crime?
    A. Unlawfully solemnizing a marriage
    B. Fraud of a civil union
    C. Identity theft
    D. Unlawful impersonation

25.____

KEY (CORRECT ANSWERS)

1. A
2. C
3. A
4. D
5. D

6. A
7. B
8. B
9. D
10. D

11. A
12. C
13. A
14. B
15. C

16. A
17. D
18. C
19. A
20. C

21. C
22. A
23. C
24. A
25. A

EXAMINATION SECTION
TEST 1

DIRECTIONS: Each question or incomplete statement is followed by several suggested answers or completions. Select the one that BEST answers the question or completes the statement. *PRINT THE LETTER OF THE CORRECT ANSWER IN THE SPACE AT THE RIGHT.*

1. Which of the following is deemed a license? 1.____
    A. An unissued learner's permit
    B. An expired license that is not renewable
    C. A learner's permit
    D. A license that has been revoked or otherwise voided

2. Which of the following conditions will result in the mandatory revocation of a license? 2.____
    A. A conviction of assault arising out of the operation of a motor vehicle
    B. A charge of menacing with a motor vehicle or motor bike
    C. An accusation of a homicide arising out of the operation of a motor vehicle
    D. A charge of homicide arising out of the operation of a motor vehicle

3. A conviction for leaving the scene of an accident without reporting will MOST likely result in the 3.____
    A. temporary suspension of motor vehicle registration
    B. temporary suspension of rights to a personalized license plate
    C. a fine of at least $1,000 but not more than $5,000 and a finite term in prison
    D. mandatory revocation of license and registration of the registered motor vehicle of the convicted

4. Jason recently moved to New York from Texas. In order for Jason to obtain a valid New York driver's license, which action must be complete? 4.____
    A. Forfeit his learner's permit   B. Pay all overdue parking tickets
    C. Surrender his Texas license   D. Surrender his New York license

Questions 5-7.

DIRECTIONS: Questions 5 through 7 are to be answered on the basis of the following fact pattern.

   Late one night Cory borrowed his mother's car and picked up three of his friends to drive to the mall. While driving, Cory turned around to grab a beer from one of his friends in the backseat. A few moments later, the car struck a pedestrian who was severely injured. Cory was later charged and convicted of assault arising out of operation of a motor vehicle.

5. Assume that Cory had a valid learner's permit. What is one consequence of his conviction?
   A. His application for a license will be suspended.
   B. He can be denied a marriage application later.
   C. He will no longer be able to pass inspection for the car.
   D. The car will need to be re-registered in Cory's mother's name.

6. Assume that Cory had a driver's license that was suspended on account of the conviction. Pursuant to the Vehicle and Traffic Law, any person whose driver's license is suspended may apply for the issuance of a(n)
   A. interim license
   B. restricted use license
   C. restricted permit
   D. interim permit

7. Which individual or entity has the power to restore Cory's license?
   A. Head of Registration
   B. Bureau of Prisons
   C. Commissioner of Motor Vehicles
   D. Commissioner of Mental Hygiene

Questions 8-10.

DIRECTIONS: Questions 8 through 10 are to be answered on the basis of the following fact pattern.

Daniel works for ABC Corp., Inc. as a long haul trucker. Daniel must maintain a commercial driver's license for his job. While on a work trip hauling supplies from New York to Nevada, he stops at a truck stop in Louisiana. Daniel attempts to sell marijuana to another trucker out of the cab of his truck who is also stopped and they are both apprehended by police. Daniel is convicted of felony attempt to distribute a controlled substance.

8. Can Daniel's commercial driver's license be revoked in New York?
   A. No, because Daniel was not convicted in New York
   B. No, because Daniel was only convicted of a minor crime
   C. Yes, because Daniel was tried by a jury of his peers
   D. Yes, because Daniel was convicted of a felony involving the use of a motor vehicle

9. Assuming Daniel's commercial driver's license is revoked, when is the earliest opportunity Daniel's license can be reinstated?
   A. 90 days   B. 120 days   C. 1 year   D. 5 years

10. If the term of reinstatement is three years, which of the following must have been inside the truck during the commission of the crime?
    A. Hazardous materials
    B. A minor person
    C. Controlled substance
    D. Unaccounted-for cargo

11. A commercial driver's license shall be suspended by the commissioner for a period of one hundred twenty days where the holder is convicted of _____ serious traffic violations.
    A. one   B. two   C. three   D. four

12. A driver with a Class E driver's license is MOST likely to operate which of the following?   12._____
    A. Sedan   B. SUV   C. Airport taxi   D. Bus or truck

Questions 13-15.

DIRECTIONS: Questions 13 through 15 are to be answered on the basis of the following fact pattern.

Jeremiah holds a Class E driver's license. Last summer, Jeremiah's friend, Mike, asked him for a ride. When Jeremiah picked up Mike, Mike asked that Jeremiah pick up Mike's girlfriend, Katrina. Jeremiah dropped both Mike and Katrina off in the Lower East Side neighborhood of New York City. Katrina was later arrested for solicitation. Jeremiah was later charged, and convicted of, promoting prostitution in the third degree.

13. Jeremiah's first violation of means that Jeremiah's Class E driver's license will be suspended for a period of   13._____
    A. five days   B. one year   C. three years   D. five years

14. If Jeremiah was convicted a second time of the same crime within a _____-year period, the likely result is _____.   14._____
    A. 3; 5-year suspension   B. 5; 10-year suspension
    C. 10; 15-year suspension   D. 10; revocation

15. Which authority and/or agency would suspend Jeremiah's license?   15._____
    A. The Head of Motor Vehicles   B. Commissioner
    C. Bureau of Prisons   D. Federal Bureau of Investigation

16. If Julie were to commit a serious violation in Seattle, what determines whether the act is considered a serious violation in New York?   16._____
    A. Whether New York deems it a serious violation
    B. Whether Washington reports it as a serious violation under the provisions of the Federal Commercial Motor Vehicle Safety Act of 1986
    C. Whether Washington State reports it as a serious violation under the provisions of the Highway Act
    D. Whether Julie deems it a serious violation

17. No person shall operate a motor vehicle while such person has _____ of one per centum or more by weight of alcohol in the person's blood.   17._____
    A. .02   B. .04   C. .06   D. .08

18. Aggravated driving while intoxicated, as opposed to driving while intoxicated, would indicate a blood alcohol level of _____ or above.   18._____
    A. .10   B. .12   C. .14   D. 18

19. Leandra's Law says that no person shall operate a motor vehicle while under the influence while a child is a passenger in the motor vehicle.
    How old must the passenger be to qualify as a child under Leandra's Law?
    A. 17 or younger
    B. 16 or younger
    C. 15 or younger
    D. 13 or older

19.____

20. A person under the age of _____ is deemed to have consumed alcohol if he or she has a blood alcohol level between .02 and 0.07.
    A. 18   B. 19   C. 21   D. 25

20.____

Questions 21-23.

DIRECTIONS: Questions 21 through 23 are to be answered on the basis of the following fact pattern.

Dawn met friends for drinks after work at a local bar last Tuesday evening. After leaving the bar, Dawn attempted to drive herself home when her friend, Bess, offered to drive her home instead. Bess had been drinking with Dawn, but consumed far less alcohol. On their way home, Bess and Dawn were pulled over and Bess was arrested for driving under the influence.

21. How long will Bess' license be suspended?
    A. Six months
    B. Eight months
    C. One year
    D. Bess has not been convicted of a crime

21.____

22. Assume that Bess has been convicted and that this is her third violation. Bess will be deemed guilty of a
    A. traffic violation
    B. traffic violation, but only if the preceding two violations occurred in the last ten years
    C. misdemeanor
    D. misdemeanor, but only if the preceding two violations occurred in the last ten years

22.____

23. Assume the same facts as above. What is the maximum fine and maximum term of imprisonment for Bess?
    A. $1,500; 180 days in jail but not both
    B. $2,000; 180 days in jail but not both
    C. $2,500 and 180 days in jail
    D. $2,500; 180 days in jail but not both

23.____

24. A person convicted of driving under the influence will also be subject to which of the following?
    A. An additional fine or term of imprisonment, determined by the judge
    B. Mandatory community service
    C. Probation or conditional discharge
    D. Wage garnishment for a period of not less than 24 months

24.____

25. Which of the following is NOT a Class E felony? 25._____
    A. Operating a school bus while under the influence with at least one student passenger
    B. Operating a motor vehicle with a gross weight above 18,000 pounds, while under the influence, which contains flammable gas
    C. Operating a motor vehicle with a gross weight above 18,000 pounds, while under the influence, which contains radioactive materials and/or explosives
    D. Operating a motor vehicle while under the influence with a child under the age of 24 as a passenger in the vehicle

KEY (CORRECT ANSWERS)

1.	C	11.	C
2.	A	12.	C
3.	D	13.	C
4.	C	14.	D
5.	A	15.	B
6.	B	16.	B
7.	C	17.	D
8.	D	18.	D
9.	C	19.	C
10.	A	20.	C

21. D
22. D
23. A
24. C
25. D

PREPARING WRITTEN MATERIAL
EXAMINATION SECTION
TEST 1

Questions 1-15.

DIRECTIONS: For each of Questions 1 through 15, select from the options given below the MOST applicable choice, and mark your answer accordingly.
    A. The sentence is correct.
    B. The sentence contains a spelling error only.
    C. The sentence contains an English grammar error only.
    D. The sentence contains both a spelling error and an English grammar error.

1. He is a very dependable person whom we expect will be an asset to this division. 1.____

2. An investigator often finds it necessary to be very diplomatic when conducting an interview. 2.____

3. Accurate detail is especially important if court action results from an investigation. 3.____

4. The report was signed by him and I since we conducted the investigation jointly. 4.____

5. Upon receipt of the complaint, an inquiry was begun. 5.____

6. An employee has to organize his time so that he can handle his workload efficiantly. 6.____

7. It was not apparent that anyone was living at the address given by the client. 7.____

8. According to regulations, there is to be at least three attempts made to locate the client. 8.____

9. Neither the inmate nor the correction officer was willing to sign a formal statement. 9.____

10. It is our opinion that one of the persons interviewed were lying. 10.____

11. We interviewed both clients and departmental personel in the course of this investigation. 11.____

12. It is concievable that further research might produce additional evidence. 12.____

13. There are too many occurences of this nature to ignore. 13.____

14. We cannot accede to the candidate's request.   14._____

15. The submission of overdue reports is the reason that there was a delay in completion of this investigation.   15._____

Questions 16-25.

DIRECTIONS: Each of Questions 16 through 25 may be classified under one of the following four categories:
    A. Faulty because of incorrect grammar or sentence structure.
    B. Faulty because of incorrect punctuation.
    C. Faulty because of incorrect spelling.
    D. Correct

Examine each sentence carefully to determine under which of the above four options it is best classified. Then, in the space at the right, write the letter preceding the option which is the BEST of the four suggested above. Each incorrect sentence contains but one type of error. Consider a sentence to be correct if it contains none of the types of errors mentioned, even though there may be other correct ways of expressing the same thought.

16. Although the department's supply of scratch pads and stationary have diminished considerably, the allotment for our division has not been reduced.   16._____

17. You have not told us whom you wish to designate as your secretary.   17._____

18. Upon reading the minutes of the last meeting, the new proposal was taken up for consideration.   18._____

19. Before beginning the discussion, we locked the door as a precautionery measure.   19._____

20. The supervisor remarked, "Only those clerks, who perform routine work, are permitted to take a rest period."   20._____

21. Not only will this duplicating machine make accurate copies, but it will also produce a quantity of work equal to fifteen transcribing typists.   21._____

22. "Mr. Jones," said the supervisor, "we regret our inability to grant you an extention of your leave of absence.   22._____

23. Although the employees find the work monotonous and fatigueing, they rarely complain.   23._____

24. We completed the tabulation of the receipts on time despite the fact that Miss Smith our fastest operator was absent for over a week.   24._____

25. The reaction of the employees who attended the meeting, as well as the reaction of those who did not attend, indicates clearly that the schedule is satisfactory to everyone concerned.

25.____

KEY (CORRECT ANSWERS)

1. D
2. A
3. A
4. C
5. A

6. B
7. B
8. C
9. A
10. C

11. B
12. B
13. B
14. A
15. C

16. A
17. D
18. A
19. C
20. B

21. A
22. C
23. C
24. B
25. D

TEST 2

Questions 1-15.

DIRECTIONS: Questions 1 through 15 consist of two sentences. Some are correct according to ordinary formal English usage. Others are incorrect because they contain errors in English usage, spelling, or punctuation. Consider a sentence correct if it contains no errors in English usage, spelling, or punctuation, even if there may be other ways of writing the sentence correctly. Mark your answer:
    A. If only sentence I is correct.
    B. If only sentence II is correct.
    C. If sentences 1 and II are correct.
    D. If neither sentence I nor II is correct.

1. I. The influence of recruitment efficiency upon administrative standards is readily apparant.
   II. Rapid and accurate thinking are an essential quality of the police officer.

2. I. The administrator of a police department is constantly confronted by the demands of subordinates for increased personnel in their respective units.
   II. Since a chief executive must work within well-defined fiscal limits, he must weigh the relative importance of various requests.

3. I. The two men whom the police arrested for a parking violation were wanted for robbery in three states.
   II. Strong executive control from the top to the bottom of the enterprise is one of the basic principals of police administration.

4. I. When he gave testimony unfavorable to the defendant loyalty seemed to mean very little.
   II. Having run off the road while passing a car, the patrolman gave the driver a traffic ticket.

5. I. The judge ruled that the defendant's conversation with his doctor was a privileged communication.
   II. The importance of our training program is widely recognized; however, fiscal difficulties limit the program's effectiveness.

6. I. Despite an increase in patrol coverage, there were less arrests for crimes against property this year.
   II. The investigators could hardly have expected greater cooperation from the public.

7. I. Neither the patrolman nor the witness could identify the defendant as the driver of the car.
   II. Each of the officers in the class received their certificates at the completion of the course.

8. I. The new commander made it clear that those kind of procedures would no longer be permitted.
    II. Giving some weight to performance records is more advisable than making promotions solely on the basis of test scores.

9. I. A deputy sheriff must ascertain whether the debtor, has any property.
    II. A good deputy sheriff does not cause histerical excitement when he executes a process.

10. I. Having learned that he has been assigned a judgment debtor, the deputy sheriff should call upon him.
    II. The deputy sheriff may seize and remove property without requiring a bond.

11. I. If legal procedures are not observed, the resulting contract is not enforseable.
    II. If the directions from the creditor's attorney are not in writing, the deputy sheriff should request a letter of instructions from the attorney.

12. I. The deputy sheriff may confer with the defendant and enter this defendants' place of business.
    II. A deputy sheriff must ascertain from the creditor's attorney whether the debtor has any property against which he may proceede.

13. I. The sheriff has a right to do whatever is necessary for the purpose of executing the order of the court.
    II. The written order of the court gives the sheriff general authority and he is governed in his acts by a very simple principal.

14. I. Either the patrolman or his sergeant are always ready to help the public.
    II. The sergeant asked the patrolman when he would finish the report.

15. I. The injured man could not hardly talk.
    II. Every officer had ought to had in their reports on time.

Questions 16-26.

DIRECTIONS: For each of the sentences given below, numbered 16 through 25, select from the following choices the MOST correct choice and print your choice in the space at the right. Select as your answer:
  A. If the statement contains an unnecessary word or expression
  B. If the statement contains a slang term or expression ordinarily not acceptable in government report writing.
  C. If the statement contains an old-fashioned word or expression, where a concrete, plain term would be more useful.
  D. If the statement contains no major faults.

16. Every one of us should try harder.

17. Yours of the first instant has been received.

18. We will have to do a real snow job on him. 18.____
19. I shall contact him next Thursday. 19.____
20. None of us were invited to the meeting with the community. 20.____
21. We got this here job to do. 21.____
22. She could not help but see the mistake in the checkbook. 22.____
23. Don't bug the Director about the report. 23.____
24. I beg to inform you that your letter has been received. 24.____
25. This project is all screwed up. 25.____

KEY (CORRECT ANSWERS)

1.	D	11.	B
2.	C	12.	D
3.	A	13.	A
4.	D	14.	D
5.	B	15.	D
6.	B	16.	D
7.	A	17.	C
8.	D	18.	B
9.	D	19.	D
10.	C	20.	D

21. B
22. D
23. B
24. C
25. B

TEST 3

DIRECTIONS: Questions 1 through 25 are sentences taken from reports. Some are correct according to ordinary English usage. Others are incorrect because they contain errors in English usage, spelling, or punctuation. Consider a sentence correct if it contains no errors in English usage, spelling, or punctuation, even if there may be other ways of writing the sentence correctly. Mark your answer:
- A. If only sentence I is correct
- B. If only sentence II is correct
- C. If sentences I and II are correct
- D. If neither sentence I nor II is correct

1. I. The Neighborhood Police Team Commander and Team Patrolmen are encouraged to give to the public the widest possible verbal and written disemination of information regarding the existence and purposes of the program.
    II. The police must be vitally interelated with every segment of the public they serve.

2. I. If social gambling, prostitution, and other vices are to be prohibited, the law makers should provide the manpower and method for enforcement.
    II. In addition to checking on possible crime locations such as hallways, roofs yards and other similar locations, Team Patrolmen are encouraged to make known their presence to members of the community.

3. I. The Neighborhood Police Team Commander is authorized to secure, the cooperation of local publications, as well as public and private agencies, to further the goals of the program.
    II. Recruitment from social minorities is essential to effective police work among minorities and meaningful relations with them.

4. I. The Neighborhood Police Team Commander and his men have the responsibility for providing patrol service within the sector territory on a twenty-four hour basis.
    II. While the patrolman was walking his beat at midnight he noticed that the clothing stores' door was partly open.

5. I. Authority is granted to the Neighborhood Police Team to device tactics for coping with the crime in the sector.
    II. Before leaving the scene of the accident, the patrolman drew a map showing the positions of the automobiles and indicated the time of the accident as 10 M. in the morning.

6. I. The Neighborhood Police Team Commander and his men must be kept apprised of conditions effecting their sector.
    II. Clear, continuous communication with every segment of the public served based on the realization of mutual need and founded on trust and confidence is the basis for effective law enforcement.

7. I. The irony is that the police are blamed for the laws they enforce when they are doing their duty.
    II. The Neighborhood Police Team Commander is authorized to prepare and distribute literature with pertinent information telling the public whom to contact for assistance.

8. I. The day is not far distant when major parts of the entire police compliment will need extensive college training or degrees.
    II. Although driving under the influence of alcohol is a specific charge in making arrests, drunkenness is basically a health and social problem.

9. I. If a deputy sheriff finds that property he has to attach is located on a ship, he should notify his supervisor.
    II. Any contract that tends to interfere with the administration of justice is illegal.

10. I. A mandate or official order of the court to the sheriff or other officer directs it to take into possession property of the judgment debtor.
    II. Tenancies from month-to-month, week-to-week, and sometimes year-to-year are termenable.

11. I. A civil arrest is an arrest pursuant to an order issued by a court in civil litigation.
    II. In a criminal arrest, a defendant is arrested for a crime he is alleged to have committed.

12. I. Having taken a defendant into custody, there is a complete restraint of personal liberty.
    II. Actual force is unnecessary when a deputy sheriff makes an arrest.

13. I. When a husband breaches a separation agreement by failing to supply to the wife the amount of money to be paid to her periodically under the agreement, the same legal steps may be taken to enforce his compliance as in any other breach of contract.
    II. Having obtained the writ of attachment, the plaintiff is then in the advantageous position of selling the very property that has been held for him by the sheriff while he was obtaining a judgment.

14. I. Being locked in his desk, the investigator felt sure that the records would be safe.
    II. The reason why the witness changed his statement was because he had been threatened.

15. I. The investigation had just began then an important witness disappeared.
    II. The check that had been missing was located and returned to its owner, Harry Morgan, a resident of Suffolk County, New York.

16. I. A supervisor will find that the establishment of standard procedures enables his staff to work more efficiently.
    II. An investigator hadn't ought to give any recommendations in his report if he is in doubt.

16.____

17. I. Neither the investigator nor his supervisor is ready to interview the witness.
    II. Interviewing has been and always will be an important asset in investigation.

17.____

18. I. One of the investigator's reports has been forwarded to the wrong person.
    II. The investigator stated that he was not familiar with those kind of cases.

18.____

19. I. Approaching the victim of the assault, two large bruises were noticed by me.
    II. The prisoner was arrested for assault, resisting arrest, and use of a deadly weapon.

19.____

20. I. A copy of the orders, which had been prepared by the captain, was given to each patrolman.
    II. It's always necessary to inform an arrested person of his constitutional rights before asking him any questions.

20.____

21. I. To prevent further bleeding, I applied a tourniquet to the wound.
    II. John Rano a senior officer was on duty at the time of the accident.

21.____

22. I. Limiting the term "property" to tangible property, in the criminal mischief setting, accords with prior case law holding that only tangible property came within the purview of the offense of malicious mischief.
    II. Thus, a person who intentionally destroys the property of another, but under an honest belief that he has title to such property, cannot be convicted of criminal mischief under the Revised Penal Law.

22.____

23. I. Very early in it's history, New York enacted statutes from time to time punishing, either as a felony or as a misdemeanor, malicious injuries to various kinds of property: piers, boos, dams, bridges, etc.
    II. The application of the statute is necessarily restricted to trespassory takings with larcenous intent: namely with intent permanently or virtually permanently to "appropriate" property or "deprive" the owner of its use.

23.____

24. I. Since the former Penal Law did not define the instruments of forgery in a general fashion, its crime of forgery was held to be narrower than the common law offense in this respect and to embrace only those instruments explicitly specified in the substantive provisions.
    II. After entering the barn through an open door for the purpose of stealing, it was closed by the defendants.

24.____

25. I. The use of fire or explosives to destroy tangible property is proscribed by the criminal mischief provisions of the Revised Penal Law.
    II. The defendant's taking of a taxicab for the immediate purpose of affecting his escape did not constitute grand larceny.

25.____

KEY (CORRECT ANSWERS)

1.	D		11.	C
2.	D		12.	B
3.	B		13.	C
4.	A		14.	D
5.	D		15.	B
6.	D		16.	A
7.	C		17.	C
8.	D		18.	A
9.	C		19.	B
10.	D		20.	C

21. A
22. C
23. B
24. A
25. A

TEST 4

Questions 1-4.

DIRECTIONS: Each of the two sentences in Questions 1 through 4 may be correct or may contain errors in punctuation, capitalization, or grammar. Mark your answer:
    A. If there is an error only in sentence I
    B. If there is an error only in sentence II
    C. If there is an error in both sentences I and II
    D. If both sentences are correct.

1.   I. It is very annoying to have a pencil sharpener, which is not in working order.   1.____
    II. Patrolman Blake checked the door of Joe's Restaurant and found that the lock has been jammed.

2.   I. When you are studying a good textbook is important.   2.____
    II. He said he would divide the money equally between you and me.

3.   I. Since he went on the city council a year ago, one of his primary concerns has been safety in the streets.   3.____
    II. After waiting in the doorway for about 15 minutes, a black sedan appeared.

Questions 4-8.

DIRECTIONS: Each of the sentences in Questions 4 through 8 may be classified under one of the following four categories:
    A. Faulty because of incorrect grammar
    B. Faulty because of incorrect punctuation
    C. Faulty because of incorrect capitalization or incorrect spelling
    D. Correct

Examine each sentence carefully to determine under which of the above four options it is BEST classified. Then, in the space at the right, print the capitalized letter preceding the option which is the BEST of the four suggested above. Each faulty sentence contains but one type of error. Consider a sentence to be correct if it contains none of the types of errors mentioned, even though there may be other correct ways of expressing the same thought.

4. They told both he and I that the prisoner had escaped.   4.____

5. Any superior officer, who, disregards the just complaints of his subordinates, is remiss in the performance of his duty.   5.____

6. Only those members of the national organization who resided in the Middle west attended the conference in Chicago.   6.____

7. We told him to give the investigation assignment to whoever was available.   7.____

8. Please do not disappoint and embarass us by not appearing in court.   8.____

Questions 9-13

DIRECTIONS: Each of Questions 9 through 13 consists of three sentences lettered A, B, and C. In each of these questions, one of the sentences may contain an error in grammar, sentence structure, or punctuation, or all three sentences may be correct. If one of the sentence in a question contains an error in grammar, sentence structure, or punctuation, print in the space at the right the capital letter preceding the sentence which contains the error. If all three sentences are correct, print the letter D.

9. A. Mr. Smith appears to be less competent than I in performing these duties. 9._____
   B. The supervisor spoke to the employee, who had made the error, but did not reprimand him.
   C. When he found the book lying on the table, he immediately notified the owner.

10. A. Being locked in the desk, we were certain that the papers would not be taken. 10._____
    B. It wasn't I who dictated the telegram; I believe it was Eleanor.
    C. You should interview whoever comes to the office today.

11. A. The clerk was instructed to set the machine on the table before summoning the manager. 11._____
    B. He said that he was not familiar with those kind of activities.
    C. A box of pencils, in addition to erasers and blotters, was included in the shipment of supplies.

12. A. The supervisor remarked, "Assigning an employee to the proper type of work is not always easy." 12._____
    B. The employer found that each of the applicants were qualified to perform the duties of the position.
    C. Any competent student is permitted to take this course if he obtains the consent of the instructor.

13. A. The prize was awarded to the employee whom the judges believed to be most deserving. 13._____
    B. Since the instructor believes his book is the better of the two, he is recommending it for use in the school.
    C. It was obvious to the employees that the completion of the task by the scheduled date would require their working overtime.

Questions 14-20.

DIRECTIONS: In answering Questions 14 through 20, choose the sentence which is BEST from the point of view of English usage suitable for a business report.

14. A. The client's receiving of public assistance checks at two different addresses were disclosed by the investigation.
    B. The investigation disclosed that the client was receiving public assistance checks at two different addresses.
    C. The client was found out by the investigation to be receiving public assistance checks at two different addresses.
    D. The client has been receiving public assistance checks at two different addresses, disclosed the investigation.

14.____

15. A. The investigation of complaints are usually handled by this unit, which deals with internal security problems in the department.
    B. This unit deals with internal security problems in the department usually investigating complaints.
    C. Investigating complaints is this unit's job, being that it handles internal security problems in the department.
    D. This unit deals with internal security problems in the department and usually investigates complaints.

15.____

16. A. The delay in completing this investigation was caused by difficulty in obtaining the required documents from the candidate.
    B. Because of difficulty in obtaining the required documents from the candidate is the reason that there was a delay in completing this investigation.
    C. Having had difficulty in obtaining the required documents from the candidate, there was a delay in completing this investigation.
    D. Difficulty in obtaining the required documents from the candidate had the affect of delaying the completion of this investigation.

16.____

17. A. This report, together with documents supporting our recommendation, are being submitted for your approval.
    B. Documents supporting our recommendation is being submitted with the report for your approval.
    C. This report, together with documents supporting our recommendation, is being submitted for your approval.
    D. The report and documents supporting our recommendation is being submitted for your approval.

17.____

18. A. The chairman himself, rather than his aides, has reviewed the report.
    B. The chairman himself, rather than his aides, have reviewed the report.
    C. The chairmen, not the aide, has reviewed the report.
    D. The aide, not the chairmen, have reviewed the report.

18.____

19. A. Various proposals were submitted but the decision is not been made.
    B. Various proposals has been submitted but the decision has not been made.
    C. Various proposals were submitted but the decision is not been made.
    D. Various proposals have been submitted but the decision has not been made.

19.____

20. A. Everyone were rewarded for his successful attempt.
    B. They were successful in their attempts and each of them was rewarded.
    C. Each of them are rewarded for their successful attempts.
    D. The reward for their successful attempts were made to each of them.

20.____

21. The following is a paragraph from a request for departmental recognition consisting of five numbered sentences submitted to a Captain for review. These sentences may or may not have errors in spelling, grammar, and punctuation:
(1) The officers observed the subject Mills surreptitiously remove a wallet from the woman's handbag and entered his automobile. (2) As they approached Mills, he looked in their direction and drove away. (3) The officers pursued in their car. (4) Mills executed a series of complicated manuvers to evade the pursuing officers. (5) At the corner of Broome and Elizabeth Streets, Mills stopped the car, got out, raised his hands and surrendered to the officers.
Which one of the following BEST classifies the above with regard to spelling, grammar, and punctuation?
    A. 1, 2, and 3 are correct, but 4 and 5 have errors.
    B. 2, 3, and 5 are correct, but 1 and 4 have errors.
    C. 3, 4, and 5 are correct, but 1 and 2 have errors.
    D. 1, 2, 3, and 5 are correct, but 4 has errors.

21.____

22. The one of the following sentences which is grammatically PREFERABLE to the others is:
    A. Our engineers will go over your blueprints so that you may have no problems in construction.
    B. For a long time he had been arguing that we, not he, are to blame for the confusion.
    C. I worked on his automobile for two hours and still cannot find out what is wrong with it.
    D. Accustomed to all kinds of hardships, fatigue seldom bothers veteran policemen.

22.____

23. The MOST accurate of the following sentences is:
    A. The commissioner, as well as his deputy and various bureau heads, were present.
    B. A new organization of employers and employees have been formed.
    C. One or the other of these men have been selected.
    D. The number of pages in the book is enough to discourage a reader.

23.____

24. The MOST accurate of the following sentences is: 24._____
    A. Between you and me, I think he is the better man.
    B. He was believed to be me.
    C. Is it us that you wish to see?
    D. The winners are him and her.

KEY (CORRECT ANSWERS)

1.	C	11.	B
2.	A	12.	B
3.	C	13.	D
4.	A	14.	B
5.	B	15.	D
6.	C	16.	A
7.	D	17.	C
8.	C	18.	A
9.	B	19.	D
10.	A	20.	B

21. B
22. A
23. D
24. A

PREPARING WRITTEN MATERIAL

PARAGRAPH REARRANGEMENT
COMMENTARY

The sentences that follow are in scrambled order. You are to rearrange them in proper order and indicate the letter choice containing the correct answer at the space at the right.

Each group of sentences in this section is actually a paragraph presented in scrambled order. Each sentence in the group has a place in that paragraph; no sentence is to be left out. You are to read each group of sentences and decide upon the best order in which to put the sentences so as to form a well-organized paragraph.

The questions in this section measure the ability to solve a problem when all the facts relevant to its solution are not given.

More specifically, certain positions of responsibility and authority require the employee to discover connection between events sometimes, apparently, unrelated. In order to do this, the employee will find it necessary to correctly infer that unspecified events have probably occurred or are likely to occur. This ability becomes especially important when action must be taken on incomplete information.

Accordingly, these questions require competitors to choose among several suggested alternatives, each of which presents a different sequential arrangement of the events. Competitors must choose the MOST logical of the suggested sequences.

In order to do so, they may be required to draw on general knowledge to infer missing concepts or events that are essential to sequencing the given events. Competitors should be careful to infer only what is essential to the sequence. The plausibility of the wrong alternatives will always require the inclusion of unlikely events or of additional chains of events which are NOT essential to sequencing the given events.

It's very important to remember that you are looking for the best of the four possible choices, and that the best choice of all may not even be one of the answers you're given to choose from.

There is no one right way to solve these problems. Many people have found it helpful to first write out the order of the sentences, as they would have arranged them, on their scrap paper before looking at the possible answers. If their optimum answer is there, this can save them some time. If it isn't, this method can still give insight into solving the problem. Others find it most helpful to just go through each of the possible choices, contrasting each as they go along. You should use whatever method feels comfortable and works for you.

While most of these types of questions are not that difficult, we've added a higher percentage of the difficult type, just to give you more practice. Usually there are only one or two questions on this section that contain such subtle distinctions that you're unable to answer confidently. And you then may find yourself stuck deciding between two possible choices, neither of which you're sure about.

PREPARING WRITTEN MATERIAL
PARAGRAPH REARRANGEMENT
EXAMINATION SECTION
TEST 1

DIRECTIONS: The sentences that follow are in scrambled order. You are to rearrange them in proper order and indicate the letter choice containing the CORRECT answer. *PRINT THE LETTER OF THE CORRECT ANSWER IN THE SPACE AT THE RIGHT.*

1. Police Officer Jenner responds to the scene of a burglary at 2106 La Vista Boulevard. He is approached by an elderly man named Richard Jenkins, whose account of the incident includes the following five sentences:
   I. I saw that the lock on my apartment door had been smashed and the door was open.
   II. My apartment was a shambles; my belongings were everywhere and my television set was missing.
   III. As I walked down the hallway toward the bedroom, I heard someone opening a window.
   IV. I left work at 5:30 P.M. and took the bus home.
   V. At that time, I called the police.
   The MOST logical order for the above sentence to appear in the report is
   A. I, V, IV, II, III   B. IV, I, II, III, V   C. I, V, II, III, IV   D. IV, III, II, V, I

   1._____

2. Police Officer LaJolla is writing an Incident Report in which back-up assistance was required. The report will contain the following five sentences:
   I. The radio dispatcher asked what my location was and he then dispatched patrol cars for back-up assistance.
   II. At approximately 9:30 P.M., while I was walking my assigned footpost, a gunman fired three shots at me.
   III. I quickly turned around and saw a white male, approximately 5'10", with black hair, wearing blue jeans, a yellow T-shirt, and white sneaker, running across the avenue carrying a handgun.
   IV. When the back-up officers arrived, we searched the area but could not find the suspect.
   V. I advised the radio dispatcher that a gunman had just fired a gun at me, and then I gave the dispatcher a description of the man
   The MOST logical order for the above sentences to appear in the report is:
   A. III, V, II, IV, I   B. II, III, V, I, IV   C. III, II, IV, I, V   D. II, V, I, III, IV

   2._____

3. Police Officer Durant is completing a report of a robbery and assault. The report will contain the following five sentences:
   I. I went to Mount Snow Hospital to interview a man who was attacked and robbed of his wallet earlier that night.
   II. An ambulance arrived at 82nd Street and 3rd Avenue and took an intoxicated, wounded man to Mount Snow Hospital
   III. Two youths attacked the man and stole his wallet.

   3._____

117

IV. A well-dressed man left Hanratty's Bar very drunk, with his wallet hanging out of his back pocket.
V. A passerby dialed 911 and requested police and ambulance assistance.
The MOST logical order for the above sentences to appear in the report is
   A. I, II, IV, III, V   B. IV, III, V, II, I   C. IV, V, II, III, I   D. V, IV, III, II, I

4. Police Officer Boswell is preparing a report of an armed robbery and assault which will contain the following five sentences:
   I. Both men approached the bartender and one of them drew a gun.
   II. The bartender immediately went to grab the phone at the bar.
   III. One of the men leaped over the counter and smashed a bottle over the bartender's head.
   IV. Two men in a blue Buick drove up to the bar and went inside.
   V. I found the cash register empty and the bartender unconscious on the floor, with the phone still dangling off the hook.
   The MOST logical order for the above sentences to appear in the report is
      A. IV, I, II, II, V   B. V, IV, III, I, II   C. IV, III, II, V, I   D. II, I, III, IV, V

5. Police Officer Mitzler is preparing a report of a bank robbery, which will contain the following five sentences:
   I. The teller complied with the instructions on the note, but also hit the silent alarm.
   II. The perpetrator then fled south on Broadway.
   III. A suspicious male entered the bank at approximately 10:45 A.M.
   IV. At this time, an undetermined amount of money has been taken.
   V. He approached the teller on the far right side and handed her a note.
   The MOST logical order for the above sentences to appear in the report is:
      A. III, V, I, II, IV   B. I, III, V, II, IV   C. III, V, IV, I, II   D. III, V, II, IV, I

6. A Police Officer is preparing an Accident Report for an accident which occurred at the intersection of East 119th Street and Lexington Avenue. The report will include the following five sentences:
   I. On September 18, while driving ten children to school, a school bus driver passed out.
   II. Upon arriving at the scene, I notified the dispatcher to send an ambulance.
   III. I notified the parents of each child once I got to the station house.
   IV. He said the school bus, while traveling west on East 119th Street, struck a parked Ford which was on the southwest corner of East 119th Street.
   V. A witness by the name of John Ramos came up to me to describe what happened.
   The MOST logical order for the above sentences to appear in the Accident Report is:
      A. I, II, V, III, IV   B. I, II, V, IV, III   C. II, V, I, III, IV   D. II, V, I, IV, III

7. A Police Officer is preparing a report concerning a dispute. The report will contain the following five sentences:
   I. The passenger got out of the back of the taxi and leaned through the front window to complain to the driver about the fare.

II. The driver of the taxi caught up with the passenger and knocked him to the ground; the passenger then kicked the driver and a scuffle ensued.
III. The taxi drew up in front of the high-rise building and stopped.
IV. The driver got out of the taxi and followed the passenger into the lobby of the apartment building.
V. The doorman tried but was unable to break up the fight, at which point he called the precinct.
The MOST logical order for the above sentences to appear in the report is
   A. III, I, IV, II, V   B. III, IV, I, II, V   C. III, IV, II, V, I   D. V, I, III, IV, II

8. Police Officer Morrow is writing an Incident Report. The report will include the following four sentences:
   I. The man reached into his pocket and pulled out a gun.
   II. While on foot patrol, I identified a suspect, who was wanted for six robberies in the area, from a wanted picture I was carrying.
   III. I drew my weapon and fired six rounds at the suspect, killing him instantly.
   IV. I called for back-up assistance and told the man to put his hands up.
   The MOST logical order for the above sentences to appear in the report is
      A. II, III, IV, I   B. IV, I, III, II   C. IV, I, II, III   D. II, IV, I, III

9. Sergeant Allen responds to a call at 16 Grove Street regarding a missing child. At the scene, the Sergeant is met by Police Officer Samuels, who gives a brief account of the incident consisting of the following five sentences:
   I. I transmitted the description and waited for you to arrive before I began searching the area.
   II. Mrs. Banks, the mother, reports that she last saw her daughter Julie about 7:30 A.M. when she took her to school.
   III. About 6 P.M., my partner and I arrived at this location to investigate a report of a missing 8-year-old girl.
   IV. When Mrs. Banks left her, Julie was wearing a red and white striped T-shirt, blue jeans, and white sneakers.
   V. Mrs. Banks dropped her off in front of the playground of P.S. 11.
   The MOST logical order for the above sentences to appear in the report is
      A. III, V, IV, II, I   B. III, II, V, IV, I   C. III, IV, I, II, V   D. III, II, IV, I, V

10. Police Officer Franco is completing a report of an assault. The report will contain the following five sentences:
    I. In the park I observed an elderly man lying on the ground, bleeding from a back wound.
    II. I applied first aid to control the bleeding and radioed for an ambulance to respond.
    III. The elderly man stated that he was sitting on the park bench when he was attacked from behind by two males.
    IV. I received a report of a man's screams coming from inside the park, and I went to investigate.
    V. The old man could not give a description of his attackers.
    The MOST logical order for the above sentences to appear in the report is
       A. IV, I, II, III, V   B. V, III, I, IV, II   C. IV, III, V, II, I   D. II, I, V, IV, III

11. Police Officer Williams is completing a Crime Report. The report contains the following five sentences:
    I. As Police Officer Hanson and I approached the store, we noticed that the front door was broken.
    II. After determining that the burglars had fled, we notified the precinct of the burglary.
    III. I walked through the front door as Police Officer Hanson walked around to the back.
    IV. At approximately midnight, an alarm was heard at the Apex Jewelry Store.
    V. We searched the store and found no one.
    The MOST logical order for the above sentences to appear in the report is
    A. I, IV, II, III, V   B. I, IV, III, V, II   C. IV, I, III, II, V   D. IV, I, III, V, II

12. Police Officer Clay is giving a report to the news media regarding someone who has jumped from the Empire State Building. His report will include the following five sentences:
    I. I responded to the 86th floor, where I found the person at the edge of the roof.
    II. A security guard at the building had reported that a man was on the roof at the 86th floor.
    III. At 5:30 P.M., the person jumped from the building.
    IV. I received a call from the radio dispatcher at 4:50 P.M. to respond to the Empire State Building.
    V. I tried to talk to the person and convince him not to jump.
    The MOST logical order for the above sentences to appear in the report is
    A. I, II, IV, III, V   B. III, IV, I, II, V   C. II, IV, I, III, V   D. IV, II, I, V, III

13. The following five sentences are part of a report of a burglary written by Police Officer Reed:
    I. When I arrived at 2400 1st Avenue, I noticed that the door was slightly open.
    II. I yelled out, *Police, don't move!*
    III. As I entered the apartment, I saw a man with a TV set passing through a window to another man standing on a fire escape.
    IV. While on foot patrol, I was informed by the radio dispatcher that a burglary was in progress at 2400 1st Avenue.
    V. However, the burglars quickly ran down the fire escape.
    The MOST logical order for the above sentences to appear in the report is
    A. I, III, IV, V, II   B. IV, I, III, V, II   C. IV, I, III, II, V   D. I, IV, III, II, V

14. Police Officer Jenkins is preparing a report for Lost or Stolen Property. The report will include the following five sentences:
    I. On the stairs, Mr. Harris slipped on a wet leaf and fell on the landing.
    II. It wasn't until he got to the token booth that Mr. Harris realized his wallet was no longer in his back pants pocket.
    III. A boy wearing a football jersey helped him up and brushed off the back of Mr. Harris' pants.
    IV. Mr. Harris states he was walking up the stairs to the elevated subway at Queensborough Plaza.
    V. Before Mr. Harris could thank him, the boy was running down the stairs to the street.

The MOST logical order for the above sentences to appear in the report is
A. IV, III, V, I, II   B. IV, I, III, V, II   C. I, IV, II, III, V   D. I, II, IV, III, V

15. Police Officer Hubbard is completing a report of a missing person. The report will contain the following five sentences:
    I. I visited the store at 7:55 P.M. and asked the employees if they had seen a girl fitting the description I had been given.
    II. She gave me a description and said she had gone into the local grocery store at about 6:15 P.M.
    III. I asked the woman for a description of her daughter.
    IV. The distraught woman called the precinct to report that her daughter, aged 12, had not returned from an errand.
    V. The storekeeper said a girl matching the description had been in the store earlier, but he could not give an exact time.
    The MOST logical order for the above sentences to appear in the report is
    A. I, III, II, V, IV   B. IV, III, II, I, V   C. V, I, II, III, IV   D. III, I, II, IV, V

16. A police officer is completing an entry in his Daily Activity Log regarding traffic summonses which he issued. The following five sentences will be included in the entry:
    I. I was on routine patrol parked 16 yards west of 170th Street and Clay Avenue.
    II. The summonses were issued for unlicensed operator and disobeying a steady red light.
    III. At 8 A.M. hours, I observed an auto traveling westbound on 170th Street not stop for a steady red light at the intersection of Clay Avenue and 170th Street.
    IV. I stopped the driver of the auto and determined that he did not have a valid driver's license.
    V. After a brief conversation, I informed the motorist that he was receiving two summonses.
    The MOST logical order for the above sentences to appear in the report is
    A. I, III, IV, V, II   B. III, IV, II, V, I   C. V, II, I, III, IV   D. IV, V, II, I, III

17. The following sentences appeared on an Incident Report:
    I. Three teenagers who had been ejected from the theater were yelling at patrons who were now entering.
    II. Police Officer Dixon told the teenagers to leave the area.
    III. The teenager said that they were told by the manager to leave the theater because they were talking during the movie.
    IV. The theater manager called the precinct at 10:20 P.M. to report a disturbance outside the theater.
    V. A patrol car responded to the theater at 10:42 P.M. and two police officers went over to the teenagers.
    The MOST logical order for the above sentences to appear in the Incident Report is
    A. I, V, IV, III, II   B. IV, I, V, III, II   C. IV, I, III, V, II   D. IV, III, I, V, II

18. Activity Log entries are completed by police officers. Police Officer Samuels has written an entry concerning vandalism and part of it contains the following five sentences:
   I. The man, in his early twenties, ran down the block and around the corner.
   II. A man passing the store threw a brick through a window of the store.
   III. I arrived on the scene and began to question the witnesses about the incident.
   IV. Malcolm Holmes, the owner of the Fast Service Shoe Repair Store, was working in the back of the store at approximately 3 P.M.
   V. After the man fled, Mr. Holmes called the police.
   The MOST logical order for the above sentences to appear in the Activity Log is
   A. IV, II, I, V, III   B. II, IV, I, III, V   C. II, I, IV, III, V   D. IV, II, V, III, I

19. Police Officer Buckley is preparing a report concerning a dispute in a restaurant. The report will contain the following five sentences:
   I. The manager, Charles Chin, and a customer, Edward Green, were standing near the register arguing over the bill.
   II. The manager refused to press any charges providing Green pay the check and leave.
   III. While on foot patrol, I was informed by a passerby of a disturbance in the Dragon Flame Restaurant.
   IV. Green paid the $15.00 check and left the restaurant.
   V. According to witnesses, the customer punched the owner in the face when Chin asked him for the amount due.
   The MOST logical order for the above sentences to appear in the report is
   A. III, I, V, II, IV   B. I, II, III, IV, V   C. V, I, III, II, IV   D. III, V, II, IV, I

20. Police Officer Wilkins is preparing a report for leaving the scene of an accident. The report will include the following five sentences:
   I. The Dodge struck the right rear fender of Mrs. Smith's 2010 Ford and continued on its way.
   II. Mrs. Smith stated she was making a left turn from 40th Street onto Third Avenue.
   III. As the car passed, Mrs. Smith noticed the dangling rear license plate #412AEJ.
   IV. Mrs. Smith complained to police of back pains and was removed by ambulance to Bellevue Hospital.
   V. An old green Dodge traveling up Third Avenue went through the red light at 40th Street and Third Avenue.
   The MOST logical order for the above sentences to appear in the report is
   A. V, III, I, II, IV   B. I, III, II, V, IV   C. IV, V, I, II, III   D. II, V, I, III, IV

21. Detective Simon is completing a Crime Report. The report contains the following five sentences:
   I. Police Officer Chin, while on foot patrol, heard the yelling and ran in the direction of the man.
   II. The man, carrying a large hunting knife, left the High Sierra Sporting Goods Store at approximately 10:30 A.M.

III. When the man heard Police Officer Chin, he stopped, dropped the knife, and began to cry.
IV. As Police Officer Chin approached the man, he drew his gun and yelled, *Police, freeze.*
V. After the man left the store, he began yelling, over and over, *I am going to kill myself!*

The MOST logical order for the above sentences to appear in the report is
A. V, II, I, IV, III   B. II, V, I, IV, III   C. II, V, IV, I, III   D. II, I, V, IV, III

22. Police Officer Miller is preparing a Complaint Report which will include the following five sentences:
    I. From across the lot, he yelled to the boys to get away from his car.
    II. When he came out of the store, he noticed two teenage boys trying to break into his car.
    III. The boys fled as Mr. Johnson ran to his car.
    IV. Mr. Johnson stated that he parked his car in the municipal lot behind Tams Department Store.
    V. Mr. Johnson saw that the door lock had been broken, but nothing was missing from inside the auto.

    The MOST logical order for the above sentences to appear in the report is
    A. IV, I, II, V, III   B. II, III, I, V, IV   C. IV, II, I, III, V   D. I, II, III, V, IV

23. Police Officer O'Hara completes a Universal Summons for a motorist who has just passed a red traffic light. The Universal Summons includes the following five sentences:
    I. As the car passed the light, I followed in the patrol car.
    II. After the driver stopped the car, he stated that the light was yellow, not red.
    III. A blue Cadillac sedan passed the red light on the corner of 79th Street and 3rd Avenue at 11:25 P.M.
    IV. As a result, the driver was informed that he did pass a red light and that his brake lights were not working.
    V. The driver in the Cadillac stopped his car as soon as he saw the patrol car, and I noticed that the brake lights were not working.

    The MOST logical order for the above sentences to appear in the Universal Summons is
    A. I, III, V, II, IV   B. III, I, V, II, IV   C. III, I, V, IV, II   D. I, III, IV, II, V

24. Detective Egan is preparing a follow-up report regarding a homicide on 170th Street and College Avenue. An unknown male was found at the scene. The report will contain the following five sentences:
    I. Police Officer Gregory wrote down the names, addresses, and phone numbers of the witnesses.
    II. A 911 operator received a call of a man shot and dispatched Police Officers Worth and Gregory to the scene.
    III. They discovered an unidentified male dead on the street.
    IV. Police Officer Worth notified the Precinct Detective Unit immediately.
    V. At approximately 9:00 A.M., an unidentified male shot another male in the chest during an argument.

The MOST logical order for the above sentences to appear in the report is
A. V, II, III, IV, I   B. II, III, V, IV, I   C. IV, I, V, II, III   D. V, III, II, IV, I

25. Police Officer Tracey is preparing a Robbery Report which will include the following five sentences:
    I. I ran around the corner and observe a man pointing a gun at a taxidriver.
    II. I informed the man I was a police officer and that he should not move.
    III. I was on the corner of 125th Street and Park Avenue when I heard a scream coming from around the corner.
    IV. The man turned around and fired one shot at me.
    V. I fired once, shooting him in the arm and causing him to fall to the ground.
    The MOST logical order for the above sentences to appear in the report is
    A. I, III, IV, II, V   B. IV, V, II, I, III   C. III, I, II, IV, V   D. III, I, V, II, IV

25.____

KEY (CORRECT ANSWERS)

1.	B		11.	D
2.	B		12.	D
3.	B		13.	C
4.	A		14.	B
5.	A		15.	B
6.	B		16.	A
7.	A		17.	B
8.	D		18.	A
9.	B		19.	A
10.	A		20.	D

21. B
22. C
23. B
24. A
25. C

TEST 2

DIRECTIONS: The sentences that follow are in scrambled order. You are to rearrange them in proper order and indicate the letter choice containing the CORRECT answer. *PRINT THE LETTER OF THE CORRECT ANSWER IN THE SPACE AT THE RIGHT*

1. Police Officer Weiker is completing a Complaint Report which will contain the following five sentences:
   I. Mr. Texlor was informed that the owner of the van would receive a parking ticket and that the van would be towed away.
   II. The police tow truck arrived approximately one half hour after Mr. Texlor complained.
   III. While on foot patrol on West End Avenue, I saw the owner of Rand's Restaurant arrive to open his business.
   IV. Mr. Texlor, the owner, called to me and complained that he could not receive deliveries because a van was blocking his driveway.
   V. The van's owner later reported to the precinct that his van had been stolen, and he was then informed that it had been towed.
   The MOST logical order for the above sentences to appear in the report is
   A. III, V, I, II, IV   B. III, IV, I, II, V   C. IV, III, I, II, V   D. IV, III, II, I, V

   1.____

2. Police Officer Ames is completing an entry in his Activity Log. The entry contains the following five sentences:
   I. Mr. Sands gave me a complete description of the robber.
   II. Alvin Sands, owner of the Star Delicatessen, called the precinct to report he had just been robbed.
   III. I then notified all police patrol vehicles to look for a white male in his early twenties wearing brown pants and shirt, a black leather jacket, and black and white sneakers.
   IV. I arrived on the scene after being notified by the precinct that a robbery had just occurred at the Star Delicatessen.
   V. Twenty minutes later, a man fitting the description was arrested by a police officer on patrol six blocks from the delicatessen.
   The MOST logical order for the above sentences to appear in the Activity Log is
   A. II, I, IV, III, V   B. II IV, III, I, V   C. II, IV, I, III, V   D. II, IV, I, V, III

   2.____

3. Police Officer Benson is completing a Complaint Report concerning a stolen taxicab, which will include the following five sentences:
   I. Police Officer Benson noticed that a cab was parked next to a fire hydrant.
   II. Dawson *borrowed* the cab for transportation purposes since he was in a hurry.
   III. Ed Dawson got into his car and tried to start it, but the battery was dead.
   IV. When he reached his destination, he parked the cab by a fire hydrant and placed the keys under the seat.
   V. He looked around and saw an empty cab with the engine running.
   The MOST logical order for the above sentences to appear in the report is
   A. I, III, II, IV, V   B. III, I, II, V, IV   C. III, V, II, IV, I   D. V, II, IV, III, I

   3.____

125

4. Police Officer Hatfield is reviewing his Activity Log entry prior to completing a report. The entry contains the following five sentences:
   I. When I arrived at Zand's Jewelry Store, I noticed that the door was slightly open.
   II. I told the burglar I was a police officer and that he should stand still or he would be shot.
   III. As I entered the store, I saw a man wearing a ski mask attempting to open the safe in the back of the store.
   IV. On December 16, 2020, at 1:38 A.M., I was informed that a burglary was in progress at Zand's Jewelry Store on East 59th Street.
   V. The burglar quickly pulled a knife from his pocket when he saw me.
   The MOST logical order for the above sentences to appear in the report is
   A. IV, I, III, V, II   B. I, IV, III, V, II   C. IV, III, II, V, I   D. I, III, IV, V, II

4.____

5. Police Officer Lorenz is completing a report of a murder. The report will contain the following five statements made by a witness:
   I. I was awakened by the sound of a gunshot coming from the apartment next door and I decided to check.
   II. I entered the apartment and looked into the kitchen and the bathroom.
   III. I found Mr. Hubbard's body slumped in the bathtub.
   IV. The door to the apartment was open, but I didn't see anyone.
   V. He had been shot in the head.
   The MOST logical order for the above sentences to appear in the report is
   A. I, III, II, IV, V   B. I, IV, II, III, V   C. IV, II, I, III, V   D. III, I, II, IV, V

5.____

6. Police Officer Baldwin is preparing an accident report which will include the following five sentences:
   I. The old man lay on the ground for a few minutes, but was not physically hurt.
   II. Charlie Watson, a construction worker, was repairing some brick work at the top of a building at 54th Street and Madison Avenue.
   III. Steven Green, his partner, warned him that this could be dangerous, but Watson ignored him.
   IV. A few minutes later, one of the bricks thrown by Watson smashed to the ground in front of an old man, who fainted out of fright.
   V. Mr. Watson began throwing some of the bricks over the side of the building.
   The MOST logical order for the above sentences to appear in the report is
   A. II, V, III, IV, I   B. I, IV, II, V, III   C. III, II, IV, V, I   D. II, III, I, IV, V

6.____

7. Police Officer Porter is completing an Incident Report concerning her rescue of a woman being held hostage by a former boyfriend. Her report will contain the following five sentences:
   I. I saw a man holding .25 caliber gun to a woman's head, but he did not see me.
   II. I then broke a window and gained access to the house.
   III. As I approached the house on foot, a gunshot rang out and I heard a woman scream.
   IV. A decoy van brought me as close as possible to the house where the woman was being held hostage.

7.____

V. I ordered the man to drop his gun, and he released the woman and was taken into custody.

The MOST logical order for the above sentences to appear in the report is
A. I, III, II, IV, V   B. IV, III, II, I, V   C. III, II, I, IV, V   D. V, I, II, III, IV

8. Police Officer Byrnes is preparing a crime report concerning a robbery. The report will consist of the following five sentences:
   I. Mr. White, following the man's instructions, opened the car's hood, at which time the man got out of the auto, drew a revolver, and ordered White to give him all the money in his pockets.
   II. Investigation has determined there were no witnesses to this incident.
   III. The man asked White to check the oil and fill the tank.
   IV. Mr. White, a gas attendant, states that he was working alone at the gas station when a black male pulled up to the gas pump in a white Mercury.
   V. White was then bound and gagged by the male and locked in the gas station's rest room.

   The MOST logical order for the above sentences to appear in the report is
   A. IV, I, III, II, V   B. III, I, II, V, IV   C. IV, III, I, V, II   D. I, III, IV, II, V

9. Police Officer Gale is preparing a report of a crime committed against Mr. Weston. The report will consist of the following five sentences:
   I. The man, who had a gun, told Mr. Weston not to scream for help and ordered him back into the apartment.
   II. With Mr. Weston disposed of in this fashion, the man proceeded to ransack the apartment.
   III. Opening the door to see who was there, Mr. Weston was confronted by a tall white male wearing a dark blue jacket and white pants.
   IV. Mr. Weston was at home alone in his living room when the doorbell rang.
   V. Once inside, the man bound and gagged Mr. Weston and locked him in the bathroom.

   The MOST logical order for the above sentences to appear in the report is
   A. III, V, II, I, IV   B. IV, III, I, V, II   C. III, V, IV, II, I   D. IV, III, V, I, II

10. A police officer is completing a report of a robbery, which will contain the following five sentences:
    I. Two police officers were about to enter the Red Rose Coffee Shop on 47th Street and 8th Avenue.
    II. They then noticed a male running up the street carrying a brown paper bag.
    III. They heard a woman standing outside the Broadway Boutique yelling that her store had just been robbed by a young man, and she was pointing up the street.
    IV. They caught up with him and made an arrest.
    V. The police officers pursued the male, who ran past them on 8th Avenue.

    The MOST logical order for the above sentences to appear in the report is
    A. I, III, II, V, IV   B. III, I, II, V, IV   C. IV, V, I, II, III   D. I, V, IV, III, II

11. Police Officer Capalbo is preparing a report of a bank robbery. The report will contain the following five statements made by a witness:
    I. Initialing, all I could see were two men, dressed in maintenance uniforms, sitting in the area reserved for bank officers.
    II. I was passing the bank at 8 P.M. and noticed that all the lights were out, except in the rear section.
    III. Then I noticed two other men in the bank, coming from the direction of the vault, carrying a large metal box.
    IV. At this point, I decided to call the police.
    V. I knocked on the window to get the attention of the men in the maintenance uniforms, and they chased the two men carrying the box down a flight of steps.
    The MOST logical order for the above sentences to appear in the report is
        A. IV, I, II, V, III   B. I, III, II, V, IV   C. II, I, III, V, IV   D. II, III, I, V, IV

12. Police Officer Roberts is preparing a crime report concerning an assault and a stolen car. The report will contain the following five sentences:
    I. Upon leaving the store to return to his car, Winters noticed that a male unknown to him was sitting in his car.
    II. The man then re-entered Winters' car and drove away, fleeing north on 2nd Avenue.
    III. Mr. Winters stated that he parked his car in front of 235 East 25th Street and left the engine running while he went into the butcher shop at that location.
    IV. Mr. Robert Gering, a witness, stated that the male is known in the neighborhood as Bobby Rae and is believed to reside at 323 East 114th Street.
    V. When Winters approached the car and ordered the man to get out, the man got out of the auto and struck Winters with his fists, knocking him to the ground.
    The MOST logical order for the above sentences to appear in the report is
        A. III, II, V, I, IV   B. III, I, V, II, IV   C. I, IV, V, II, III   D. III, II, I, V, IV

13. Police Officer Robinson is preparing a crime report concerning the robbery of Mr. Edwards' store. The report will consist of the following five sentences:
    I. When the last customer left the store, the two men drew revolvers and ordered Mr. Edwards to give them all the money in the cash register.
    II. The men proceeded to the back of the store as if they were going to do some shopping.
    III. Janet Morley, a neighborhood resident, later reported that she saw the men enter a green Ford station wagon and flee northbound on Albany Avenue.
    IV. Edwards complied after which the gunmen ran from the store.
    V. Mr. Edwards states that he was stocking merchandise behind the store counter when two white males entered the store.
    The MOST logical order for the above sentences to appear in the report is
        A. V, II, III, I, IV   B. V, II, I, IV, III   C. II, I, V, IV, III   D. III, V, II, I, IV

14. Police Officer Wendell is preparing an accident report for a 6-car accident that occurred at the intersection of Bath Avenue and Bay Parkway. The report will consist of the following five sentences:
   I. A 2016 Volkswagen Beetle, traveling east on Bath Avenue, swerved to the left to avoid the Impala, and struck a 2014 Ford station wagon which was traveling west on Bath Avenue.
   II. The Seville then mounted the curb on the northeast corner of Bath Avenue and Bay Parkway and struck a light pole.
   III. A 2013 Buick Lesabre, traveling northbound on Bay Parkway directly behind the Impala, struck the Impala, pushing it into the intersection of Bath Avenue and Bay Parkway.
   IV. A 2015 Chevy Impala, traveling northbound on Bay Parkway, had stopped for a red light at Bath Avenue.
   V. A 2017 Toyota, traveling westbound on Bath Avenue, swerved to the right to avoid hitting the Ford station wagon, and struck a 2017 Cadillac Seville double-parked near the corner.
   The MOST logical order for the above sentences to appear in the report is
   A. IV, III, V, II, I   B. III, IV, V, II, I   C. IV, III, I, V, II   D. III, IV, V, I, II

14.____

15. The following five sentences are part of an Activity Log entry Police Officer Rogers made regarding an explosion:
   I. I quickly treated the pedestrian for the injury.
   II. The explosion caused a glass window in an office building to shatter.
   III. After the pedestrian was treated, a call was placed to the precinct requesting additional police officers to evacuate the area.
   IV. After all the glass settled to the ground, I saw a pedestrian who was bleeding from the arm.
   V. While on foot patrol near 5th Avenue and 53rd Street, I heard a loud explosion.
   The MOST logical order for the above sentences to appear in the report is
   A. II, V, IV, I, III   B. V, II, IV, III, I   C. V, II, I, IV, III   D. V, II, IV, I, III

15.____

16. Police Officer David is completing a report regarding illegal activity near the entrance to Madison Square Garden during a recent rock concert. The report will obtain the following five sentences:
   I. As I came closer to the man, he placed what appeared to be tickets in his pocket and began to walk away.
   II. After the man stopped, I questioned him about *scalping* tickets.
   III. While on assignment near the Madison Square Garden entrance, I observed a man apparently selling tickets.
   IV. I stopped the man by stating that I was a police officer.
   V. The man was then given a summons, and he left the area.
   The MOST logical order for the above sentences to appear in the report is
   A. I, III, IV, II, V   B. III, I, IV, V, II   C. III, IV, I, II, V   D. III, I, IV, II, V

16.____

17. Police Officer Sampson is preparing a report containing a dispute in a bar. The report will contain the following five sentences:
   I. John Evans, the bartender, ordered the two men out of the bar.
   II. Two men dressed in dungarees entered the C and D Bar at 5:30 P.M.
   III. The two men refused to leave and began to beat up Evans.
   IV. A customer in the bar saw me on patrol and yelled to me to come separate the three men.
   V. The two men became very drunk and loud within a short time.
   The MOST logical order for the above sentences to appear in the report is
      A. II, I, V, III, IV   B. II, III, IV, V, I   C. III, I, II, V, IV   D. II, V, I, III, IV

18. A police officer is completing a report concerning the response to a crime in progress. The report will include the following five sentences:
   I. The officers saw two armed men run out of the liquor store and into a waiting car.
   II. Police Officers Lunty and Duren received the call and responded to the liquor store.
   III. The robbers gave up without a struggle.
   IV. Lunty and Duren blocked the getaway car with their patrol car.
   V. A call came into the precinct concerning a robbery in progress at Jane's Liquor Store.
   The MOST logical order for the above sentence to appear in the report is
      A. V, II, I, IV, III   B. II, V, I, III, IV   C. V, I, IV, II, III   D. I, V, II, III, IV

19. Police Officers Jenkins is preparing a Crime Report which will consist of the following five sentences:
   I. After making inquirie in the vicinity, Smith found out that his next door neighbor, Viola Jones, had seen two local teenagers, Michael Heinz and Vincent Gaynor, smash his car's windshields with a crowbar.
   II. Jones told Smith that the teenagers live at 8700 19th Avenue.
   III. Mr. Smith heard a loud crash at approximately 11:00 P.M., looked out of his apartment window, and saw two white males running away from his car.
   IV. Smith then reported the incident to the precinct, and Heinz and Gaynor were arrested at the address given.
   V. Leaving his apartment to investigate further, Smith discovered that his car's front and rear windshields had been smashed.
   The MOST logical order for the above sentences to appear in the report is
      A. III, IV, V, I, II   B. III, V, I, II, IV   C. III, I, V, II, IV   D. V, III, I, II, IV

20. Sergeant Nancy Winston is reviewing a Gun Control Report which will contain the following five sentences:
   I. The man fell to the floor when hit in the chest with three bullets from 22 caliber gun.
   II. Merriam's 22 caliber gun was seized, and he was given a summons for not having a pistol permit.
   III. Christopher Merriam, the owner of A-Z Grocery, shot a man who attempted to rob him.
   IV. Police Officer Franks responded and asked Merriam for his pistol permit, which he could not produce.

V. Merriam phoned the police to report he had just shot a man who had attempted to rob him.

The MOST logical order for the above sentences to appear in the report is
A. III, I, V, IV, II   B. I, III, V, IV, II   C. III, I, V, II, IV   D. I, III, II, V, IV

21. Detective John Manville is completing a report for his superior regarding the murder of an unknown male who was shot in Central Park. The report will contain the following five sentences:
   I. Police Officers Langston and Cavers responded to the scene.
   II. I received the assignment to investigate the murder in Central Park from Detective Sergeant Rogers.
   III. Langston notified the Detective Bureau after questioning Jason.
   IV. An unknown male, apparently murdered, was discovered in Central Park by Howard Jason, a park employee, who immediately called the police.
   V. Langston and Cavers questioned Jason.

   The MOST logical order for the above sentences to appear in the report is
   A. I, IV, V, III, II   B. IV, I, V, II, III   C. IV, I, V, III, II   D. IV, V, I, III, II

21.____

22. A police officer is completing a report concerning the arrest of a juvenile. The report will contain the following five sentences:
   I. Sanders then telephoned Jay's parents from the precinct to inform them of their son's arrest.
   II. The store owner resisted, and Jay then shot him and ran from the store.
   III. Jay was transported directly to the precinct by Officer Sanders.
   IV. James Jay, a juvenile, walked into a candy store and announced a hold-up.
   V. Police Officer Sanders, while on patrol, arrested Jay a block from the candy store.

   The MOST logical order for the above sentences to appear in the report is
   A. IV, V, II, I, III   B. IV, II, V, III, I   C. II, IV, V, III, I   D. V, IV, II, I, III

22.____

23. Police Officer Olsen prepared a crime report for a robbery which contained the following five sentences:
   I. Mr. Gordon was approached by this individual who then produced a gun and demanded the money from the cash register.
   II. The man then fled from the scene on foot, southbound on 5th Avenue.
   III. Mr. Gordon was working at the deli counter when a white male, 5'6", 150-160 lbs., wearing a green jacket and blue pants, entered the store.
   IV. Mr. Gordon complied with the man's demands and handed him the daily receipts.
   V. Further investigation has determined there are no other witnesses to this robbery.

   The MOST logical order for the above sentences to appear in the report is
   A. I, III, IV, V, II   B. I, IV, II, III, V   C. III, IV, I, V, II   D. III, I, IV, II, V

23.____

24. Police Officer Bryant responded to 285 E. 31st Street to take a crime report of a burglary of Mr. Bond's home. The report will contain a brief description of the incident, consisting of the following five sentences:
   I. When Mr. Bond attempted to stop the burglar by grabbing him, he was pushed to the floor.
   II. The burglar had apparently gained access to the home by forcing open the 2nd floor bedroom window facing the fire escape.
   III. Mr. Bond sustained a head injury in the scuffle, and the burglar exited the home through the front door.
   IV. Finding nothing in the dresser, the burglar proceeded downstairs to the first floor, where he was confronted by Mr. Bond who was reading in the dining room.
   V. Once inside, he searched the drawers of the bedroom dresser.
   The MOST logical order for the above sentences to appear in the report is
      A. V, IV, I, II, III   B. II, V, IV, I, III   C. II, IV, V, III, I   D. III, II, I, V, IV

25. Police Officer Derringer responded to a call of a rape-homicide case in his patrol area and was ordered to prepare an incident report, which will contain the following five sentences:
   I. He pushed Miss Scott to the ground and forcibly raped her.
   II. Mary Scott was approached from behind by a white male, 5'7", 150-160 lbs. wearing dark pants and a white jacket.
   III. As Robinson approached the male, he ordered him to stop.
   IV. Screaming for help, Miss Scott alerted one John Robinson, a local grocer, who chased her assailant as he fled the scene.
   V. The male turned and fired two shots at Robinson, who fell to the ground mortally wounded.
   The MOST logical order for the above sentences to appear in the report is
      A. IV, III, I, II, V   B. II, IV, III, V, I   C. II, IV, I, V, III   D. II, I, IV, III, V

KEY (CORRECT ANSWERS)

1. B
2. C
3. C
4. A
5. B

6. A
7. B
8. C
9. B
10. A

11. C
12. B
13. B
14. C
15. D

16. D
17. D
18. A
19. B
20. A

21. C
22. B
23. D
24. B
25. D

READING COMPREHENSION
UNDERSTANDING AND INTERPRETING WRITTEN MATERIAL

EXAMINATION SECTION
TEST 1

DIRECTIONS: Each question or incomplete statement is followed by several suggested answers or completions. Select the one that BEST answers the question or completes the statement. *PRINT THE LETTER OF THE CORRECT ANSWER IN THE SPACE AT THE RIGHT.*

Questions 1-5.

DIRECTIONS: Questions 1 through 5 are to be answered on the basis of the following passage.

    The laws with which criminal courts are concerned contain threats of punishment for infraction of specified rules. Consequently, the courts are organized primarily for implementation of the punitive societal reaction of crime. While the informal organization of most courts allows the judge to use discretion as to which guilty persons actually are to be punished, the threat of punishment for all guilty persons always is present. Also, in recent years a number of formal provisions for the use of non-punitive and treatment methods by the criminal courts have been made, but the threat of punishment remains, even for the recipients of the treatment and non-punitive measures. For example, it has become possible for courts to grant probation, which can be non-punitive, to some offenders, but the probationer is constantly under the threat of punishment, for, if he does not maintain the conditions of his probation, he may be imprisoned. As the treatment reaction to crime becomes more popular, the criminal courts may have as their sole function the determination of the guilt or innocence of the accused persons, leaving the problem of correcting criminals entirely to outsiders. Under such conditions, the organization of the court system, the duties and activities of court personnel, and the nature of the trial all would be decidedly different.

1. Which one of the following is the BEST description of the subject matter of the above passage?
The

    A. value of non-punitive measures for criminals
    B. effect of punishment on guilty individuals
    C. punitive functions of the criminal courts
    D. success of probation as a deterrent of crime

1.____

2. It may be INFERRED from the above passage that the present traditional organization of the criminal court system is a result of

    A. the nature of the laws with which these courts are concerned
    B. a shift from non-punitive to punitive measures for correctional purposes
    C. an informal arrangement between court personnel and the government
    D. a formal decision made by court personnel to increase efficiency

2.____

3. All persons guilty of breaking certain specified rules, according to the above passage, are subject to the threat of

   A. treatment
   B. punishment
   C. probation
   D. retrial

4. According to the above passage, the decision whether or not to punish a guilty person is a function USUALLY performed by

   A. the jury
   B. the criminal code
   C. the judge
   D. corrections personnel

5. According to the above passage, which one of the following is a possible effect of an increase in the *treatment reactions to crime?*

   A. A decrease in the number of court personnel
   B. An increase in the number of criminal trials
   C. Less reliance on probation as a non-punitive treatment measure
   D. A decrease in the functions of the court following determination of guilt

Questions 6-8.

DIRECTIONS: Questions 6 through 8 are to be answered on the basis of the following passage.

A glaring exception to the usual practice of the judicial trial as a means of conflict resolution is the utilization of administrative hearings. The growing tendency to create administrative bodies with rule-making and quasi-judicial powers has shattered many standard concepts. A comprehensive examination of the legal process cannot neglect these newer patterns.

In the administrative process, the legislative, executive, and judicial functions are mixed together, and many functions, such as investigating, advocating, negotiating, testifying, rule making, and adjudicating, are carried out by the same agency. The reason for the breakdown of the separation-of-powers formula is not hard to find. It was felt by Congress, and state and municipal legislatures, that certain regulatory tasks could not be performed efficiently, rapidly, expertly, and with due concern for the public interest by the traditional branches of government. Accordingly, regulatory agencies were delegated powers to consider disputes from the earliest stage of investigation to the final stages of adjudication entirely within each agency itself, subject only to limited review in the regular courts.

6. The above passage states that the usual means for conflict resolution is through the use of

   A. judicial trial
   B. administrative hearing
   C. legislation
   D. regulatory agencies

7. The above passage IMPLIES that the use of administrative hearing in resolving conflict is a(n) _____ approach.

   A. traditional
   B. new
   C. dangerous
   D. experimental

8. The above passage states that the reason for the breakdown of the separation-of-powers formula in the administrative process is that

A. Congress believed that certain regulatory tasks could be better performed by separate agencies
B. legislative and executive functions are incompatible in the same agency
C. investigative and regulatory functions are not normally reviewed by the courts
D. state and municipal legislatures are more concerned with efficiency than with legality

Questions 9-10.

DIRECTIONS: Questions 9 and 10 are to be answered SOLELY on the basis of the information given in the following paragraph.

An assumption commonly made in regard to the reliability of testimony is that when a number of persons report upon the same matter, those details upon which there is an agreement may, in general, be considered as substantiated. Experiments have shown, however, that there is a tendency for the same errors to appear in the testimony of different individuals, and that, quite apart from any collusion, agreement of testimony is no proof of dependability.

9. According to the above paragraph, it is commonly assumed that details of an event are substantiated when

   A. a number of persons report upon them
   B. a reliable person testifies to them
   C. no errors are apparent in the testimony of different individuals
   D. several witnesses are in agreement about them

10. According to the above paragraph, agreement in the testimony of different witnesses to the same event is

    A. evaluated more reliably when considered apart from collusion
    B. not the result of chance
    C. not a guarantee of the accuracy of the facts
    D. the result of a mass reaction of the witnesses

Questions 11-12.

DIRECTIONS: Questions 11 and 12 are to be answered SOLELY on the basis of the information given in the following paragraph.

The accuracy of the information about past occurrence obtainable in an interview is so low that one must take the stand that the best use to be made of the interview in this connection is a means of finding clues and avenues of access to more reliable sources of information. On the other hand, feelings and attitudes have been found to be clearly and correctly revealed in a properly conducted personal interview.

11. According to the above paragraph, information obtained in a personal interview

    A. can be corroborated by other clues and more reliable sources of information revealed at the interview
    B. can be used to develop leads to other sources of information about past events
    C. is not reliable
    D. is reliable if it relates to recent occurrences

12. According to the above paragraph, the personal interview is suitable for obtaining

   A. emotional reactions to a given situation
   B. fresh information on factors which may be forgotten
   C. revived recollection of previous events for later use as testimony
   D. specific information on material already reduced to writing

Questions 13-15.

DIRECTIONS: Questions 13 through 15 are to be answered on the basis of the following paragraph.

Admissibility of handwriting standards (samples of handwriting for the purpose of comparison) as a basis for expert testimony is frequently necessary when the authenticity of disputed documents may be at issue. Under the older rules of common law, only that writing relating to the issues in the case could be used as a basis for handwriting testimony by an expert. Today, most jurisdictions admit irrelevant writings as standards for comparison. However, their genuineness, in all instances, must be established to the satisfaction of the court. There are a number of types of documents, however, not ordinarily relevant to the issues which are seldom acceptable to the court as handwriting standards, such as bail bonds, signatures on affidavits, depositions, etc. These are usually already before the court as part of the record in a case. Exhibits written in the presence of a witness or prepared voluntarily for a law enforcement officer are readily admissible in most jurisdictions. Testimony of a witness who is considered familiar with the writing is admissible in some jurisdictions. In criminal cases, it is possible that the signature on the fingerprint card obtained in connection with the arrest of the defendant for the crime currently charged may be admitted as a handwriting standard. In order to give the defendant the fairest possible treatment, most jurisdictions do not admit the signatures on fingerprint cards pertaining to prior arrests. However, they are admitted sometimes. In such instances, the court usually requires that the signature be photographed or removed from the card and no reference be made to the origin of the signature.

13. Of the following, the types of handwriting standards MOST likely to be admitted in evidence by most jurisdictions are those

   A. appearing on depositions and bail bonds
   B. which were written in the presence of a witness or voluntarily given to a law enforcement officer
   C. identified by witnesses who claim to be familiar with the handwriting
   D. which are in conformity with the rules of common law only

14. The PRINCIPAL factor which generally determines the acceptance of handwriting standards by the courts is

   A. the relevance of the submitted documents to the issues of the case
   B. the number of witnesses who have knowledge of the submitted documents
   C. testimony that the writing has been examined by a handwriting expert
   D. acknowledgment by the court of the authenticity of the submitted documents

15. The MOST logical reason for requiring the removal of the signature of a defendant from fingerprint cards pertaining to prior arrests, before admitting the signature in court as a handwriting standard, is that

A. it simplifies the process of identification of the signature as a standard for comparison
B. the need for identifying the fingerprints is eliminated
C. mention of prior arrests may be prejudicial to the defendant
D. a handwriting expert does not need information pertaining to prior arrests in order to make his identification

Questions 16-20.

DIRECTIONS: Questions 16 through 20 are to be answered SOLELY on the basis of the information contained in the following paragraph.

A statement which is offered in an attempt to prove the truth of the matters therein stated, but which is not made by the author as a witness before the court at the particular trial in which it is so offered, is hearsay. This is so whether the statement consists of words (oral or written), of symbols used as a substitute for words, or of signs or other conduct offered as the equivalent of a statement. Subject to some well-established exceptions, hearsay is not generally acceptable as evidence, and it does not become competent evidence just because it is received by the court without objection. One basis for this rule is simply that a fact cannot be proved by showing that somebody stated it was a fact. Another basis for the rule is the fundamental principle that in a criminal prosecution the testimony of the witness shall be taken before the court, so that at the time he gives the testimony offered in evidence he will be sworn and subject to cross-examination, the scrutiny of the court, and confrontation by the accused.

16. Which of the following is hearsay? 16.____
   A(n)

   A. written statement by a person not present at the court hearing where the statement is submitted as proof of an occurrence
   B. oral statement in court by a witness of what he saw
   C. written statement of what he saw by a witness present in court
   D. re-enactment by a witness in court of what he saw

17. In a criminal case, a statement by a person not present in court is 17.____

   A. *acceptable* evidence if not objected to by the prosecutor
   B. *acceptable* evidence if not objected to by the defense lawyer
   C. *not acceptable* evidence except in certain well-settled circumstances
   D. *not acceptable* evidence under any circumstances

18. The rule on hearsay is founded on the belief that 18.____

   A. proving someone said an act occurred is not proof that the act did occur
   B. a person who has knowledge about a case should be willing to appear in court
   C. persons not present in court are likely to be unreliable witnesses
   D. permitting persons to testify without appearing in court will lead to a disrespect for law

19. One reason for the general rule that a witness in a criminal case must give his testimony in court is that

    A. a witness may be influenced by threats to make untrue statements
    B. the opposite side is then permitted to question him
    C. the court provides protection for a witness against unfair questioning
    D. the adversary system is designed to prevent a miscarriage of justice

20. Of the following, the MOST appropriate title for the above passage would be

    A. WHAT IS HEARSAY?
    B. RIGHTS OF DEFENDANTS
    C. TRIAL PROCEDURES
    D. TESTIMONY OF WITNESSES

21. A person's statements are independent of who he is or what he is. Statements made by a person are not proved true or false by questioning his character or his position. A statement should stand or fall on its merits, regardless of who makes the statement. Truth is determined by evidence only. A person's character or personality should not be the determining factor in logic. Discussions should not become incidents of name calling.
    According to the above, whether or not a statement is true depends on the

    A. recipient's conception of validity
    B. maker's reliability
    C. extent of support by facts
    D. degree of merit the discussion has

Question 22-25.

DIRECTIONS: Questions 22 through 25 are to be answered on the basis of the following passage.

The question, whether an act, repugnant to the Constitution, can become the law of the land, is a question deeply interesting to the United States; but, happily, not of an intricacy proportioned to its interest. It seems only necessary to recognize certain principles, supposed to have been long and well-established, to decide it. That the people have an original right to establish, for their future government, such principles as, in their opinion, shall most conduce to their own happiness, is the basis on which the whole American fabric has been erected. The exercise of this original right is a very great exertion; nor can it, nor ought it, to be frequently repeated. The principles, therefore, so established are deemed fundamental; and as the authority from which they proceed is supreme, and can seldom act, they are designed to be permanent.

22. The BEST title for the above passage would be

    A. PRINCIPLES OF THE CONSTITUTION
    B. THE ROOT OF CONSTITUTIONAL CHANGE
    C. ONLY PEOPLE CAN CHANGE THE CONSTITUTION
    D. METHODS OF CONSTITUTIONAL CHANGE

23. According to the above passage, original right is

    A. fundamental to the principle that the people may choose their own form of government
    B. established by the Constitution

C. the result of a very great exertion and should not often be repeated
D. supreme, can seldom act, and is designed to be permanent

24. Whether an act not in keeping with Constitutional principles can become law is, according to the above passage,

   A. an intricate problem requiring great thought and concentration
   B. determined by the proportionate interests of legislators
   C. determined by certain long established principles, fundamental to Constitutional Law
   D. an intricate problem, but less intricate than it would seem from the interest shown in it

25. According to the above passage, the phrase *and can seldom act* refers to the

   A. principle enacted early into law by Americans when they chose their future form of government
   B. original rights of the people as vested in the Constitution
   C. original framers of the Constitution
   D. established, fundamental principles of government

KEY (CORRECT ANSWERS)

1.	C	11.	B
2.	A	12.	A
3.	B	13.	B
4.	C	14.	D
5.	D	15.	C
6.	A	16.	A
7.	B	17.	C
8.	A	18.	A
9.	D	19.	B
10.	C	20.	A

21. C
22. B
23. A
24. D
25. A

TEST 2

DIRECTIONS: Each question or incomplete statement is followed by several suggested answers or completions. Select the one that BEST answers the question or completes the statement. *PRINT THE LETTER OF THE CORRECT ANSWER IN THE SPACE AT THE RIGHT.*

Questions 1-3.

DIRECTIONS: Questions 1 through 3 are to be answered SOLELY on the basis of the following paragraph.

The police laboratory performs a valuable service in crime investigation by assisting in the reconstruction of criminal action and by aiding in the identification of persons and things. When studied by a technician, physical things found at crime scenes often reveal facts useful in identifying the criminal and in determining what has occurred. The nature of substances to be examined and the character of the examination to be made vary so widely that the services of a large variety of skilled scientific persons are needed in crime investigations. To employ such a complete staff and to provide them with equipment and standards needed for all possible analysis and comparisons is beyond the means and the needs of any but the largest police departments. The search of crime scenes for physical evidence also calls for the services of specialists supplied with essential equipment and assigned to each tour of duty so as to provide service at any hour.

1. If a police department employs a large staff of technicians of various types in its laboratory, it will affect crime investigations to the extent that

    A. most crimes will be speedily solved
    B. identification of criminals will be aided
    C. search of crime scenes for physical evidence will become of less importance
    D. investigation by police officers will not usually be required

2. According to the above paragraph, the MOST complete study of objects found at the scenes of crimes is

    A. always done in all large police departments
    B. based on assigning one technician to each tour of duty
    C. probably done only in large police departments
    D. probably done in police departments of communities with low crime rates

3. According to the above paragraph, a large variety of skilled technicians is useful in criminal investigations because

    A. crimes cannot be solved without their assistance as part of the police team
    B. large police departments need large staffs
    C. many different kinds of tests on various substances can be made
    D. the police cannot predict what methods may be tried by wily criminals

Questions 4-6.

DIRECTIONS: Questions 4 through 6 are to be answered SOLELY on the basis of the following passage.

Probably the most important single mechanism for bringing the resources of science and technology to bear on the problems of crime would be the establishment of a major prestigious science and technology research program within a research institute. The program would create interdisciplinary teams of mathematicians, computer scientists, electronics engineers, physicists, biologists, and other natural scientists, psychologists, sociologists, economists, and lawyers. The institute and the program must be significant enough to attract the best scientists available, and, to this end, the director of this institute must himself have a background in science and technology and have the respect of scientists. Because it would be difficult to attract such a staff into the Federal government, the institute should be established by a university, a group of universities, or an independent nonprofit organization, and should be within a major metropolitan area. The institute would have to establish close ties with neighboring criminal justice agencies that would receive the benefit of serving as experimental laboratories for such an institute. In fact, the proposal for the institute might be jointly submitted with the criminal justice agencies. The research program would require, in order to bring together the necessary *critical mass* of competent staff, an annual budget which might reach 5 million dollars, funded with at least three years of lead time to assure continuity. Such a major scientific and technological research institute should be supported by the Federal government.

4. Of the following, the MOST appropriate title for the foregoing passage is

   A. RESEARCH - AN INTERDISCIPLINARY APPROACH TO FIGHTING CRIME
   B. A CURRICULUM FOR FIGHTING CRIME
   C. THE ROLE OF THE UNIVERSITY IN THE FIGHT AGAINST CRIME
   D. GOVERNMENTAL SUPPORT OF CRIMINAL RESEARCH PROGRAMS

5. According to the above passage, in order to attract the best scientists available, the research institute should

   A. provide psychologists and sociologists to counsel individual members of interdisciplinary teams
   B. encourage close ties with neighboring criminal justice agencies
   C. be led by a person who is respected in the scientific community
   D. be directly operated and funded by the Federal government

6. The term *critical mass,* as used in the above passage, refers MAINLY to

   A. a staff which would remain for three years of continuous service to the institute
   B. staff members necessary to carry out the research program of the institute successfully
   C. the staff necessary to establish relations with criminal justice agencies which will serve as experimental laboratories for the institute
   D. a staff which would be able to assist the institute in raising adequate funds

Questions 7-9.

DIRECTIONS: Questions 7 through 9 are to be answered SOLELY on the basis of the following paragraph.

The use of modern scientific methods in the examination of physical evidence often provides information to the investigator which he could not otherwise obtain. This applies particularly to small objects and materials present in minute quantities or trace evidence because the quantities here are such that they may be overlooked without methodical searching, and often special means of detection are needed. Whenever two objects come in contact with one another, there is a transfer of material, however slight. Usually, the softer object will transfer to the harder, but the transfer may be mutual. The quantity of material transferred differs with the type of material involved and the more violent the contact the greater the degree of transference. Through scientific methods of determining physical properties and chemical composition, we can add to the facts observable by the investigator's unaided senses, and thereby increase the chances of identification.

7. According to the above paragraph, the amount of material transferred whenever two objects come in contact with one another

   A. varies directly with the softness of the objects involved
   B. varies directly with the violence of the contact of the objects
   C. is greater when two soft, rather than hard, objects come into violent contact with each other
   D. is greater when coarse-grained, rather than smooth-grained, materials are involved

8. According to the above paragraph, the PRINCIPAL reason for employing scientific methods in obtaining trace evidence is that

   A. other methods do not involve a methodical search of the crime scene
   B. scientific methods of examination frequently reveal physical evidence which did not previously exist
   C. the amount of trace evidence may be so sparse that other methods are useless
   D. trace evidence cannot be properly identified unless special means of detection are employed

9. According to the above paragraph, the one of the following statements which BEST describes the manner in which scientific methods of analyzing physical evidence assists the investigator is that such methods

   A. add additional valuable information to the investigator's own knowledge of complex and rarely occurring materials found as evidence
   B. compensate for the lack of important evidential material through the use of physical and chemical analyses
   C. make possible an analysis of evidence which goes beyond the ordinary capacity of the investigator's senses
   D. identify precisely those physical characteristics of the individual which the untrained senses of the investigator are unable to discern

Questions 10-13.

DIRECTIONS: Questions 10 through 13 are to be answered SOLELY on the basis of the information contained in the following paragraph.

Under the provisions of the Bank Protection Act of 1968, enacted July 8, 1968, each Federal banking supervisory agency, as of January 7, 1969, had to issue rules establishing minimum standards with which financial institutions under their control must comply with respect to the installation, maintenance, and operation of security devices and procedures, reasonable in cost, to discourage robberies, burglaries, and larcenies, and to assist in the identification and apprehension of persons who commit such acts. The rules set the time limits within which the affected banks and savings and loan associations must comply with the standards, and the rules require the submission of periodic reports on the steps taken. A violator of a rule under this Act is subject to a civil penalty not to exceed $100 for each day of the violation. The enforcement of these regulations rests with the responsible banking supervisory agencies.

10. The Bank Protection Act of 1968 was designed to

    A. provide Federal police protection for banks covered by the Act
    B. have organizations covered by the Act take precautions against criminals
    C. set up a system for reporting all bank robberies to the FBI
    D. insure institutions covered by the Act from financial loss due to robberies, burglaries, and larcenies

11. Under the provisions of the Bank Protection Act of 1968, each Federal banking supervisory agency was required to set up rules for financial institutions covered by the Act governing the

    A. hiring of personnel
    B. punishment of burglars
    C. taking of protective measures
    D. penalties for violations

12. Financial institutions covered by the Bank Protection Act of 1968 were required to

    A. file reports at regular intervals on what they had done to prevent theft
    B. identify and apprehend persons who commit robberies, burglaries, and larcenies
    C. draw up a code of ethics for their employees
    D. have fingerprints of their employees filed with the FBI

13. Under the provisions of the Bank Protection Act of 1968, a bank which is subject to the rules established under the Act and which violates a rule is liable to a penalty of NOT _____ than $100 for each _____.

    A. more; violation   B. less; day of violation
    C. less; violation   D. more; day of violation

Questions 14-17.

DIRECTIONS: Questions 14 through 17 are to be answered SOLELY on the basis of the following passage.

Specific measures for prevention of pilferage will be based on careful analysis of the conditions at each agency. The most practical and effective method to control casual pilferage is the establishment of psychological deterrents.

One of the most common means of discouraging casual pilferage is to search individuals leaving the agency at unannounced times and places. These spot searches may occasionally detect attempts at theft, but greater value is realized by bringing to the attention of individuals the fact that they may be apprehended if they do attempt the illegal removal of property.

An aggressive security education program is an effective means of convincing employees that they have much more to lose than they do to gain by engaging in acts of theft. It is important for all employees to realize that pilferage is morally wrong no matter how insignificant the value of the item which is taken. In establishing any deterrent to casual pilferage, security officers must not lose sight of the fact that most employees are honest and disapprove of thievery. Mutual respect between security personnel and other employees of the agency must be maintained if the facility is to be protected from other more dangerous forms of human hazards. Any security measure which infringes on the human rights or dignity of others will jeopardize, rather than enhance, the overall protection of the agency.

14. The $100,000 yearly inventory of an agency revealed that $50 worth of goods had been stolen; the only individuals with access to the stolen materials were the employees. Of the following measures, which would the author of the above passage MOST likely recommend to a security officer?

    A. Conduct an intensive investigation of all employees to find the culprit.
    B. Make a record of the theft, but take no investigative or disciplinary action against any employee.
    C. Place a tight security check on all future movements of personnel.
    D. Remove the remainder of the material to an area with much greater security.

15. What does the passage imply is the percentage of employees whom a security officer should expect to be honest?

    A. No employee can be expected to be honest all of the time
    B. Just 50%
    C. Less than 50%
    D. More than 50%

16. According to the above passage, the security officer would use which of the following methods to minimize theft in buildings with many exits when his staff is very small?

    A. Conduct an inventory of all material and place a guard near that which is most likely to be pilfered
    B. Inform employees of the consequences of legal prosecution for pilfering
    C. Close off the unimportant exits and have all his men concentrate on a few exits
    D. Place a guard at each exit and conduct a casual search of individuals leaving the premises

17. Of the following, the title BEST suited for this passage is

    A. CONTROL MEASURES FOR CASUAL PILFERING
    B. DETECTING THE POTENTIAL PILFERER
    C. FINANCIAL LOSSES RESULTING FROM PILFERING
    D. THE USE OF MORAL PERSUASION IN PHYSICAL SECURITY

Questions 18-24.

DIRECTIONS: Questions 18 through 24 are to be answered SOLELY on the basis of the following passage.

Burglar alarms are designed to detect intrusion automatically. Robbery alarms enable a victim of a robbery or an attack to signal for help. Such devices can be located in elevators, hallways, homes and apartments, businesses and factories, and subways, as well as on the street in high-crime areas. Alarms could deter some potential criminals from attacking targets so protected. If alarms were prevalent and not visible, then they might serve to suppress crime generally. In addition, of course, the alarms can summon the police when they are needed.

All alarms must perform three functions: sensing or initiation of the signal, transmission of the signal and annunciation of the alarm. A burglar alarm needs a sensor to detect human presence or activity in an unoccupied enclosed area like a building or a room. A robbery victim would initiate the alarm by closing a foot or wall switch, or by triggering a portable transmitter which would send the alarm signal to a remote receiver. The signal can sound locally as a loud noise to frighten away a criminal, or it can be sent silently by wire to a central agency. A centralized annunciator requires either private lines from each alarmed point, or the transmission of some information on the location of the signal.

18. A conclusion which follows LOGICALLY from the above passage is that 18.____

    A. burglar alarms employ sensor devices; robbery alarms make use of initiation devices
    B. robbery alarms signal intrusion without the help of the victim; burglar alarms require the victim to trigger a switch
    C. robbery alarms sound locally; burglar alarms are transmitted to a central agency
    D. the mechanisms for a burglar alarm and a robbery alarm are alike

19. According to the above passage, alarms can be located 19.____

    A. in a wide variety of settings
    B. only in enclosed areas
    C. at low cost in high-crime areas
    D. only in places where potential criminals will be deterred

20. According to the above passage, which of the following is ESSENTIAL if a signal is to be received in a central office? 20.____

    A. A foot or wall switch
    B. A noise-producing mechanism
    C. A portable reception device
    D. Information regarding the location of the source

21. According to the above passage, an alarm system can function WITHOUT a 21.____

    A. centralized annunciating device
    B. device to stop the alarm
    C. sensing or initiating device
    D. transmission device

22. According to the above passage, the purpose of robbery alarms is to 22.____

    A. find out automatically whether a robbery has taken place
    B. lower the crime rate in high-crime areas
    C. make a loud noise to frighten away the criminal
    D. provide a victim with the means to signal for help

23. According to the above passage, alarms might aid in lessening crime if they were   23._____

    A. answered promptly by police
    B. completely automatic
    C. easily accessible to victims
    D. hidden and widespread

24. Of the following, the BEST title for the above passage is   24._____

    A. DETECTION OF CRIME BY ALARMS
    B. LOWERING THE CRIME RATE
    C. SUPPRESSION OF CRIME
    D. THE PREVENTION OF ROBBERY

25. Although the rural crime reporting area is much less developed than that for cities and   25._____
    towns, current data are collected in sufficient volume to justify the generalization that
    rural crime rates are lower than those or urban communities.
    According to this statement,

    A. better reporting of crime occurs in rural areas than in cities
    B. there appears to be a lower proportion of crime in rural areas than in cities
    C. cities have more crime than towns
    D. crime depends on the amount of reporting

KEY (CORRECT ANSWERS)

1. B	11. C
2. C	12. A
3. C	13. D
4. A	14. B
5. C	15. D
6. B	16. B
7. B	17. A
8. C	18. A
9. C	19. A
10. B	20. D

21. A
22. D
23. D
24. A
25. B

POLICE SCIENCE NOTES

BASIC FUNDAMENTALS OF INVESTIGATION OF CRIME AND CRIMINAL OFFENSES

CONTENTS

		Page
A.	*CRIME*	1
	1. Definition of Crime	1
	2. Investigation of Crime	1
	3. Proof of Crime	1
B.	*CRIMINAL OFFENSES*	2
	1. Larceny and Wrongful Appropriation	2
	2. Burglary and Housebreaking	3
	3. Robbery	4
	4. Assault	4
	5. Murder/Homicide	5
	6. Manslaughter	8
	7. Maiming	8
	8. Attempted Suicide	9
	9. Sodomy	9
	10. Rape and Carnal Knowledge	9
	11. Forgery	10
	12. Counterfeiting	10
	13. Narcotic Violations	11
	14. Perjury	12
	15. Arson	12
C.	*BASIC QUESTIONS IN INVESTIGATION*	13
	1. WHO questions	13
	2. WHAT questions	13
	3. WHERE questions	14
	4. WHEN questions	14
	5. HOW questions	14
	6. WHY questions	14
D.	*SOURCES OF INFORMATION*	15
	I. Developing Sources of Information	15

		Page
II.	Personnel Sources	15
	1. Complainants	15
	2. Informants	15
	3. Witnesses	16
	4. Suspects	16
III.	Information Sources	16
	1. Newspapers and Periodicals	16
	2. Department of the Army Records	16
	3. Department of the Air Force Records	16
	4. Department of the Navy Records	16
	5. Treasury Department Records	17
	6. Department of Justice Records	17
	7. United States Postal Service Records	17
	8. Veterans Administration Records	17
	9. State Records	18
	10. County and City Records	18
	11. Private Detective Bureaus	18
	12. Other Record Sources	18

POLICE SCIENCE NOTES

BASIC FUNDAMENTALS OF INVESTIGATION OF CRIME AND CRIMINAL OFFENSES

A. CRIME

1. DEFINITION OF CRIME

A crime is an act or omission of an act prohibited or enjoined by law for the protection of the public and punishable by the state in a judicial proceeding in its own name.

Crimes are classified according to the degree of seriousness. Under the Criminal Code of the United States, a felony is a crime for which the punishment may be death or imprisonment for more than one year. (State criminal codes contain similar or equivalent definitions.)

Those crimes for which the maximum penalty may not exceed imprisonment for one year are classified as misdemeanors.

The police officer is concerned with three general classes of crime:
    a. Crimes Against the Person. - Offenses that are directed primarily against the physical person of another.
    b. Crimes Against Property. - Offenses that are directed primarily against property.
    c. Crimes Against the Government. - Offenses that are primarily directed against the peace and dignity of the government rather than against the person or property of an individual.

2. INVESTIGATION OF CRIME

To investigate a criminal offense effectively and efficiently, the police officer must be familiar with the elements of the offense. He must ascertain whether a crime has, in fact, been committed and must be cognizant of the evidence required to establish the commission of such crime.

As a guide to the investigator, some of the major offenses, their definitions, and the elements required for proof are set forth in this section. The purpose of the suggestions given is to provide a general checklist for the investigator; the suggestions appearing under a given offense may also be used in the investigation of other crimes.

A complete investigation requires that six basic questions concerning the crime, the subject, and the victim be answered fully. They are: Who? What? Where? When? How? Why? For subsidiary questions which may be employed to elucidate these basic questions, see Part C of this section.

3. PROOF OF CRIME

Generally, with regard to each offense, it must be proved, beyond a reasonable doubt by competent and relevant evidence, that the offense was committed, that the accused committed it, that he had the requisite criminal intent at the time or was negligent to the required degree, and that he is a person" subject to the jurisdiction. Since only evidence which is legally admissible may be introduced in a trial, the procurement of such evidence by the police investigator is of great importance.

B. CRIMINAL OFFENSES

1. LARCENY AND WRONGFUL APPROPRIATION

    a. Definition. - Any person is guilty of *larceny* if he wrongfully takes, obtains, or withholds, by any means whatever, from the possession of the true owner or of any other person any money, personal property, or article of value of any kind, with intent permanently to deprive or defraud another person of the use and benefit of property or to appropriate the same to his own use or the use of any person other than the true owner.
    Wrongful appropriation is defined in the same way as larceny, except that the wrongful taking, obtaining, or withholding need be with intent to deprive, defraud, or appropriate only temporarily. A charge of wrongful appropriation is necessarily included in a charge of larceny.

    b. Proof of Larceny. - The elements of proof required are:
        (1) That the accused wrongfully took, obtained, or withheld from the possession of the true owner or of any other person the property described in the specification.
        (2) That such property belonged to a certain person named or described.
        (3) That such property was of the value alleged, or of some value.
        (4) The facts and circumstances of the case, showing that the taking, obtaining, or withholding by the accused was with intent permanently to deprive or defraud another person of the use of any person other than the true owner.

    c. Proof of Wrongful Appropriation. - The elements of proof required are the same as those required of larceny except the facts and circumstances of the case must show that the taking, obtaining, or withholding by the accused was with intent to temporarily deprive or defraud.

    d. Suggestions. - The method of investigation of larceny and wrongful appropriation is similar to that of burglary and robbery. The investigator should determine:
        (1) The date and hour of the offense.
        (2) The description of property taken, including a complete list of items and their value.
        (3) The owner of the property, the possessor of it at the time of the offense, and the proof of ownership.
        (4) The location of the property at the time of the theft.
        (5) The complete details of how the theft was accomplished.
        (6) Who knew the location and the value of the stolen property.
        (7) Who is suspected.
        (8) The facts pertaining to the description of the suspects.
        (9) Whether the property was carried away by the thief.
        (10) Whether the thief intended to deprive the owner permanently of the property.
        (11) Whether the thief intended to deprive the owner temporarily of the property.
        (12) Whether the stolen article was personal or government property.
        (13) If the property was obtained under false pretenses, and obtain the details thereof.
        (14) All the documents and other evidence connected with the offense.

2. BURGLARY AND HOUSEBREAKING

   a. Definitions. - *Burglary* is the breaking and entering, in the nighttime, of the dwelling house of another person, with intent to commit murder, manslaughter, rape and carnal knowledge, larceny and wrongful appropriation, robbery, forgery, maiming, sodomy, or arson.
   Housebreaking is unlawfully entering the building or structure of another person with intent to commit a criminal offense therein. The offense is broader than burglary in that the place entered is not required to be a dwelling house.

   b. Proof of Burglary. - To constitute burglary, it must be proved that:
      (1). The accused broke and entered the certain dwelling house of a certain other person, as specified.
      (2) Such breaking and entering were done in the nighttime.
      (3) The facts and circumstances of the case (such as the actual commission of the offense) show that such breaking and entering were done with the intent to commit the alleged offense therein.

   c. Proof of Housebreaking. - To prove a charge of housebreaking, the investigator must show that:
      (1) The accused unlawfully entered a certain building or structure of a certain other person, as specified.
      (2) The facts and circumstances show that there was an intent to commit a criminal offense therein.

   d. Suggestions. - The following suggestions are presented without regard to the legal distinction between burglary and house-breaking. The purpose is to suggest courses of inquiry where a structure has been entered with criminal intent. The investigator should:
      (1) Record the address or location, and the description of the structure entered.
      (2) Note the date and hour of entry.
      (3) Search the building and immediate area carefully, if property was taken.
      (4) Determine where the owners or occupants were at the time of the crime.
      (5) Ascertain when the owners or occupants left the premises, whether all the doors and windows were secured, and where the keys were kept.
      (6) Develop information pertaining to any recent visitors to the premises. Obtain descriptions of all ostensible visitors, tradesmen, and utilities inspectors. Ascertain whether the crime was committed by someone inside or outside the premises, whether the premises were occupied at the time, whether the entry was gained by force, and, if it were an outside job, how the criminal entered.
      (7) Examine the locks to determine whether entry was effected by the picking of a lock, by the taking of wax impressions, or by the use of skeleton keys or other burglar tools.
      (8) Prepare photographs and sketches of the building, and indicate the place of entry.
      (9) Compile a complete list of the property stolen, and include detailed descriptions of any identifying data.
      (10) Describe all recovered property. Record where, when, and how it was recovered, and whether the owner identified it.
      (11) Establish whether the thief limited himself to one kind of property or whether he took a variety of items.
      (12) Ascertain whether the criminal conducted a systematic search, whether that search indicated that he possessed a knowledge of the area, and whether he knew where to look for the property.

(13) Examine the area carefully for fingerprints and their location and also examine the surrounding area for tire tracks and footprints.

(14) Record all the available details of the thief's characteristics and habits. Describe his method and system of operation.

(15) Check modus operand files to see if similar methods were employed in other burglaries.

(16) Search pawnshops and secondhand shops for loot. Check express offices for evidence of recent shipments.

(17) Describe any tools recovered at the scene. Were any tools recovered from the person of the suspect or his dwelling? Have a laboratory comparison made of any recovered tools and tool marks found at the crime scene.

(18) Obtain a complete description of any person seen loitering about the premises. Did anyone observe the criminal leaving the premises? Were any clues observed in or around the premises?

3. ROBBERY

   a. Definition. - *Robbery* is the taking with intent to steal of anything of value from the person or in the presence of another against his will, by force or violence or fear of immediate or future injury to his person or property or the person or property of a relative or member of his family, or of anyone in his company at the time of the robbery.

   b. Proof. - The elements of proof required are:
      (1) The larceny of the property by the accused, as alleged. (No proof of specific value need be determined.)
      (2) That the larceny was from the person or in the presence of the person alleged to have been robbed.
      (3) That the taking was by force and violence, or by putting in fear, as alleged.

   c. Suggestions. - Many of the suggestions included under larceny and wrongful appropriation, may be useful in the investigation of robbery. If the force employed amounted to physical violence, the suggestions outlined under assault may be used.

4. ASSAULT

   a. Definition. - An *assault* is an attempt or offer with unlawful force or violence to do bodily harm to another, whether or not the attempt or offer is consummated. An assault may consist of a culpably negligent act or omission which foreseeably might and does cause another reasonably to fear that force will at once be applied to his person. An *aggravated assault* is an assault committed with a dangerous weapon or other means of force likely to produce death or grievous bodily harm or with intent to inflict greivous bodily harm with or without a weapon. *Battery* is an assult in which the attempt or offer to do bodily harm is consummated by the infliction of such harm.

   b. Proof. - The elements of proof required are:
      (1) That the accused attempted or offered with unlawful force or violence to do bodily harm to a certain person, as alleged.
      (2) That, in the case of a consummated assault, the accused, intentionally or otherwise, did bodily harm to such person with a certain weapon, unlawful force, or violence.

c. Suggestions. - The following are suggestions for developing information on assaults:
 (1) Was a description of the assault obtained?
 (2) What was the extent of the injuries, if any?
 (3) What was the purpose of the assault?
 (4) Did the suspect make any threats prior to the assault?
 (5) What was the intent of the offender? Robbery? Murder? Rape? Manslaughter? Bodily harm?
 (6) What are the complete facts and circumstances surrounding the assault?
 (7) Did the offender employ a weapon?
 (8) How was the weapon employed?
 (9) Was any other offense committed in addition to the assault? Describe.
 (10) Was there intent on the part of the offender to inflict corporal hurt on the victim?
 (11) Was there a battery? Obtain proof, if possible.
 (12) Who else or what else was involved?
 (13) If assailant is unknown, was a complete description or portrait parle obtained?
 (14) Was the assault successful? If not, what prevented its completion?
 (15) Was assailant too drunk to entertain specific intent?
 (16) Was any weapon or other pertinent evidence left at the scene? Was a laboratory examination deemed advisable and made? Was the scene of attack photographed, and/or sketches prepared?

5. MURDER/HOMICIDE   5._____

 a. The killing of a human being is unlawful when done without justification or excuse. The determination of whether an unlawful killing constitutes *murder* or a lesser offense depends upon the circumstances under which it occurred.
  (1) Justification. - A murder committed in the proper performance of a legal duty is justifiable.
  (2) Excuse. - A homicide which is the result of an accident or a misadventure in doing a lawful act or in a lawful manner which is done in self-defense is excusable.
  (3) Premeditation. - Premeditated murder is murder committed after the formulation of a specific intent to kill someone and consideration of the act intended. A murder is not premeditated unless the thought of taking a life is consciously conceived, and the act or omission by which it was taken was intended.
  (4) Intent to kill or inflict great bodily harm. - An unlawful killing, without premeditation, is also murder when the person has either the intent to kill, or intent to inflict great bodily harm.
  (5) Act inherently dangerous with wanton disregard of human life. - Engaging in an act inherently dangerous to others, without any intent to cause the death of, or great bodily harm to, any particular person, or even with a wish that death may not be caused may also constitute murder if the performance of the act shows a wanton disregard for human life.
  (6) Commission of certain offenses. - A homicide committed during the perpetration or attempted perpetration of burglary, sodomy, rape, robbery, or aggravated arson also constitutes murder, and it is immaterial that the slaying may be unintentional or even accidental.

b. Proof. - The elements of proof required are:
   (1) That the victim named or described is dead.
   (2) That his death resulted from the act or omission of the accused, as alleged.
   (3) Facts and circumstances showing that the accused had a premeditated design to kill; or intended to kill or inflict great bodily harm; or was engaged in an act inherently dangerous to others, evincing a wanton disregard of human life; or was engaged in the perpetration or attempted perpetration of burglary, sodomy, rape, robbery, or aggravated arson.
c. Suggestions. - The following are suggestions for developing evidence in murder investigations and may be of assistance in manslaughter investigations:
   (1) Obtain name, address, and organization of the deceased.
   (2) Who discovered the body what other persons were present at the scene of the crime who can identify the body of the deceased? Record names and addresses for future reference.
   (3) Question available witnesses.
   (4) Ascertain the date and exact time of the discovery of the crime.
   (5) Was the deceased alive when first found?
   (6) Describe the exact location of the body when found was the body moved before the investigator arrived and, if so, by whom, why, and what change was made in the body's position?
   (7) Describe the position and appearance of the body.
   (8) Photograph the body as found, if possible, and photograph surrounding area, where necessary.
   (9) Record the condition of the weather, the visibility, the direction and force of the wind, and the illumination afforded the scene by the sun, moon, street lamps, or other sources of light.
   (10) Arrange, if possible, to have a medical examiner or physician make a brief preliminary examination of the body before it is moved. Record his name.
   (11) With the assistance of the Medical Examiner obtain a complete autopsy report which should show the following:
      (a) List of all apparent injuries, dirt, blood, or other marks on the body.
      (b) Complete physical description of the body.
      (c) Medical opinion as to time and cause of death.
   (12) When body is moved, mark position. Search area underneath and around body.
   (13) Arrange to obtain victim's clothing and make a careful search of it. Describe in notes. Preserve and identify for use as evidence.
   (14) Conduct a thorough search of the crime scene.
   (15) Search any suspects and their residence, when necessary.
   (16) Prepare necessary photographs, sketches, and notes.
   (17) Describe the crime scene in detail.
   (18) Collect all available evidence, taking precautions to identify and preserve it.
   (19) Submit any bullets, shells, weapons, hairs, bloodstains, fingernail scrapings, empty bottles, suspicious chemicals, fingerprints, footprints, and documents to a criminal laboratory for analysis.
   (20) Search scene and victim's effects for diaries, journals, letters, addresses, telephone numbers, or other documents which may reveal information about the crime.
   (21) Record the location, color, shape, size, and density of any blood spots found; collect, preserve, and identify them.

(22) Record the location, appearance, condition, and ownership of each article of clothing found at the crime scene.

(23) What is the general appearance of the exterior and interior of the scene of the crime? In what condition are the furniture, rugs, window curtains, and articles on tables? Are there any injuries, marks, scars, stains, or other soiling of furniture, carpets, curtains, and window sills? Were telephone wires cut? Did a search of the crime scene uncover strands of hair, cloth, buttons, and cigarette butts? Were these traces left by the victim, by the murderer, or by someone else?

(24) Do the premises contain any clues as to the motive, identity, means of entry, or methods of the culprit?

(25) How did the murderer escape?

(26) Does a reconstruction and search of the route of the murderer reveal footprints, damaged vegetation, articles dropped while fleeing, or traces along the road?

(27) What are the names, descriptions, addresses, peculiarities and habits of associates of the probable murderer? Where may the murderer be found? What is the description of the vehicle he used? Was he wounded or otherwise injured? What were his probable means and direction of escape and place of rendezvous? Has a general alarm been turned in for his apprehension?

(28) Was robbery, revenge, anger, jealousy, profit, sadism, sex motives, insanity, or self-defense a possible motive for the crime?

(29) Was the crime preceded by a quarrel or assault? Who participated? Where were they at the time of the homicide?

(30) What were the character, background, habits, and haunts of the deceased, the suspects, and of their associates?

(31) Were any unguarded statements made by the witnesses and bystanders?

(32) Were the suspects armed shortly before the crime? Were they seen at or near the scene of the crime under suspicious circumstances at the time of its occurrence?

(33) What were the movements of suspects during the days preceding the crime and on the day of the crime?

(34) What were the suspects' actions and demeanor subsequent to the crime? Did they take flight or go into hiding? Did they make any false statements?

(35) What persons frequently visit the suspects at their homes and their places of employment?

(36) What are suspects' channels of communication and what information passes through them?

(37) What movements are made by suspects' associates, sweethearts, and family?

(38) From whom do they receive mail?

(39) Were weapons, ammunition, empty shells, stains or other incriminating facts disclosed by a search of the suspect's residence? From whom, by whom, and when were the weapons secured?

(40) What were the location and condition of all weapons or incriminating evidence found in the suspect's residence or office?

(41) If the suspect has been apprehended, did a search of the clothing and fingernails reveal any blood or particles which would connect him with the scene of the crime?

(42) Secure evidence of all statements by accused both before and after crime.

(43) Check all statements for truth.
(44) Obtain dying declaration of victim, if possible. List persons present, and record time declaration was made.
(45) Interview all close associates of deceased for possible leads.

6. MANSLAUGHTER

   a. Definition. -
      (1) *Voluntary manslaughter.* - An unlawful killing done in the heat of sudden passion caused by provocation, although done with an intent to kill or inflict great bodily harm, is not murder but voluntary manslaughter.
      (2) *Involuntary manslaughter.* - Involuntary manslaughter is an unlawful homicide committed with an intent to kill or inflict great bodily harm. It is an unlawful killing by culpable negligence, or while perpetrating or attempting to perpetrate an offense other than burglary, sodomy, rape, robbery, or aggravated arson, directly affecting the person. It is a degree of carelessness greater than simple negligence.
   b. Proof. - The elements of proof required are:
      (1) That the victim named or described is dead.
      (2) That his death resulted from the act or omission of the accused, as alleged.
      (3) Facts and circumstances showing that the homicide amounted in law to the degree of manslaughter alleged.
   c. Suggestions. - The investigation of manslaughter may be conducted in the same manner as homicide.

7. MAIMING

   a. Definition. - *Maiming* is the inflicting upon the person of another an injury which seriously disfigures his person by any mutilation thereof, or destroys or disables any member or organ of his body or seriously diminishes his physical vigor by the injury of any member or organ. As described above, the injury must be of a substantially permanent nature even though there is a possibility that the victim may eventually recover. However, if the injury be done under circumstances which would justify or excuse homicide, the offense is not committed.
   b. Proof. - The elements of proof required are:
      (1) That the accused inflicted upon a certain person the injury alleged.
      (2) That the injury seriously disfigured his person, or destroyed or disabled an organ or member, or seriously diminished his physical vigor by the injury to an organ or member.
      (3) Facts and circumstances showing that the accused had an intent to injure, disfigure, or disable the person.
   c. Suggestions. - The investigation of maiming is similar to the investigation of an assault. Reference may be made to the suggestions heretofore outlined relative to investigations of assaults. In addition thereto, an investigation of the offense of maiming should include:
      (1) A detailed description of the particular loss or permanent injury suffered.
      (2) A determination as to whether same was self-inflicted, or inflicted upon request of the victim.

8. ATTEMPTED SUICIDE

   a. Definition. - *Attempted suicide* is the attempt to intentionally take one's own life. It is a violation of law and may be prosecuted as such.
   b. Proof. - The elements of proof required are:
      (1) That the accused inflicted upon himself a certain injury in the manner alleged.
      (2) The facts and circumstances indicating that such injury was intentionally inflicted for the purpose of effecting his own death.
   c. Suggestions. - The investigation of attempted suicide is similar to the investigation of homicide. The investigator should arrange for psychiatric examinations and use the suggestions outlined in paragraph 5c. The motive must be established and may often be determined through the subject's associates.

9. SODOMY

   a. Definition. - *Sodomy* is defined as engaging in unnatural carnal copulation, either with another person of the same or opposite sex, or with an animal. Any penetration, however slight, is sufficient to complete the offense.
   b. Proof. - That the accused engaged in unnatural carnal copulation with a certain other person or with an animal, as alleged.
   c. Suggestions. - The crime of sodomy is difficult to prove because of the usual privacy of the offense and the scarcity of physical evidence. The report of a psychiatric examination will facilitate the action of separation from a job. In investigating the crime of sodomy, the following suggestions may prove helpful. The investigator should:
      (1) Secure factual evidence of the crime, avoid hearsay or circumstantial evidence, and procure signed statements from witnesses.
      (2) Send all physical evidence collected to the laboratory for analysis.
      (3) Obtain the results of a psychiatric examination of the offenders.

10. RAPE AND CARNAL KNOWLEDGE

    a. Definition. - *Rape* is defined as the commission of an act of sexual intercourse by a person with a female not his wife, by force, and without her consent. It may be committed on a female of any age. *Carnal knowledge* is defined as the commission of an act of sexual intercourse under circumstances not amounting to rape by a person with a female not his wife who has not attained the age of 16 years. As in rape, any penetration is sufficient to complete the offense. It is no defense that the accused is ignorant or misinformed as to the true age of the female. It is the fact of the girl's age and not his knowledge or belief which fixes his criminal responsibility.
    b. Proof. - The elements of proof required are:
       (1) That the accused had sexual intercourse with a certain female not his wife.
       (2) That the act was done by force and without her consent; or
       (3) That she had not attained the age of 16 years.
    c. Suggestions. - To develop evidence in rape and carnal knowledge investigations, the investigator should:
       (1) Note the time and place of the offense.
       (2) Record the name, age, address, employment, marital status, and family relationships of the victim.
       (3) Obtain the name, social security, organization, marital status, and family relationships of the accused. Obtain a complete description, and also consult the modus operand! file for possible leads if the accused is unknown.

(4) Procure a complete written statement from the victim.
(5) Discreetly obtain information concerning the reputation of the victim as to truth and veracity, and her reputation as to morals and integrity.
(6) Arrange for an immediate physical examination of the victim by a medical officer, for evidence of injury, sexual relationship, blood, or semen.

11. FORGERY

   a. Definition. - *Forgery* is the intent to defraud by false making or altering any signature to, or any part of, any writing which would, if genuine, apparently impose a legal liability on another or change his legal right or liability to his prejudice, or the uttering, offering, issuing, or transferring, with intent to defraud, of such a writing known by the offender to be so or altered,
   b. Proof. - The elements of proof required are:
   (1) That a certain signature or writing was falsely made or altered, as alleged.
   (2) That the signature or writing was of a nature which would, if genuine, apparently impose a legal liability on another or change his legal right or liability to his prejudice.
   (3) That it was the accused who so falsely made or altered such signature or writing; or uttered, offered, issued, or transferred it, knowing it to have been so made or altered.
   (4) The facts and circumstances showing the intent of the accused thereby to defraud.

12. COUNTERFEITING

   a. Definition. - *Counterfeiting* originally was the offense of unlawfully making currency or coin for the purpose of passing the product as true money. By statute, in the United States at the present time, it includes other closely related offenses. The proof in each case varies with the nature of the particular offense charged. Generally speaking the offense usually includes the making of any currency, coin, securities, or obligations of the United States, or of any other country; reproducing or drawing stamps, official seals, possessing such reproductions; making or possessing plates, dies, hubs, or stamps for such reproductions, and dealing in any of the foregoing.
   b. Proof. - The United States Secret Service usually assumes charge of counterfeiting cases. The police criminal investigator, however, collects as much information as possible prior to the transfer of the case. To constitute counterfeiting, it must be proved that the accused possessed, dealt in, or attempted to pass as genuine any of the contraband articles enumerated above, as alleged.
   c. Suggestions. - In the investigation of this offense, the investigator may follow the suggestions outlined for the investigation of forgery. In addition to those suggestions, the investigator should:
   (1) Compare the suspected paper money with genuine money. Ascertain the difference in the types of paper and ink as well as in sharpness and contrast. Examine all details carefully and contrast scrolls, seals, letters, numbers, portraits, and ink distribution. Often the portrait is lacking in expression, the hair lacking in detail, and is unnaturally white. If available in sufficient quantity, stack paper money in order to determine any uneven cutting.

(2) Compare counterfeit coins with genuine coins by dropping them on a hard surface and noting any differences in the ring. Note the ease with which they can be cut; whether they feel greasy, have uneven corrugated edges, or blacken upon the application of a weak nitric acid solution containing silver nitrate.

(3) Identify all the participants in transactions involving the use of counterfeit money, and the nature of their activities.

(4) Ascertain the manufacturer of the money and the source of materials.

(5) Obtain the actual engraving tools, plates, printing presses, inks, papers, molds, materials, and byproducts of the manufacturing process, or information pertaining thereto.

13. NARCOTIC VIOLATIONS

   a. Definition. - The unauthorized use, possession, sale, purchase, or receipt of narcotic drugs is a violation of the -law. The use, possession, or sale of narcotic drugs is regulated by Federal law and is enforced by the Bureau of Narcotics of the Treasury Department. The Bureau of Narcotics may request the assistance of criminal investigators in obtaining evidence of narcotic law violations.

   b. Proof. - To constitute a *narcotic violation,* it must be proved that:
      (1) The accused received, had in his possession, purchased, used, dealt in, or introduced into groups, certain narcotics as alleged.
      (2) Such acts of the accused were unauthorized.

   c. Suggestions. - It is suggested that the investigator consult the Bureau of Narcotics before taking action. The investigator should:
      (1) In the United States: Notify appropriate agency and refrain from continuing investigation until coordination has been ' established.
      (2) In foreign countries:
         (a) Determine source:
            1. Interrogation of subject
            2. Surveillance
            3. Undercover
            4. By type of drug
         (b) Determine scope of distribution:
            1. Buyers
            2. Sellers
            3. Number of persons involved
            4. Locale of sales
      (3) Handling persons under the influence of drugs:
         (a) When a person is apprehended for the suspected use of narcotics, the authorities should keep the subject under observation. He may be rational at the time of apprehension but may suddenly become violent. Quite frequently it may be advisable to secure the subject with handcuffs or other means of restraint.
         (b) A complete search should be accomplished as soon as possible after the apprehension. Suspects have been known to swallow drugs rather than have such incriminating evidence found in their possession.
         (c) Where the subject is addicted to an opiate, manifestations of withdrawal symptoms will appear between eight and twelve hours after cessation of administration of the drugs. It is advisable to keep the subject under observation by a medical officer.

14. PERJURY

   a. Definition. - *Perjury* is the willful and corrupt giving, in a judicial proceeding or course of justice, and upon a lawful oath or in any form allowed by law to be substituted for an oath, any false testimony material to the issue or matter of inquiry.
   b. Proof. - Elements of proof required are:
      (1) That the accused took an oath or its equivalent in that proceeding or course of action, as alleged.
      (2) That the oath was administered to the accused in a matter in which an oath was required or authorized by law, as alleged.
      (3) That the oath was administered by a person having authority to do so.
      (4) That upon such oath, he gave the testimony alleged.
      (5) That the testimony was material; and
      (6) Facts and circumstances that such testimony showed that the accused did not believe such testimony to be true.
   c. Suggestions. - To develop evidence in perjury investigations, the investigator should:
      (1) Identify the judicial proceedings or course of justice in which the alleged perjury was committed.
      (2) Determine that the oath or lawful substitute was duly administered to the offender by a person qualified to do so.
      (3) Secure a copy of the transcript of the testimony given by the offender. If such is not available, take statements from witnesses as to substance of testimony.
      (4) Obtain, if possible, documentary proof that the testimony given was false.
      (5) Ascertain that the testimony of the offender was material to the issue.
      (6) Determine whether the offender intentionally gave false testimony, and whether the offender was familiar with the true facts when the false testimony was given.
      (7) Determine what the offender gained by giving false testimony, or what he would have lost by giving true testimony.
      (8) Interrogate the offender and attempt to secure a statement. Even a statement of denial will be useful in developing the case.

15. ARSON

   a. Definition. - *Aggravated arson* is defined as the willful and malicious burning or setting on fire of an inhabited dwelling, or of any other structure, movable or immovable, wherein, to the knowledge of the offender, there is, at the time, a human being. *Simple arson* is the willful and malicious burning or setting fire to the property of another under circumstances not amounting to aggravated arson. In aggravated arson, danger to human life is the essential element; in simple arson, it is injury to the property of another.
   b. Proof. - The elements of proof required are:
      (1) That the accused burned or set on fire the inhabited dwelling or other structure, as alleged.
      (2) That such dwelling or structure was of value and belonged to a certain person, as alleged.
      (3) Facts and circumstances showing that the act was willful and malicious, and, if in an inhabited dwelling, facts and circumstances that the accused had knowledge there was a human being in the structure at the time.

c. Suggestions. - The following are suggestions for developing evidence in arson investigations. The investigator should:
   (1) Proceed to the scene and complete the investigation as soon as possible.
   (2) Determine who observed the fire first, and obtain an account of what was observed.
   (3) Ascertain the details concerning the point of origin and the spread of the fire.
   (4) If the fire was incendiary in origin, establish the means employed to spread it, any simultaneous ignition points, and any evidence of the use of inflammable liquids.
   (5) Confirm whether inflammable objects were normally present in the burned building.
   (6) Study all possible fire hazards in the building, and determine whether they were basic factors in the fire under investigation.
   (7) Examine the debris in the vicinity, and also charrings and ashes. Suspicious specimens should be sent to the laboratory for analysis.
   (8) Check whether there were any previous fires in the building, or attempts to start fires.
   (9) Inspect fire-extinguishing devices to see whether they have been tampered with.
   (10) Ascertain who had a personal interest in the fire, and in what manner.
   (11) Consider whether the fire originated from natural causes without human aid, whether a human being was involved directly or indirectly, or whether actual arson has been committed.
   (12) Eliminate the possibility of natural causes, such as lightning, action of the sun, explosions, animals causing an accident, spontaneous combustion, or from actions involving a human being directly or indirectly, such as faulty stoves, flues, or circuits.
   (13) Ascertain whether or not the accused had knowledge that there was a human being in the structure at the time.

C. BASIC QUESTIONS IN INVESTIGATION

1. WHO questions

   a. WHO discovered the crime?
   b. WHO reported the crime?
   c. WHO saw or heard anything of importance?
   d. WHO had a motive for committing the crime?
   e. WHO committed the crime?
   f. WHO helped the perpetrator?
   g. With WHOM did the suspect associate?
   h. With WHOM are the witnesses associated?

2. WHAT questions

   a. WHAT happened?
   b. WHAT crime was committed?
   c. WHAT are the elements of the crime?
   d. WHAT were the actions of the suspect?
   e. WHAT do the witnesses know about the case?
   f. WHAT evidence was obtained?
   g. WHAT was done with the evidence?

- h. WHAT tools were employed?
- i. WHAT weapons were utilized?
- j. WHAT knowledge, skill, or strength was necessary to commit the crime?
- k. WHAT means of transportation was used in the commission of the crime?
- l. WHAT was the motive?
- m. WHAT was the modus operandi?

3. WHERE questions

    - a. WHERE was the crime discovered?
    - b. WHERE was the crime committed?
    - c. WHERE were the suspects seen?
    - d. WHERE were the witnesses during the crime?
    - e. WHERE was the victim found?
    - f. WHERE were the tools and weapons obtained?
    - g. WHERE did the suspect live?
    - h. WHERE did the victim live?
    - i. WHERE did the suspect spend his leisure time?
    - j. WHERE is the suspect now?
    - k. WHERE is the suspect likely to go?
    - l. WHERE was the suspect apprehended?

4. WHEN questions

    - a. WHEN was the crime committed?
    - b. WHEN was the crime discovered?
    - c. WHEN was notification received?
    - d. WHEN did the police arrive at the scene?
    - e. WHEN was the victim last seen?
    - f. WHEN was the suspect apprehended?

5. HOW questions

    - a. HOW was the crime committed?
    - b. HOW did the suspect get to the scene?
    - c. HOW did the suspect get away?
    - d. HOW did the suspect get the information necessary to enable him to commit the crime?
    - e. HOW was the crime discovered?
    - f. HOW did the suspect secure the tools and weapons?
    - g. HOW were the tools and weapons utilized?
    - h. HOW much damage was done?
    - i. HOW much property was stolen?
    - j. HOW much skill, knowledge, and strength was necessary to commit the crime?

6. WHY questions

    - a. WHY was the crime committed?
    - b. WHY were the particular tools utilized?
    - c. WHY was the particular method employed?
    - d. WHY are the witnesses reluctant to talk?
    - e. WHY was the crime reported?

15

D. SOURCES OF INFORMATION

I. Developing Sources of Information

A source of information is any person, object, or recorded data utilized by a police investigator in the conduct of an investigation.

A successful investigation depends largely upon locating, developing, and following through on as many sources of dependable information as possible.

Investigators must know all sources of information in their working area and must constantly strive to develop new sources. Persons who are reliable sources of information should be treated with tact, diplomacy, and consideration, and every effort should be made to instill and maintain confidence and complete collaboration.

II. Personnel Sources

1. COMPLAINANTS

A complainant is a person who notifies a law enforcement agency of an actual or suspected crime or offense. He is usually the victim, witness, or discoverer of a crime.

2. INFORMANTS

An informant is a person who openly gives information to police. The good informant is a person who can produce pertinent information when it is needed. A confidential informant is a person who confidentially provides police with information with the understanding that his identity will not be revealed.

    a. Safeguarding Identity. - Although the information gained may be furnished other investigative agencies, the identity of an informant is furnished only when absolutely necessary. To preserve secrecy, each confidential informant should be assigned a number, symbol, or fictitious name, to be used in all references to him and in official reports.

    b. Investigator-Informant Relationship. - To develop and maintain close collaboration with informants, members of an investigative office should observe the following:

    (1) Treat informants fairly.
    (2) Be scrupulously exact in all transactions.
    (3) Express appreciation for information given.
    (4) Investigate all reports or leads from informants and record them for future reference as circumstances indicate.
    (5) Secure all possible information from an anonymous informant before the conversation ends. (Anonymous persons who volunteer information by telephone rarely call twice.)
    (6) Protect the interests of the informant.
    (7) Be absolutely truthful and make no promise or commitment which cannot be fulfilled.
    (8) Make no attempt to force information from informants.

3. WITNESSES

The best source of information in any incident is the person who actually witnessed it. The investigator must make every effort to locate all witnesses to every incident, and, by thorough and detailed interview, elicit from them all possible information pertaining to the case.

4. SUSPECTS

Suspects, when properly interrogated, may be valuable sources of information.

III. Information Sources

1. NEWSPAPERS AND PERIODICALS

Newspapers and periodicals maintain permanent files of individual news items pertaining to persons and incidents. These files are termed "morgues" and may be consulted by the investigator.

2. DEPARTMENT OF THE ARMY RECORDS

Official Department of the Army records pertaining to military personnel provide a valuable source of information for the investigator's use. Some of the agencies which maintain personnel records are:
   a. Office of The Adjutant General. - The Adjutant General maintains records of all organizations, and of officers and enlisted personnel who are or have been in the military service of the United States.
   b. Office of The Provost Marshal General. - The Office of The Provost Marshal General maintains records of all investigations conducted by criminal investigators of major crimes committed by military personnel and civilians subject to the Articles of the Uniform Code of Military Justice.
   c. Counter Intelligence Corps. - The Counter Intelligence Corps (CIC) maintains records of investigations of subversive activity within the Army, including civilians employed by the Army.
   d. Army Security Agency. - The Army Security Agency (ASA) maintains records of investigations of Army communication security violations.
   e. Office of The Inspector General. - The Office of The Inspector General maintains records of investigations conducted by inspectors general.

3. DEPARTMENT OF THE AIR FORCE RECORDS

In the Department of the Air Force, the Office of Special Investigations (OSI) maintains records of all investigations conducted on major offenses, including criminal and subversive, occurring within the Air Force.

4. DEPARTMENT OF THE NAVY RECORDS

In the Department of the Navy, the Office of Naval Intelligence (ONI) maintains records of investigations conducted by Naval Intelligence.

5. TREASURY DEPARTMENT RECORDS

The Treasury Department has five law enforcement divisions, each maintaining files and records relative to the functions it performs:
   a. United States Secret Service. - The United States Secret Service suppresses counterfeiting and protects the person of the President and members of his family.
   b. Bureau of Narcotics. - The Bureau of Narcotics investigates violations of the narcotic laws.
   c. Bureau of Internal Revenue.
      (1) The Intelligence Unit investigates violations of Federal income tax laws.
      (2) The Alcohol Tax Unit investigates violations of the laws relating to manufacture, storage, and sale of alcoholic beverages and enforces the National Firearms Act.
   d. Bureau of Customs. - The Bureau of Customs enforces the customs laws, supervises the importation of articles into the United States, and apprehends smugglers.
   e. Coast Guard. - The Coast Guard enforces the laws of the United States in the coastal areas and navigable waters of the United States. During time of peace, this department is a branch of the Treasury Department. During time of war, it becomes a branch of the Department of the Navy.

6. DEPARTMENT OF JUSTICE RECORDS

   a. Federal Bureau of Investigation.- The Federal Bureau of Investigation (FBI) enforces all Federal violations not specifically assigned to some other Federal law enforcement agency. It maintains complete files, including an extensive fingerprint file, and a scientific laboratory for analyzing and identifying evidence.
   b. Immigration and Naturalization Service,- The Immigration and Naturalization Service has photographs, fingerprints, and brief biographies of immigrants, their residence and employment addresses, and the status of their naturalization.

7. UNITED STATES POSTAL SERVICE

U.S. Postal Service will provide the investigator with all the information which appears on the outside of envelopes in the United States mail addressed to a particular individual. This service is known as a "mail cover" and may be continued for a specific period agreed upon by the investigator and the postal authorities. Mail may not be read except by censors or when seized pursuant to a search warrant. In securing a search warrant for mail, the investigator should confer with the local postal inspector. At military establishments, the postal officer should be consulted for assistance. Tracings of covers of envelopes may be obtained on request; however, a postal inspector, either civilian or military, should be consulted on the subject.

8. VETERANS ADMINISTRATION RECORDS

The Veterans Administration maintains records on former members of the United States military forces.

9. STATE RECORDS

State police are responsible for investigation of violations of State laws within their respective States and maintain appropriate records. A State patrol is usually vested only with the authority of peace officers and is restricted to the enforcement of the provisions of the vehicle act and maintaining appropriate records. Some States have a central body of highly trained investigators, available to any law enforcement agency within the State to assist in the solution of criminal cases in especially designated fields of investigation. Vehicle license bureaus have a record of the issuance of license plates and drivers licenses.

10. COUNTY AND CITY RECORDS

The Sheriff's department is usually responsible for the enforcement of criminal laws and the vehicular code within a county and the maintenance of records pertaining thereto. The Bureau of Vital Statistics maintains complete records of births, deaths, marriages, divorces, changes of names, and adoptions. District attorneys' offices have records of criminals or suspected criminals and other information which may be of value. Municipal police are responsible for the enforcement of all laws and ordinances within a city or town and have established records sections.

11. PRIVATE DETECTIVE BUREAUS

Private detective bureaus conduct investigations and may serve as a source of information. However, the investigator should use discretion in discussing official cases with private detectives.

12. OTHER RECORD SOURCES

   a. Employment agencies have records of applicants and former ap-licants and a record of past employment for each individual.
   b. The American Red Cross has certain types of information of a domestic nature.
   c. The American Social Hygiene Association has information regarding vice, gambling, and liquor control.
   d. Transportation companies have records of reservations of passengers and bills of lading.
   e. Insurance company clearing houses have records on all persons who have had life insurance or fire insurance policies.
   f. Water, electric, and gas companies have records of names and addresses. They are often the first agencies to obtain such information on persons newly arrived in a community.
   g. Automobile associations are able to furnish information regarding the registration and ownership of members' automobiles and, on some occasions, past or planned trips.
   h. Hotel associations maintain files on certain types of criminals, such as bad check passers, gamblers, and confidence men. Hotels maintain registers of all persons residing at the hotels and records of valuables checked by patrons.
   i. Hospital records reveal information of past and present patients, including names, addresses, injuries, and medical histories. In some localities the law requires that certain types of wounds be reported to the police.
   j. City directories contain names, addresses, and occupations of members of families living in a city at the time the information for the directory was collected. Earlier editions will reveal past information.

k. Banks have records of past and present financial transactions with customers or former customers and may supply other general information.
l. Finance companies have records of loans which may include a considerable amount of information relative to the persons securing loans.
m. Commercial credit bureaus maintain extensive files on persons who have made use of personal credit. Information includes addresses, bank accounts, charge accounts, records of judgments, assets, and financial standing.
n. Telephone companies will furnish addresses and telephone numbers of subscribers, as well as names and telephone numbers of subscribers when addresses are known.

CRIMINAL INVESTIGATION

TECHNIQUE OF INTERVIEWS AND INTERROGATION

TABLE OF CONTENTS

		Page
1.	General	1
2.	Purpose of Interview	1
3.	Preparation for Interview	1
4.	Time of Interview	2
5.	Place of Interview	2
6.	Introduction of the Investigator	2
7.	Control Over Interviews	2
8.	Rights of Person Interviewed	2
9.	Attitude and Demeanor of Investigator	2
10.	Types of Approaches	3
11.	Interview of Complainants	3
12.	Interview of Victims	3
13.	Interview of Witnesses	3
14.	Types of Witnesses	4
15.	Assistance to Witnesses in Descriptions	4
16.	Credibility of Witnesses	4
17.	Evaluation During Interview	5
18.	Interview Notes	5
19.	Purpose of Interrogation	5
20.	Preparation for Interrogation	6
21.	Classification of Suspects	6
22.	Length of Interrogation	6
23.	Persons at Interrogation	7
24.	Interrogation Checklist	7
25.	Introduction of Investigator	7
26.	Rights of Person Being Interrogated	7
27.	Attitude of Investigator	8
28.	Types of Approach	8
29.	Interrogation Notes	9
30.	Scientific Aids to Interrogation	9
31.	Lie Detecting Set	9
32.	Narco-Analysis	10

CRIMINAL INVESTIGATION

TECHNIQUE OF INTERVIEWS AND INTERROGATION

1. **GENERAL**
   The successful investigation of criminal offenses depends in a great measure upon the effective questioning of complainants, witnesses, informants, suspects, and other persons encountered during the course of an investigation. Questioning is divided into two broad classifications: *interviews*, which are conducted to learn facts from persons who may have knowledge of a wrongful act but who are not themselves implicated; and *interrogations*, which are conducted to learn facts and to obtain admissions or confessions of wrongful acts from persons who are implicated in a wrongful act. Persons who have been interviewed may later be interrogated. An interrogation is not necessarily confined to individuals suspected of criminal acts, but may include persons who may have been accessories, or who may have knowledge of the crime which, for various motives, they are reluctant to admit. It is usually advisable to take statements from persons being interviewed or interrogated. When an interview or interrogation develops information that will have definite value as evidence, that information or evidence must be recorded in a written, signed, and witnessed statement, or preserved through mechanical recording.

2. **PURPOSE OF INTERVIEW**
   An interview is an informal questioning to learn facts. The successful investigation of crime requires that the investigator be able to learn, through personal questioning, what the person interviewed has observed through his five senses: sight, hearing, taste, smell, and touch. Each individual interviewed is presumed to possess certain information that may lead to the solution of a crime. Effective interviewing requires that the interviewer make full use of all the knowledge of human nature he possesses, so that the individual interviewed will disclose all that he knows about the matter in question. If a person does not possess knowledge of the crime, the interview should establish that fact. Pertinent negative evidence is as much a part of a complete investigation as positive information.

3. **PREPARATION FOR INTERVIEW**
   Interviews other than those conducted at the scene of the crime should be planned carefully and thoroughly to prevent repetition of the interview. The investigator must review thoroughly all developments in the investigation prior to the interview. He must also consider the relationship of the person to be interviewed to the investigation; i.e., complainant, victim, witness, or informant. An effective interviewer combines his knowledge of human nature with all available information about the person to be interviewed, such as education, character, reputation, associates, habits, and past criminal record. This background information is used advantageously in the interview. The investigator should estimate the extent and kind of information that he may expect to elicit. He should prepare, by noting pertinent facts to be developed, to detect inconsistencies and discrepancies in the statements of the person being interviewed, to evaluate them, and to require their clarification. The investigator should prepare a plan for the interview

which takes into consideration the information available to him about the person to be interviewed: the time, place, and environment for the interview; as well as the legal proof to be developed in the crime.

4. **TIME OF INTERVIEW**
An interview should be conducted as soon as possible after the discovery of a crime. The investigator should take as much time as is required for a complete and thorough interview.

5. **PLACE OF INTERVIEW**
When possible, the place of the interview should be so selected as to assure a favorable environment. When possible, the interview should be conducted in a comfortable room and in an environment familiar to the person interviewed. The person to be interviewed should never be brought to the investigator.

6. **INTRODUCTION OF THE INVESTIGATR**
Usually the investigator and the person to be interviewed are strangers. The investigator should introduce himself, present his credentials (when appropriate), and begin by making a general statement regarding the purpose of the interview. The introduction should be made in such a manner as to establish a cordial relationship between the investigator and the person being interviewed.

7. **CONTROL OVER INTERVIEWS**
An investigator must maintain absolute control of the interview at all times. He must be careful not to elicit false information through improper questioning. He may permit digression or discussion of matters seemingly unrelated to the crime in order to place the person interviewed at ease but he must not permit the person being interviewed to become evasive. If the person interviewed should become so evasive as to obscure the purpose of the interview, effective results may be obtained by a more formal type of questioning, taking notes, or by the aggressiveness of the investigator.

8. **RIGHTS OF PERSON INTERVIEWED**
Although an investigator has no legal power to compel a person being interviewed to divulge information, he may, if he is clever and alert, induce him to disclose what he knows. When an interview develops into an interrogation, the investigator must warn the person being interviewed of his rights (Par. 26).

9. **ATTITUDE AND DEMEANOR OF INVESTIGATOR**
The attitude and demeanor of an investigator contributes immeasurably to the success or failure of an interview. The investigator should be friendly, yet businesslike. He should endeavor to lead the person being interviewed into talkativeness. He should then direct the conversation toward the investigation. The individual being interviewed should be permitted to give an uninterrupted account while the investigator makes mental notes of omissions, inconsistencies, or discrepancies that require clarification by later questioning. The investigator should strive to turn to advantage the subject's prejudices. He rarely reveals the precise objective of an interview, and usually obtains a more accurate account

from the person interviewed if he claims only to be attempting to establish facts. He should avoid a clash of personalities; acts of undue familiarity; the use of profanity or violent expressions such as "kill," "steal," "confess," "murder"; improbable stories; or distracting mannerisms such as pacing the floor or fumbling with objects.

10. **TYPES OF APPROACHES**
The *indirect* approach employed in interviewing consists of discussion carried on in a conversational tone that permits the person being interviewed to talk without having to answer direct questions. The *direct* approach consists of direct questioning as in interrogations (Par. 28a). The use of interrogation technique often succeeds when the person interviewed fears or dislikes police officers, fears retribution from a criminal, desires to protect a friend or relative, is impudent, or, for diverse reasons, is unwilling to cooperate with the investigator. Unreliable persons or liars should always be permitted to give their version of an incident. They may, through contradiction or denial, trip themselves into admissions through which the true facts may be obtained. When interviewing shy or nervous persons, the investigator may be obliged to obtain information piecemeal. He should interview in the normal environment of such persons and should be as casual and calm as possible. The talkative person should be allowed to speak freely and to use his own expressions, but should be confined to the subject by appropriate questions. When persons pretend to know nothing about an incident, the investigator should ask many questions, any one which, if answered, will refute their claim that they know nothing at all. Disinterested persons may divulge more information if their personal interest can be aroused by an indirect approach. Investigators should always attempt to put uneducated witnesses at ease and to help them express themselves as best they can, but should not put word into their mouths. Flattery is most often successful when alcoholics or braggarts are interviewed. Information gained from such individuals must be corroborated.

11. **INTERVIEW OF COMPLAINANTS**
In interviewing complainants, the investigator should be considerate, understanding, tactful, and impartial, regardless of the motive for the complaint, and should inform the complainant that appropriate action will be initiated promptly.

12. **INTERVIEW OF VICTIMS**
When interviewing victims, the investigator must consider their emotional state, particularly in crimes of violence. Frequently, victims have unsupported beliefs regarding the circumstances connected with the crime. Their observations may be partial and imperfect because of excitement and tension. It is imperative that the investigator obtain from the victim an accurate account of the circumstances that existed immediately before, during, and after the incident. The investigator should consider the reputation of the victim in determining the credibility of his complaint.

13. **INTERVIEW OF WITNESSES**
The investigator must frequently assist witnesses to recall and relate facts exactly as they observed them. He must know what affect a person's ability to observe and describe acts,

articles, or circumstances related to a crime (CH. 3). He should lead witnesses toward accurate statements of fact by assisting them to recall in detail their experiences.

14. TYPES OF WITNESSSES

In general, children from 7 to 12 years of age are good observers, although their testimony may be inadmissible in court. Teenage children are also good observers but may exaggerate. Young adults are often poor witnesses; middle-aged and older persons are the best witnesses. Persons differ in their physical and mental characteristics as well as in their experience and training. These differences may cause them to notice only those aspects of a situation in which they may have had a particular experience. As a consequence, they differ in their observations, interpretations, and descriptions. If a witness cannot recall what he has observed, poor memory may be the cause. Preoccupation of a witness may often prevent him from recalling exactly what occurred. Lack of education may make it difficult for a witness to describe what he observed; such a person is sometimes reluctant to divulge information because of embarrassment over his diction. That which has been observed, because of exaggeration, misrepresentation, or inaccurate interpretation, may result in faulty information; i.e., a squeal of joy may be misinterpreted as a scream of terror. The emotions of witnesses before, during, and after an incident, and when interviewed, greatly affect their recall of events as they actually occurred. A frightened witness may recall events differently than a calm, unruffled person. Witnesses may exaggerate more each time their observations are repeated.

15. ASSISTANCE TO WITNESSES IN DESCRIPTIONS

The investigator should provide certain indexes to assist witnesses in describing size, height, weight, distance, and colors. The eye-level method of determining height may be used as standard. By asking a witness to tell how far another person's eyes were above or below his own, the investigator may obtain an estimate of height. Speed is difficult to estimate accurately; even opinions based on long experience may be subject to influence by noise, light, weather, and other conditions. Age is difficult for witnesses to judge because of differences among races, nationalities, and individuals; if selected individuals are used for comparison, they must be chosen carefully. In situations which are strange or which involve unusual circumstances, the witness may have no standards or associations on which to base his judgment and may be unable to utilize the standards presented for comparison. A detailed review or reconstruction of events will sometimes help the witness to recall events, but the investigator must be careful to avoid confusing the actual event with the reconstruction.

16. CREDIBILITY OF WITNESSES

Credibility of a witness is usually governed by his character and is evidenced by his reputation for veracity. Personal or financial reason or previous criminal activity may cause a witness to give false information to avoid being implicated. Hope of gain by informants or prisoners; political, racial, or religious factors; and hatred for the police or the suspect are some of the reasons why a witness may make a false statement. Age, sex, physical and mental abnormalities, loyalty, revenge, social and economic status, indulgence in alcohol, and the influence of other persons are some of the many factors which may affect the accuracy, willingness, or ability with which witnesses observe, interpret, and describe occurrences.

17. **EVALUATION DURING INTERVIEW**

    During an interview, the investigator must evaluate continuously the mannerisms and the emotional state of the person in terms of the information developed. The manner in which a person relates his story or answers questions may indicate that he is not telling the truth or is concealing information. Evasiveness, hesitation, or unwillingness to discuss situations may signify a lack of cooperation. The relation of body movements to the emotional state of persons must be carefully considered by the investigator. A dry mouth indicated by the wetting of the lips, fidgeting, or vague movements of the hands may indicate nervousness or deception. A "cold sweat" or pale face may indicate fear. A slight gasp, holding the breath, or an unsteady voice may indicate that the knowledge of the investigator has shocked the person being interviewed. The pumping of the heart may be observed by the pulse in the neck. A ruddy or flushed face may be an indication of anger or embarrassment, not necessarily guilt, and may also indicate that the matter under discussion is of vital importance, or that some information is being withheld. Although such symptoms are not necessarily valid indications of guilt or innocence and may be a manifestation of the physical condition or health of the individual, they are often related to the emotional state of the person.

18. **INTERVIEW NOTES**

    Complete notes are essential to effective investigation and reporting. Normally, most people have no objection to note-taking; however, the investigator should not take notes until he has had an opportunity to gage the person's reactions, since note-taking may create a reluctance to divulge information. If he does not take notes, the investigator should record, at the first opportunity after the interview, all pertinent information while it is fresh in his mind. Notes on interviews should contain the case number; hour, date, and place of interview; complete identification of the person interviewed; names of other persons present; and a resume of the interview.

19. **PURPOSE OF INTERROGATION**

    The interrogation should take place immediately if the suspect is surprised or apprehended in the act of committing a crime. In all other instances, interrogation should be conducted only after sufficient information has been secured and the background of the suspect has been thoroughly explored. The purpose of interrogation of a suspect is to obtain an admission or confession of his wrongful acts and a written, signed, and witnessed statement, and to establish the facts of a crime or to develop information which will enable the investigator to obtain direct, physical, or other evidence to prove or disprove the truth of an admission or confession. A confession is an acknowledgment of guilt, whereas an admission is a self-incriminatory statement falling short of an acknowledgment of guilt. The securing of confessions or acknowledgments of guilt does not complete the investigation of a crime. A statement made by one conspirator during the conspiracy and in pursuance of it is admissible in evidence against his co-conspirators as tending to prove the fact of the matter stated. In interrogation, the investigator seeks to learn the identity of accomplices and details of any other crime in which the suspect may have been involved.

20. **PREPARATION FOR INTERROGATION**
    a. Preparation for interrogation should be thorough. The investigator should base his plan for interrogation on background data, information, or direct evidence received from victims and witnesses, physical evidence, and reconstruction of the crime scene. The plan, which should be written, should take into consideration the various means for testing the truthfulness of the suspect and for gaining a psychological advantage over him through the use of known facts and proper use of time, place, and environment. Unless the investigator interrogates a suspect immediately following the commission of a crime, or desires to question him without previous notification, he should be interrogated at criminal investigation headquarters, where recordings may be made or stenographic notes may be taken.
    b. During interrogation, the subject should be seated in a plain chair placed where his movements and physical reactions may be observed easily. The interrogation room should be plainly but comfortably furnished, without items that may cause distraction. Recording devices, one-way mirrors, and similar equipment should appear as normal furnishings. Tables, desks, and other furnishings should be located where they will not impair the interrogator's observation of the suspect.

21. **CLASSIFICATION OF SUSPECTS**
    Background information and the facts established in an investigation enable the investigator to classify persons to be interrogated as follows:
    a. Known offenders, whose guilt is reasonably certain on the basis of the evidence available
    b. Persons whose guilt is doubtful or uncertain because of the evidence or lack of evidence.
    c. Material witnesses, accessories, and persons who have knowledge of the crime but may not themselves be guilty of a crime. Persons to be interrogated may be further classified as those readily influenced by sympathy or understanding; and those readily influenced by the use of an attitude of suspicion and obvious disbelief.

22. **LENGTH OF INTERROGATION**
    No time limit is placed on the duration of interrogation except that it shall not be so long and under such conditions as to amount to duress. Questioning for many hours without food, sleep, or under glaring lights has been held to constitute such duress as to invalidate a confession. The suspect may be questioned at length in an attempt to break down his resistance, or he may be questioned for short periods daily as a test of his consistency. The interrogator should always consider the physical condition of the person being interrogated as well as his emotional stability. Once the suspect has begun to reveal pertinent information, the interrogator should not be interrupted.

23. PERSONS AT INTERROGATION

An interrogation usually should be conducted in complete privacy. A person under interrogation is not inclined to reveal confidences to a public gathering. Witnesses to a confession may be called in to hear the reading of the statement and the declaration that it is the subject's statement, to witness the signing by the subject, and to affix their own signatures. Some investigative agencies advocate the presence of a witness at all times during an interrogation, particularly during the period of warning of rights and at such other periods when corroborative testimony might be needed or desirable. When a woman is questioned, the interrogator should provide witnesses, preferably women, in order to avoid charges of compromise which an unscrupulous woman may later interject a mitigating circumstance.

24. INTERROGATION CHECKLIST

Before beginning an interrogation, the investigator should check his preparation against the following questions:
a. Has the crime scene been carefully and adequately searched for real evidence?
b. Have all persons known to have knowledge of the crime been questioned?
c. Has all possible evidence been obtained?
d. Has the person to be interrogated been searched?
e. Have all files been checked for pertinent information?
f. Is background investigation complete?
g. Is the interrogation room properly prepared for the interrogation?
h. Is the interrogation plan complete?
i. Have the elements of legal proof been checked?
j. Are all details of the investigation firmly fixed in the investigator's mind?
k. What information should be elicited from the individual to be interrogated?

25. INTRODUCTION OF INVESTIGATOR

Prior to any interrogation, the investigator may introduce and identify himself by presenting his credentials if the person to be interrogated questions the authority of the investigator. After the introduction, the person to be interrogated should be informed in general terms of the investigation being conducted. The investigator, however, should not disclose his knowledge of the case, nor should he prematurely disclose any fact of the case.

26. RIGHTS OF PERSON BEING INTERROGATED

The investigator should begin interrogation by explaining to the person to be questioned his rights under the Fifth Amendment to the Constitution of the United States. If he is a civilian, and under Article 31 of the Uniform Code of Military Justice, if he is a military person. The person to be questioned is informed that he need not answer any question which may tend to incriminate him but that, if he chooses to answer any question, such answer may be used in testimony against him. Throughout the questioning the investigator must refrain from threats, violence, or promise of reward. In response to a request by the person being questioned for legal counsel, the investigator should courteously but firmly refuse and state that the Uniform Code of Military Justice does not provide for counsel prior to charges being preferred against a soldier.

27. ATTITUDE OF INVESTIGATOR

Because of the importance of admissions or confessions, the investigator must become skilled in the art of interrogation. He must master a variety of questioning techniques, learn to judge the psychological strength of weakness of others, and learn to take advantage of his own particular abilities in questioning any suspect or reluctant witness. He must not presume guilt of the persons being interrogated without sufficient proof. He must act as naturally as possible under the circumstances. If a suspect begins admitting criminal acts, the investigator must not become overeager or condescending. The interrogator should, when it is necessary to stir the emotions of another to confess a wrongful act, permit his own emotions to be stirred.

28. TYPES OF APPROACH

He adapts his approach to the character and background of the person to be interrogated, the known facts of the crime, and the real evidence available. The investigator may use any of the following type approaches or any combination of them:

a. The *direct approach* is normally employed where guilt is reasonably certain. The investigator assumes an air of confidence concerning the guilt of the offender and points out the evidence indicative of guilt. He outwardly sympathizes with the offender and indicates that anyone else might have done the same thing under similar circumstances. He urges the offender to tell the truth, avoids threatening words or insinuation, and develops a detailed account of the crime from premeditation to commission. He may ask questions such as the following: "Tell me all you know about this. When did you get the idea of doing it? Why did you do it? How did you do that? Where did you get the money?" In dealing with habitual criminals whose guilt is reasonably certain and who apparently have no feeling of wrongdoing, the investigator must convince them that their guilt can be or is established by the testimony of witnesses or available evidence. Investigators must never make promises of leniency or clemency as these promises might vitiate confessions obtained as a result of the interrogation.

b. The *indirect approach* is normally employed in interrogating a person who has knowledge of the crime. The investigator must proceed cautiously. He requests the individual being interrogated to tell all he knows about the incident. He then requires an explanation of discrepancies or distortions and endeavors to lead the individual being interrogated into admissions of truth. When facts indicative of guilt are developed, the investigator casually asks question to determine through the offender's reactions whether he will acknowledge or deny guilt. When guilt appears probable, the investigator reverts to direct questioning to obtain an admission or confession.

c. The *emotional approach* is designed to arouse any play upon the emotions of a person. Body actions may indicate the presence of nervous tension. The investigator points out these signs of nervous tension to the person under interrogation. The investigator may discuss the moral seriousness of the offense, emphasize the penalty, and appeal to the suspect's pride or ego, fear, like or dislike, or his hate and desire for revenge. This approach may lead to emotional breakdown and a confession.

d. *Subterfuge* is employed to induce guilty persons to confess when all other approaches have failed. Considerable care should be exercised in the employment of subterfuge. If the person to be interrogated recognizes the approach as subterfuge, further efforts to obtain an admission or confession may be futile. Examples of subterfuge are:

(1) *Hypothetical Story.* A fictitious crime, varying only in minute details from the offense of which the subject is suspected, is related to him. The investigator later visits the subject and asks him to write out details of the hypothetical story as related. If the subject is guilty, he often includes details of the crime under investigation, but not mentioned by the investigator in his fictitious story. When confronted with these inconsistencies, the suspect may make a confession.

(2) *Signed False Statement.* When evidence indicates, but is not conclusive, that a certain person may be guilty of a crime, he may be requested to make a sworn written statement. After he has made a false written statement, the discrepancies contained therein are pointed out to him in an attempt to gain a true confession.

(3) *"Cold Shoulder."* This term designates a technique of subterfuge keynoted by indifference. The person suspected is invited to come to the investigator's office. If he accepts the invitation, he is taken either to the office or the crime scene. The investigator, or those accompanying the person subject to this type of interrogation, say nothing to him or to each other, and await his reactions. This technique may cause the suspect to surmise that the investigator has evidence adequate to prove his guilt.

(4) *Playing One Suspect Against Another.* When two or more persons are suspected of having been involved in a crime, the person believed to have the weakest character is interrogated first. The others are interrogated separately and informed that their partner has accused them of the crime. A confession, shown to the others involved, may influence them to attempt to protect themselves by confessing.

(5) *Contrasting Personalities.* This technique employs two investigators, one determined and the other sympathetic and understanding. The interrogation is so arranged that the person under interrogation will play into the hands of one or the other.

29. INTERROGATION NOTES

The taking of notes during an interrogation may be essential in order to record all pertinent information; however, the effect of note-taking on the success of the interrogation must be considered. If notes are not taken during the interrogation, the investigator should record all pertinent data immediately after the interrogation.

30. SCIENTIFIC AIDS TO INTEROGATION

Scientific aids are available to the investigator to assist in the investigation of criminal offenses. These aids are normally employed to develop information from persons who are suspected of committing a crime. They may also be used to check the validity and completeness of information given by complainants, witnesses, and victims.

31. LIE DETECTING SET

Lie detecting set examinations can be conducted only by operators trained in the use of the instrument. The lie detecting set is an instrument which records the body changes that accompany emotions and is used to develop information, to determine if a person has knowledge of an offense, and to obtain an admission or confession of guilt. The provisions of Article 31, Uniform Code of Military Justice, and the Fifth Amendment to the Constitution of the United States apply to persons who are requested to submit to an examination by a lie detecting set. Investigators should obtain written consent from all persons subjected to lie detecting set examinations, acknowledging that they have been informed of their rights and that they agree to submit voluntarily to such an examination. A copy of this statement should be included in the case file folder. In general, graphs obtained during a lie detecting set examination are not admissible as evidence in court. However, the operator is usually permitted to testify relative to the questions asked, and the answers given. Oral or written admissions or confessions obtained as a consequence of the examination may be admitted into evidence, if they meet legal requirements.

32. **NARCO-ANALYSIS**

Narco-analysis is the term employed to define the questioning of a person under the influence of drugs (truth serums). Scopolamine, sodium amytal, and sodium pentothal are the drugs most commonly used. When properly administered, these drugs tend to overcome inhibitions. The use of narco-analysis as an investigative technique has not found general acceptance. Admissions or confessions obtained through the use of truth serums are not admissible as evidence in court. The information obtained may be used only to develop the investigation. The subject must be warned of his rights, and a written statement obtained wherein the subject acknowledges the warning and voluntarily agrees to the narco-analysis. *No person may be compelled to submit to such an examination. It must be conducted only when a qualified medical officer if available to administer the drugs and to witness the examination.*

POLICE SCIENCE NOTES

COLLECTION, IDENTIFICATION AND PRESERVATION OF EVIDENCE

The Definition and importance of Evidence

Definition

Evidence can be defined as "any medium of proof or probative matter, legally presented at the trial of any issue, by the participants of the trial and through the medium of witnesses, records, documents, objects, etc., for the purpose of inducing belief in the minds of the court and the jurors as to its creditability and contention." In more general terms, evidence is anything that can be legally presented to indicate the guilt of a criminal act or to aid in determining the truth about any fact in question.

Importance

The primary importance of evidence is the aid it offers in the identification of the guilty party and in his successful prosecution. Because of this, the proper collection, identification, and preservation of evidence make up a vital part of police operations. Cases may be won or lost depending upon the proficiency of the police department in this area.

Evidence is the means by which the patrolman or investigator can aid the prosecutor in giving the court a complete picture of the crime and its commission. It explains the facts that the officer uses to determine that the accused is guilty. Properly prepared and presented, evidence may serve the same purpose as taking the court and the jury to the scene of the crime and reconstructing the events which led to the commission of the crime charged.

In order to insure that this vital function is performed properly, most departments have specialists known as criminal investigators to collect, search and properly evaluate evidence. The reason for this is that such specialization saves time and leaves the patrolman free to resume his primary duties once the investigator arrives at the scene. However, since the general patrolman or the auxiliary policeman will usually be the first to arrive at the scene and therefore is crucial to the outcome of the criminal investigation, it is important that they have an adequate understanding of evidence and be skilled in its preservation and protection. The need for developing adequate investigative skills is especially crucial in those departments without a specialist and where the officers are expected to conduct their own investigation.

Classification of Evidence

Evidence may be divided into three major classifications:

DIRECT evidence directly establishes the main fact of issue. It applies immediately to the fact to be proven or disproven and is usually what a person sees, hears, or knows.

CIRCUMSTANTIAL evidence tends to prove or disprove the fact in issue by other facts leading to a presumption of the truth or falsity of the main fact. The essence here is inference-establishing a factor or circumstance from which a court may infer another fact. It may be real evidence or things which may be said to "speak for themselves." Ownership of the murder weapon, the fingerprints thereon, and the inability of the accused to account for his actions at the time of the crime would be matters of circumstantial evidence.

REAL OR PHYSICAL evidence comprises those tangible objects introduced at the trial which speak for themselves and need no explanation, just identification. Examples of real evidence would be guns, fingerprints, and bloodstains. Real evidence can be further divided into:

FIXED OR IMMOVABLE evidence which by its very nature cannot be moved from the crime scene. It includes such objects as latent fingerprints, tool marks, doors, windows, wall plaster, etc. Of course, fingerprints may be lifted, casts made of foot and tire marks, and photographs taken of the entire scene; but the actual object remains incapable of being transported to the courtroom.

MOVABLE evidence which can be preserved intact for examination at headquarters and presentation in the courtroom. This includes such objects as bullets, tools, hair, documents, clothing, and many other similar objects.

Chain of Custody - The Cardinal Rule of Evidence

In order for the evidence to be properly admitted into court, its location and holder must be accurately established from the time the officer or investigator finds the evidence until it is presented in court. If the whereabouts of the evidence cannot be established, even for a moment, the court will rule it is inadmissible. The reason for this is because if it can be shown that the evidence was out of responsible hands or unaccountable for, then it is also likely that the evidence could have been tampered with thereby negating its validity and leaving the court no alternative but to dismiss it. Therefore, in order to overcome the questions presented by the defense and to impress the judge and jury that the evidence has been properly protected, the police officer must establish an accurate "chain of custody" for each piece of evidence presented in court.

Perhaps the best method of maintaining an accurate chain of custody is through the use of receipts. If the evidence is to be out of the officer's hand for even a minute he should demand a receipt containing: the time, date, and place where the exchange occurred, to whom the evidence was given, and for what purpose. Likewise, if the officer receives any evidence for transportation or for other purposes he should fill out and give a receipt to the person giving him the evidence.

Collection of Evidence

Two points to be remembered by all personnel concerned with the collection of evidence are: (1) there, is rarely a major crime committed without some kind of evidence being left at the scene, and (2) nothing at a crime scene is too significant to be overlooked. The ultimate success of any investigation will depend on the acumen of the officers in searching the scene, recognizing evidence, and preserving it.

Preliminary Activities at the Crime Scene

The first officer at the crime scene who will usually be either the beat patrolman or the auxiliary policeman should:
1. Assist the injured when necessary.
2. Notify the proper experts and equipment to conduct a proper crime scene examination.
3. Obtain pertinent data from the witnesses and any suspects, keeping them separated if possible.
4. Use the most effective means possible to protect the crime scene from any intrusions by unauthorized personnel.
5. Arrest any perpetrators caught at or near the scene.
6. Assist the investigator when he arrives to examine the scene.

The investigator or whoever is in charge of the investigation should determine from the initial officer what has been done and what needs to be done before taking command of the situation. He will then conduct a thorough investigation of the scene and question all witnesses, victims, and suspects at the scene.

Examination of the Crime Scene

Usually the first person to be admitted to the crime scene is the photographer who will take as many photographs as necessary to insure proper coverage of the scene for further study and analysis. While the photographer is shooting the scene, the investigator will make a sketch of the scene to supplement the photographs by adding the dimensions of height, distances, and locations of the scene. Notes should also be made of the camera's position, characteristics, and the weather conditions that affect the camera's settings.

The next step in the process is the search of the crime scene area which presents various problems, especially when the area is extensive. It is essential that proper consideration be given to all aspects of the search problems before proceeding, in order that the search can be made as complete and as thorough as possible. The general organization of the search party will be determined by the size and type of the area to be covered, available personnel, and the equipment with which the party must work. It is important that the search party be divided into manageable units with each unit aware of just what area it is responsible for searching.

The number of men necessary to conduct a search will largely depends on the conditions existing at the time. Search parties may consist of as many as a hundred men, but should never be less than two. Regardless of how many people conduct the search, a careful and methodical effort must be exerted, the search should proceed according to plan, and the searchers should search for one thing at a time. If the search is going to be for fingerprints then the search should be for fingerprints only until they are all found or there is good reason to believe that there are none. Then the search can be for bloodstains or hair, and so on down the line. The searchers may note the presence and location of one piece of evidence while looking for another piece, but the evidence noted should not be touched until the searchers are specifically looking for it. It is also a good practice to have each man responsible for a particular duty during the search. He can be a note taker, sketcher, evidence collector, or whatever else is necessary. Then when the search starts again he should be switched to another duty. This helps keep the persons alert, and insure adequate coverage of the scene. Never search a crime scene just once; always go over and over the scene until everyone is satisfied that all the evidence has been found. However, do not handle evidence more than is necessary.

The Identification of Evidence

To insure the proper chain of custody of any evidence found during the search it is necessary that every piece of evidence be marked for identification by the person who found it. Others who witness its finding should also mark the evidence of witness. If the evidence does not provide sufficient suitable area for more than a single mark it should be marked by the finding officer and witnessed by other persons. The characteristics of the mark should be recorded in the notes of the officer as well as the witnesses.

The following steps should be followed in the marking of any evidence:

1. Each bit of evidence should be appropriately marked at the time it is removed from its original position. No piece of evidence should be removed from the position in which it was found until after it has been photographed, sketched, processed for latent fingerprints, and listed in the investigator's notebook.

2. The mark "X" should never be used to identify evidence. The identifying mark should be one that is characteristic and easily identifiable. Using the written initials of the finder is considered best. The mark used and its position as well as any serial numbers or distinctive marks present on the object should be recorded in the officer's notebook for further reference.

3. Whenever possible mark the object itself, taking extreme care to prevent any destruction of the value of the evidence. Unless evidence or the article itself prohibits it, the marks made on all articles of a similar nature should be in the same direction.

4. Always mark the container in which the object is being placed as well as the object. If the object cannot be marked then seal the container and mark the seal as well as the container.

Proper marking and the keeping of notes on the evidence found during the course of an investigation will make it possible for the officer to positively identify each piece of evidence at the time it is presented in court. Using a mark which is characteristic and one that will not have been accidentally placed on the evidence, as well as knowing just where to locate the mark on the evidence is of great value to the officer witness. He will be poised and confident in his manner of handling the evidence and the judge and jury will be more impressed as to the value of the evidence presented.

Preservation and transportation of Evidence Preservation

Each article of evidence should be placed in an appropriate container depending on the nature and size of the evidence. It is recommended that the container used should be larger than necessary to normally accommodate the evidence article, so as to prevent it from being crushed or squeezed by other articles. However, the container should not be so large as to cause damage to the evidence from excessive movement. The containers should be new and clean and each article of evidence should be packed in a separate container. This is especially necessary where evidence might have foreign matter adhering to it. Should any matter adhering to the evidence fall or become separated from the article during or after packing, it will be found in the container in which the article was packed.

Transporting the Article

The transportation of the sealed evidence to the laboratory should be accompanied by the officer who collected the evidence. It has to be shipped to a laboratory, the safest and most practical method of delivery should be used and in the case of perishables, the speediest method possible should be employed.

The contents of any container should be clearly listed on the package or label. If several individual packages are packed into a single large container, the larger container should be labeled to show the content of the individual containers. This would be in addition to the labels on the individual containers. The information contained on the package should include: (1) contents of the package, (2) name of the person from whom the property was taken or where it was found, (3) the number of the case on which the evidence has a bearing, (4) the date and time it was found, (5) the name of the officer who found or received it and (6) the article to be subjected to laboratory examination, and (7) the type of examination suggested.

Storage of Evidence

One of the most important phases of maintaining the value of the evidence is its storage. The evidence must be stored in such a manner that there is no question as to actual possession.

In some departments the officer has to store the evidence in his personal locker, in others, special wall lockers are set aside for the storage of evidence with keys only available to the officer in charge of each watch and the officer who has evidence to store.

Probably the best arrangement would be for the department to have a property room with an officer from each watch in charge. After obtaining evidence the officer could then place it in the property room and receive a receipt for it. This room should have the proper facilities for storing evidence along with a strict security apparatus to keep all people except the officer of each watch in charge of it from entering.

This way the evidence could be properly stored according to its needs and the officer can be assured that the evidence has been under strict control and carefully guarded until it is needed in the laboratory or in the courtroom. He can then maintain the chain of evidence and assure the court and jury the evidence was given the best of care and handled by responsible personnel.

Conclusion

The identification, collection, and preservation of evidence are of crucial importance to the execution of police responsibilities. The auxiliary policeman will be expected to take part in these duties when the occasion arises. His specific duties will naturally depend upon the department with which he is allied. However, in most departments because of the presence of specialists in the area of criminal investigation his main duties will be the protection of the scene and assisting the specialists where necessary. Regardless of what his duties are, the auxiliary policeman should constantly strive to gain further knowledge about this field for his own benefit. In a natural or manmade disaster he may be the only representative of the law left within an entire area and, at that time, his knowledge of proper investigative techniques will help continue law and order in society.

The auxiliary officer should remember that there are always clues at a crime scene and that everything within a crime scene is significant. Only knowledge, experience, and patience will bring these clues into the open and these take time to develop. He should never forget the importance of maintaining the chain of custody by issuing and receiving receipts. Above all, he should be constantly aware of the importance of evidence and should constantly try to improve his own skills in its identification, collection, and preservation.

www.ingramcontent.com/pod-product-compliance
Lightning Source LLC
Chambersburg PA
CBHW081814300426
44116CB00014B/2350